Asian Tragedies in the Americas

Asian Tragedies in the Americas

Chinese, Japanese, and Korean Stories

Won K. Yoon

LEXINGTON BOOKS
Lanham • Boulder • New York • London

Published by Lexington Books
An imprint of The Rowman & Littlefield Publishing Group, Inc.
4501 Forbes Boulevard, Suite 200, Lanham, Maryland 20706
www.rowman.com

6 Tinworth Street, London SE11 5AL, United Kingdom

Copyright © 2021 by The Rowman & Littlefield Publishing Group, Inc.

All rights reserved. No part of this book may be reproduced in any form or by any electronic or mechanical means, including information storage and retrieval systems, without written permission from the publisher, except by a reviewer who may quote passages in a review.

British Library Cataloguing in Publication Information Available

Library of Congress Control Number: 2020950147

ISBN 978-1-7936-2853-4 (cloth)
ISBN 978-1-7936-2855-8 (pbk)
ISBN 978-1-7936-2854-1 (electronic)

*To the peoples of East Asian ancestry in the Americas,
lest their pioneers' struggles and sufferings be forgotten*

Contents

Preface		ix
Introduction		1
1	Western Encounters and Encroachments in East Asia	13
2	A Floating Hell in Devil's Throat	41
3	The Coolie Mart and Bitter Sugar in Cuba	61
4	A One-Way Passage to a Peruvian Hell	83
5	Paper Children: The Enticement of Gold Mountain	103
6	Koreans in Thorny Henequen Fields in Yucatan	131
7	A Korean Picture Marriage: The Lure of Hawaii	157
8	Peruvian Japanese in US Relocation Camp	181
9	An Empire Never Defeated: The Japanese in Brazil	203
10	Japanese War Brides Following GI Husbands	223
Conclusion		245
Bibliography		247
Index		255
About the Author		261

Preface

When I was working on my previous book, *Global Pulls on the Korean Communities in Sao Paulo and Buenos Aires* (2015), I wanted to understand the two largest Korean communities in South America as a part of a much larger East Asian community. In South America, the Korean community has been much smaller and younger than the Chinese or the Japanese community. The establishment of the first Korean communities in Sao Paulo and Buenos Aires were almost a century behind the first Chinese communities in Havana and Lima. Similarly, the Japanese community and the Korean community in Sao Paulo were established almost half a century apart.

Without knowing the experiences of the two older and larger East Asian communities in South America, I thought I might not be able to fairly understand the experiences of Korean immigrants who had moved to the continent in the 1960s and the 1970s. Most residents of the host countries cannot or do not distinguish the three East Asian groups. In their eyes, Chinese, Japanese, and Koreans are simply Orientals or Asians from the same geographical region.

In the process of expanding my knowledge on the East Asian communities, I came across some rare stories in Chinese and Japanese past. To me, it was a wake-up call. I then wondered how many East Asians on both sides of the Pacific Ocean might have known about the rare stories of their own ethnic communities in the Americas let alone people of the host countries.

I decided to tell a much larger story of East Asian communities by combining Chinese, Japanese, and Korean experiences in the Americas. That was how the idea of this book was conceived. No sooner had I finished my previous project than I started working on this one. I was compelled to write this book with a sense of mission that the rare stories need to be told to a wider public in Asia and the Americas.

The readers may deepen their understanding of the East-West relations in the nineteenth and twentieth centuries through the early East Asian immigrants' experiences. The insights gained from this book may help in bridging the two most important regions of the world in the twenty-first century: East Asia and North America. Furthermore, the readers may better grasp the complicated relations between the United States at one end and China and Japan at the other end. Many helped in the improvement of the manuscript. My colleague, Dr. Andrew Howe, read the manuscript and provided valuable suggestions for improvement. Sam Yoon checked the manuscript in the early stage and spotted errors and inadequacies. Lee Ja-Kyung deserves special recognition for her pioneering research on the long-forgotten henequen Koreans in Yucatan, Mexico. Eric Kunztman, the acquisition editor of Asian Studies at Lexington Books, recognized the value of the book proposal and shared my enthusiasm for the project. Alex Rallo, Kasey Bedhun, and Catherine Herman at the publisher guided me in every step of the final publication process. Dr. Myungki Hong, the director of M & L Hong Foundation, provided a grant to support my travel and other expenses for the book project. Last, my wife and others in the family understood my excuses and limited participation in the family activities. Their encouragement kept me going.

Unexpectedly, the COVID-19 pandemic disrupted the final preparation for the publication of this manuscript. With a sigh of relief, I am grateful to everyone involved in the book project at Lexington Books/Rowman & Littlefield for their extra efforts under the unusual circumstances.

—Won K. Yoon, Riverside, California

Introduction

The Americas were "discovered" by Europeans in their pursuit of wealth in Asia, especially in India and China. For millennia, the original migrants from Asia inhabited the vast lands that were hidden to Europeans on the other side of the Atlantic Ocean, until the end of the fifteenth century and the arrival of the first explorers. In the course of expanding their settlement of the New World, European immigrants to North and South America and their descendants caused havoc upon the original inhabitants (Native Americans or Indians).

From the beginning, European settlers viewed the newly discovered continents as a source of economic exploitation and colonial expansion. To that end, European colonists brought African slaves for hard labor beginning in the sixteenth century. When slavery was challenged and eventually abolished, plantation owners, mine operators, construction companies, and governments turned to Asia for new sources of cheap labor. This transition overlapped the phase-out of African slavery and the introduction of Asian laborers is critical to understanding the genesis of Asian tragedy in the Americas. During the phase-out, Asian labor recruits replaced freed slaves in some countries and supplemented the shrinking slave labor force in others. For instance, Asian laborers worked side by side with black slaves in Cuba and former slaves in Peru. In these places, they were treated no better than the slaves. The coexistence of slavery and an indentured labor system in the Americas made it easier to exploit and mistreat Asian laborers. By the end of the nineteenth century, slavery was completely phased out throughout the Americas after nearly four hundred years of the New World's dependency on this labor model. It took nearly one hundred years to complete the emancipation process in North and South America. The first emancipation took place in Haiti (1804) through slave revolts; slavery ended in Cuba in 1886 and

Brazil in 1888, respectively. President Abraham Lincoln proclaimed emancipation for American slaves in 1863 during the middle of the Civil War (1861–1865). Generally, America was slower in freeing slaves than their counterparts in Latin America. In fact, some early Chinese labor recruits came to the Americas aboard ships that had been used prior to transporting African slaves, and some of them worked for slave owners or former slave owners. Even after official abolition, the memory of slavery and old habits in dealing with slaves lingered, affecting the treatment of indentured foreign workers from Asia. This dynamic was similar to the post–Civil War South in the United States, where racial mistreatment lasted for generations after abolishment. More than 150 years, or about six generations later, the United States is still struggling with the legacy of slavery.

ASIAN TRAGEDIES

In the Americas, the Asian tragedies described in this book have been eclipsed in Western consciousness for three reasons. First of all, the overwhelming tragedies faced by black slaves and indigenous people were far graver and long-lasting. In relative terms, the suffering of the later and much smaller groups from Asia seemed to be insignificant and did not draw the attention of the news media or general public. Second, such tragedies have been eclipsed by the myth of a "model minority"[1] or "middle minority"[2] that enveloped Asian immigrants. The tragedies of the distant past have been forgotten in the stories of "Asian success." In addition, the economic ascendancy of Asian nations has mitigated the gravity of pain experienced by these early immigrants. Finally, the obscurity of Asian tragedies reflects "the silent minority"[3] symptom. As seen in the case of the massive Japanese American internment during the Pacific War, former internees and their descendants have remained relatively silent about the injustice of the US government upon its citizens. In history, unspoken past is an unknown reality. Nonetheless, these Asian tragedies were real. Besides the overlapped timing of slavery, either continuing in some cases or phased out in others, and the introduction of Chinese laborers in particular, other sociocultural and personal conditions contributed to such tragedies.

First of all, during the Chinese coolie trade period (1847–1874), problems began at the outset. From Macao or Hong Kong to Lima or Havana, the transportation of Chinese labor recruits took anywhere from four months to a year, and the average mortality rate during the long voyage was about 12 percent.[4] This mark was higher than the average mortality rate of 10 percent[5] that occurred during the transportation of slaves from West Africa to the Americas. On a few occasions, some transport ships experienced greater than a 50 percent[6] mortality rate. The causes of death during either the Pacific or

Indian-Atlantic Ocean crossing included sickness, suicide, and violence during the frequent mutinies mounted by angry Chinese.

Second, most early Asian laborers engaged in dangerous, difficult, and dirty work in the Americas. In today's vernacular, they were 3D jobs in agriculture, mining, and construction. That was the reason why countries in the Americas wanted to bring foreign laborers in the first place. Newly independent nations or old colonies in the Americas depended on either African slave labor or Asian indentured workers for physically demanding jobs. Such dangerous, difficult, and dirty work took its toll on the Asian laborers, both physically and mentally. Working conditions affected the health of workers resulting in sickness and death. Suicide rates among the early Chinese laborers, for example, were many times higher than those of Cubans.[7]

Third, a lack of normal family life was another source of suffering among many early Asian immigrants. The majority chose to come alone regardless of their marital status at home. If married, they left their wives and children behind, promising to return. As a result, labor recruits were dominantly male and the sex ratio was extremely skewed. Chinese women comprised less than 5 percent of the total Chinese admitted into the United States in the early years of immigration.[8] This ratio might have been even more lopsided in other nations in the Americas. Many early Asian laborers had no one to turn to for emotional and social support, as they had no families of their own. A laborer's life without a family was far more unbearable in a hostile, foreign land.

Fourth, most early Asian labor recruits came to the Americas with the mindset of sojourners.[9] When they left their homeland, they had no intention of settling down permanently in a strange place. They were pushed by difficulties at home rather than pulled by the attractions of unknown places. Moreover, their destinations in the New World included some of the furthest places on earth, heightening the sense of separation from loved ones at home. With going home in mind, they cared less about adapting to their host countries. Such an attitude led to an almost insulated existence, and these sojourner laborers remained as perpetual strangers in foreign countries. Alienation and isolation resulted in an unhealthy social life.

Fifth, the members of host countries mistreated Asian laborers with almost no fear of punishment from local authorities, much less from the home governments of the migrant workers. Although the host governments had rules and regulations on the treatment of foreign laborers, the abuse of these workers was hardly enforced and punished. At the same time, Asian nations were too weak and too far away to protect their citizens who were scattered throughout the Americas. Without legal guardians and protection, early Asian laborers were easy prey. To make the situation worse, the general public's anti-Asian sentiment stirred the atmosphere. In the United States, boiling anti-Chinese sentiment and fear mongering of the impending "yellow peril," particularly in California, led to the 1882 prohibition of new Chinese immigrants.

Sixth, as many Asian labor recruits, if not all, came from low socioeconomic backgrounds, they conveyed less than a desirable first impression to the people of their host countries. With little or no education, let alone cultural sophistication, peasants and day laborers had a hard time adjusting to the life of strange new places. The lack of social capital and skills on the part of Asian laborers reinforced the racial prejudice of white residents, and the prevalent anti-Asian sentiment fueled racial hatred.

Seventh, misunderstandings caused by miscommunication exacerbated management-labor relations, which often led to anger and hostility between the two groups. With no one advocating for or defending Asian laborer rights, conflicts sometimes ended with violence. Usually interpreters accompanied labor recruits to their destinations, yet each shipload was divided into different workplaces. In the early years, the management and workers were almost completely ignorant of one other.

Finally, mistreatment in the form of racial discrimination initiated by governments resulted in personal tragedy. For example, the exclusion laws against Chinese and the removal acts against people of Japanese ancestry in the United States and in some Latin American countries following the Pearl Harbor attack caused tremendous damage to Asian communities. Besides discriminatory acts undertaken by central governments, some local authorities also introduced rules and regulations targeting Asians. In sum, hard labor in a foreign land, extreme loneliness, mistreatment, and exploitation caused many labor recruits to experience tragedy. Although Japanese and Korean immigrants in the early part of the twentieth century faced less severe circumstances than did of the Chinese, they had their share of hardships and suffering.

THE FIRST ONE HUNDRED YEARS

Early East Asian immigration to the Americas took place between the mid-nineteenth and mid-twentieth centuries. It began in the years between the First and Second Opium Wars (1839–1842; 1856–1860) and ended with the Pacific War (1941–1945), a subset of World War II. This approximately one hundred-year period was characterized by Western imperial activity in Asia. Most Asian nations, especially those in South Asia and Southeast Asia, were under European colonial rule. It was clearly a time of European dominance and Asian submission. As far as Asia was concerned, it was a century of humiliation. This period was one of the most tumultuous eras in East Asian history. Dynasties ended in Korea in 1910 and China in 1911, respectively. A sequence of different dynasties had spanned more than two thousand years in

China and 1,500 years in Korea. Such a long political tradition of monarchial rule came to an end when the West disturbed and destabilized these nations.

Japan was an exception, a closed nation for almost two hundred years until the Black Fleet of America appeared in Tokyo Bay in 1854. The island nation went through a major national transformation through the Meiji Reform, which began in 1868. Among the three East Asian nations, Japan seemed to have benefited the most from its contact with the West. While maintaining political continuity and stability by strengthening the position of its emperor, Japan became a major modern power to the extent of eventually challenging Western dominance in 1941 with an attack on Pearl Harbor and other nations throughout the Pacific. The irony was that Japan's neighboring nations, China and Korea, were victimized by a Japan that had gained knowledge and means through Westernization. China lost a portion of its territory, including Manchuria, Inner Mongolia, Taiwan, and some urban districts, to Japan. Korea became a Japanese colony until the end of the Pacific War. In the wars that marked the beginning and the end of this one hundred-year period, China and Japan were the losers. The winners were Great Britain in the Opium War and the United States in the Pacific War. Directly or indirectly, these military outcomes affected the flow of immigration and the life of East Asians in the Americas. In particular, the effects of the Pacific War on people of Japanese ancestry in the Americas were evident in the mistreatment by their host governments.

THE AMERICAN DOMINO EFFECT

Most nations in the Americas mistreated early Asian immigrants, to varying degrees. However, some nations were more responsible for mistreatment than others due to their position and influence in the hemisphere. Among the sovereign nations in the Americas, excluding twenty European territories (including those of the United Kingdom, France, the Netherlands, Denmark, and Norway), the United States has been the most powerful and influential. The country founded on the ideals of freedom, equality, and justice, however, was not so fair toward those from East Asia during this period. Other nations in the Western hemisphere often rationalized or justified their mistreatment of East Asians by citing the example of the United States. It was more so among small, less powerful countries. During the one hundred-year period, many US policies were largely restrictive to East Asians. The US Congress passed two exclusion laws in less than fifty years: the Chinese Exclusion Act of 1882 and the Oriental Exclusion Act of 1924. It was very clear that the US did not welcome Asian immigration other than when it suited their labor needs. These messages of exclusion from a dominant nation had an impact upon other American nations. Second, the US government legally prohibited

Asian immigrants from becoming naturalized American citizens until 1952. From the nation's origins, only white immigrants were eligible for naturalization, according to the Naturalization Act of 1790. For more than one hundred years, Asian immigrants had lived as perpetual foreigners in their own country of residence, although citizenship by birth was applicable to their American-born children. Finally, a dozen Latin American nations collaborated with the United States in deporting to the US people of Japanese ancestry during the Pacific War.[10] Following the US government's removal and internment of more than one hundred thousand people, other nations were ready to cooperate. Some grabbed the opportunity to get rid of their Japanese residents.[11]

Besides federal legislative actions and the presidential executive order against Asian residents, state and municipal governments passed all sorts of laws and regulations against Asians. Some examples included prohibition against interracial marriage,[12] limitation on property ownership, school segregation, special taxes for certain business practices, and so forth. The United States sent out negative messages on Asian immigrants to the rest of the Americas. The nation known for championing human dignity and rights was selective.

THE LAGGARD

The asymmetric relations between East Asia and the West in terms of economic and military power during this one hundred-year period affected the lives of early Asian immigrants to the Americas. The major cause of power imbalance between the two spheres can be traced to the Industrial Revolution,[13] among other reasons. While Western nations advanced rapidly in science and technology, the tradition-bound East Asian nations resisted the modern influences of the West. China, Japan, and Korea, heavily influenced and shaped by Confucianism and Buddhism, attempted to close their doors to the encroachment of the West.[14] In addition, scientific and technological advancements in the West were often associated with inherent superiority of the white race, thus justifying the "civilized" West leading the "uncivilized" rest of the world. In the binary world of "white" and "colored," East Asians were regarded as colored, and thus inferior. Such a racial perception affected the nature of relations between host white residents, including mestizos, and early East Asian immigrant laborers in the Americas.

In the Americas, East Asian immigrants were commonly called Orientals, a derogatory term almost comparable to calling blacks Negros or worse.[15] The Orient refers to the East, as opposed to Occident, which refers to the West. Yet Westerners used the term with negative connotations of racial contempt. Thus, Asian tragedies in the Americas contained not only aspects of scientific knowledge but also a racial dimension. The combination of these two was potent in how Westerners perceived these Asian laborers. Superior technology combined with a supposedly superior inherent capability provided a base for contempt. On the other hand, most Eastern rulers in the nineteenth century did not think they would need to embrace new Western ideas or technologies, as they felt self-sufficient and self-contained. By all means, they wanted to preserve internal harmony and equilibrium by blocking out any external influences and foreign elements. Especially, the Middle Kingdom of China saw itself as the center of the world, and as a great, proud nation, it was not interested in the teachings of "barbarians"[16] from the far corners of the earth. In the early phase of East-West contact, arrogant Chinese elites summarily dismissed anything Western regardless of its veracity or utility.[17] As a result, East Asia lagged considerably behind the West in modern scientific and technological development. Thus, Western nations could easily neutralize the resistance of East Asian nations with superior navigation and military technology.

For a long time, however, China was the envy of Europe. Europeans knew something about the faraway Middle Kingdom through the merchants who conveyed back fine Chinese goods. It was the most dynamic place in terms of innovation and productivity. "In 1500, the GDP of East Asia was three times that of Western Europe and as late as 1820, it was two and a half times bigger."[18] Then, the region became "Eastern Slaves for Western Profits."[19] In the beginning, Europeans approached China with curiosity, then with ambition for commercial, religious, and political gain. The demands of the West following the defeat of China in the Opium Wars revealed their true intentions. This brief description of the backdrop for early East Asian immigration, especially context for the Chinese "coolie" laborers, may provide some clues as to the suffering of Asian immigrants in the Americas. Their painful, often tragic, stories may also be understood in the context of international relations between East Asia and the Americas in the nineteenth and twentieth centuries up to the time of the Pacific War.

THE SIGNIFICANCE OF THIS BOOK

This book is significant for a number of reasons. First, early Asian immigrants to the Americas covered the whole world by crossing the Pacific Ocean to the east (San Francisco or Lima) or the Indian Ocean then Atlantic Ocean to the west (Havana) in the age of international travel by ships. Many epic-scale stories involve whites, blacks, and Asians on three continents (Asia, North America, and South America). Second, this book presents a wide range of East Asian experiences in the Americas during a clearly defined historical period. Unlike most books focused on a single national group in a single resident country (e.g., Japanese in Peru), this book presents the whole spectrum of East Asian experiences in the Americas, from the United States to Brazil. Third, no book before has focused on the theme of human tragedies among the East Asian immigrants to the Americas. Although most stories of these early immigrants are sad and painful, this book is intentional in focusing on the theme of tragedy. Fourth, about one-third of the stories are related to Asian women, a rare feature in most books on early Asian immigrant groups. Early East Asian immigrants were dominantly males for cultural and other reasons. Fifth, even a few anthological books[20] on Asian immigrant groups pay scant attention, or none at all, to Korean experiences. Because the Chinese and Japanese immigrant communities were much larger and with a longer history than that of the Koreans, the latter have often been left out. The West has shown interest in China and Japan while the much smaller Korea has been overshadowed by its two powerful neighbors. In this book, early Korean immigrant experiences in the Americas receives proportional attention. Sixth, another significance is the framing of the time period. As previously described, the approximately one hundred–year period between the Opium War and the Pacific War is more than a temporal happenstance. China challenged Great Britain in the Opium War and Japan challenged the United States in the Pacific War. In both cases, the Asian nations were defeated, thereby resulting in coining the term "century of humiliation" for East Asia. Finally, retelling the tragic human stories of the mid-nineteenth and the early twentieth centuries is relevant as China, Japan, and Korea have become twenty-first century power players in international politics, economy, and culture. As Garten succinctly put it, "Asia is again ascending."[21] One-time, labor-supplying nations mired in poverty have reversed their place in the world. Readers of this book may realize a shift in global power center. It may also provide insight and inspiration to readers in many struggling countries, especially in the global south.

THE APPROACH

This book attempts to contextualize the relationship of the two regions of the world through individual and collective stories that are relatively unknown. The stories are terrible, including the cruelty of the transport of Chinese "coolies," Chinese laborers in Cuba and Peru, Korean slaves in Yucatan, the Japanese deported from Peru to the United States during the Pacific War, and so forth. In contrast, a few comically sad stories, such as Chinese paper sons and daughters, the denial of the Japanese defeat in the Pacific War, present tragic elements nevertheless. Half of the East Asian stories in this book are related to Chinese immigrants as they came to the Americas much earlier and in larger numbers than those of either Japan or Korea. The sociocultural atmosphere of the nineteenth-century Americas, when the Chinese arrived, was far more prejudiced and discriminatory than when Japanese and Koreans came in the early decades of the twentieth century. An initial chapter is provided for those who are unfamiliar with the history of encounters between East Asia and the West. This chapter offers a general backdrop, and includes the social conditions of China, Japan, and Korea before the encroachment of Western powers.

The stories in this book are presented in chronological order to indicate changes over time, with some inevitable overlaps. Efforts were made to tell the stories as they had happened. To that end, the sources of specific numbers or events are indicated in each chapter's notes section. Some story segments are amplified by inserting extra information related to other groups. For example, the transportation of the Chinese coolies from South China to Cuba is compared with the trans-Atlantic voyages of the African slaves from the coasts of West Africa to the Atlantic coast of the Americas. In the same manner, the purchase price of Chinese coolies in the Americas was compared with the purchase price of African slaves during the same time frame. Readers may find such comparative information valuable in gauging the suffering and humiliation of the early Chinese coolies vis-à-vis that of the African slaves. Thus, each story is presented in the larger context of historical time and sociocultural space where possible. For the same reason, each East Asian group is related to the other two wherever justifiable.

The number of chapters allocated to each East Asian group may require an explanation. In this book, four chapters are focused on Chinese, three on Japanese, and two on Korean immigrants. Among the three East Asian groups, Chinese and Japanese experiences have received far more attention by scholars and lay people alike. This proportional reality may reflect the size of the immigrant population and the length of their residence in the Americas. Older and larger Chinese and Japanese communities have received far more attention than the smaller and younger Korean community. In addition, the varying intensity of Western curiosity and interest in the three Asian countries, especially in the early phases of such encounters, may have also affected the extent of scholarly research and public attention. Finally, the rising international status and influence of modern-day China and Japan may have stimulated more studies on these nations and their overseas communities. There is a general rule of thumb on the ratio of publications related to Chinese, Japanese, and Koreans: 5, 4, and 1, respectively.

In brief, chapter 1 describes the history of encounters between West and East Asia. It shows how China, Japan, and Korea were initially approached, then eventually forced to yield to the West. Chapters 2 through 4 involve the suffering of Chinese coolies during their long transport, on the sugarcane plantations of Cuba, and in the *guano* mines of Peru. Chapter 5 is sadly comic and focused on the deception tactics used by many Chinese to come to the United States. Chapters 6 and 7 are related to Korean experiences in Yucatan, Mexico, and picture marriage of Korean women with Korean sugarcane laborers in Hawaii. The last three chapters are on Japanese experiences during and after the Pacific War. Chapter 8 involves the wartime detention of Peruvian Japanese in American relocation camps during World War II, while Chapter 9 describes the denial of the Japanese defeat in World War II by many Japanese residents in Brazil. The final chapter involves the story of Japanese war brides who followed their American GI husbands to America during the post-war years.

Each chapter ends with a section of reflections. The implications of the tragic past are sought in the context of present times and situations. Although history tends to repeat itself, it is important to avoid the same human tragedies by learning from the past. In that sense, all history is contemporary. Throughout the book, East Asia refers to China, Japan, and Korea. Although Mongolia is a part of East Asia, immigration from that country to the Americas has been negligible. The land-locked, sparsely populated nomadic nation never promoted overseas immigration as did the other three Pacific-rim nations. Politically speaking, China in the present tense refers only to mainland China, excluding Taiwan, Hong Kong, and Macao.

In this book, early East Asian immigrants are those who came to North and South America up to the time of the Pacific War (or World War II). They are differentiated from those who came to the Americas in the 1960s and thereafter.[22] Unlike the early East Asians who came mainly for hard physical labor, most during the second wave of immigration have come with a variety of occupations, including many professionals such as engineers, scientists, nurses, doctors, and the like. Moreover, host governments have carefully screened applicants in terms of education, language skills, and job skills. Most of these immigrants, if not all, flew over the Pacific Ocean aboard modern jet airplanes. In the second half of the twentieth century, Koreans, then Chinese, came in large numbers. In the twenty-first century, however, most Japanese and Koreans have lost interest in immigrating to any part of the Americas. The economic advancement of East Asia has drastically changed the cross-Pacific immigration trend. East Asian immigration may follow the pattern of the European immigration to the Americas, slowly declining over the years.

NOTES

1. Madeline Y. Hsu, *Dreaming of Gold, Dreaming of Home: Transnationalism and Migration Between the United States and South China, 1882–1943* (Stanford: Stanford University Press, 2000), 183. Madeline Y. Hsu, *The Good Immigrants: How the Yellow Peril Became the Model Minority* (Princeton: Princeton University Press, 2015), 21–22.

2. This term refers to Asian American's middle-range position in terms of socioeconomic status. It also implies its racial position in the middle between whites and blacks in America.

3. The silent minority refers to Asian American tendency to remain silent about the injustice upon them in the past. The Chinese Exclusion Act and Japanese internment during the Pacific War are examples of the past injustice.

4. Arnold J. Meagher, *The Coolie Trade: The Traffic of Chinese Laborers to Latin America 1847–1874* (Arnold J. Meagher, 2008), 169.

5. Meg Greene and Mark G. Malvasi, "Middle Passage: Did the Treatment of Slaves During the Middle Passage Produce Excessively High Mortality Rates?" in *History in Dispute vol. 13: Slavery in the Western Hemisphere, Circa 1500–1888*, ed. Mark G. Malvasi (Detroit: St. James Press, 2003), 129–37.

6. Evelyn Hu-De Hart, "La Trata Amarilla: The Yellow Trade and the Middle Passage, 1847–1884," in *Many Middle Passages: Forced Migration and the Making of the Modern World*, ed. Emma Christopher, Cassandra Pybus, and Marcus Rediker (Berkeley: University of California Press, 2007), 166–83.

7. Kathleen Lopez, *Chinese Cubans: A Transnational History* (Chapel Hill: The University of North Carolina Press, 2013), 39.

8. For instance, Chinese women admitted into the United States between 1870 and 1882 comprised only the annual average of 3.2 percent. During the thirteen-year period, the lowest percentages of Chinese women admission were 0.3 percent in 1882, 0.6 percent in 1881, and 0.7 percent in 1877. See Erika Lee, *At America's Gate* (Chapel Hill: The University of North Carolina Press, 2003), 117–18.

9. Lee, *At America's Gate*, 122.

10. Lika C. Miyake, "Forsaken and Forgotten: The U.S. Internment of Japanese Peruvians During World War II," *Asian American Law Journal* 9 (January 2002): 163–93.

11. C. Harvey Gardiner, *Pawns in a Triangle of Hate: The Peruvian Japanese and the United States* (Seattle: University of Washington Press, 1981), 19.

12. The US Supreme Court ruled that the prohibition of intermarriage violates the Equal Right Protection Act in the case of *Loving vs. Virginia* in 1967.

13. The invention of the steam engine in Great Britain was a turning-point in differentiating Europe and East Asia. With technological advancement, especially in navigation and weapons, the West had encroached East Asia.

14. Japan and Korea had imposed their lock-down policy against Westerners in 1644 and 1864, respectively.

15. Tess Owen, "The Words 'Oriental' and 'Negro' Can No Longer Be Used in US Federal Laws," *Vice News*, May 21, 2016, accessed January 25, 2018, news.vice.com/the-words-oriental-and-negro-can-no-longer-be-used-in-us-federal-laws.

16. D. E. Mungello, *The Great Encounter of China and the West, 1500–1800* (New York: Rowman & Littlefield, 2009), 4–5.

17. J. D. Frodsham, *The First Chinese Embassy to the West: The Journal of Kuo Sung Tao, Liu His-Hung, and Chang Te-Yi* (Oxford: Claredon Press, 1974), xxv.

18. Jeffrey E. Garten, *From Silk to Silicon: The Story of Globalization through Ten Extraordinary Lives* (New York: Harper, 2016), 28–29.

19. Michael J. Green, *By More Than Providence: Grand Strategy and American Power in the Asia Pacific Since 1783* (New York: Columbia University Press, 2017), 230.

20. Some examples may include Erika Lee, *The Making of Asia America: A History* (New York: Simon & Schuster Paperbacks, 2015); W. Anderson and Robert G. Lee, ed. *Displacement and Diasporas: Asians in the Americas* (New Brunswick, NJ: Rutgurs University Press, 2005); Roshini Rusatomji-Kerns with R. Srikanth and L. M. Strobel, ed. *Encounters: People of Asian Descent in the Americas* (New York: Rowman & Littlefield, 1999); Luz M. M. Montiel, *Asiatic Migrations in Latin America* (Mexico: El Colegio De Mexico, 1981).

21. Garten, *From Silk to Silicon*, 29.

22. The US Congress passed the Immigration Amendment Act in 1965 whereby each Asian country could send up to twenty thousand annually to the United States. It was the reversal of the Oriental Exclusion Act of 1924.

Chapter One

Western Encounters and Encroachments in East Asia

For more than a millennium, Europe was connected with China through the overland Silk Road. This route, often called the spine of Asia, covered the Near East, Persia, Central Asia, and China traversing formidable mountains, deserts, and steppes. Through multi-stage relay trades, goods and ideas moved between the West and the East. The west-bound land route often ended at the port cities of the eastern Mediterranean coast. From there, merchandise was transported by ships to Mediterranean countries in Europe and North Africa, including Rome. Besides the overland Silk Road, goods were sometimes transported by ships via the South China Sea, Indian Ocean, then either the Persian Gulf or Red Sea before reaching the major ports of the Arabian Peninsula or Egypt.

When the Mongols ruled China, Central Asia, Northern India, Persia, and Central and Eastern Europe including Russia, the Silk Road became vital for the administration of the largest contiguous empire ever. It served as an information and commercial highway for the vast empire. Thus, maintaining a well-running, safe Silk Road was in the empire's best interest. It was not an accident that Europeans began to appear more frequently in China during the Yuan Dynasty (1271–1368) under the Mongol's rule. Rooted in a nomadic life in open steppes, the Mongol rulers were inclusive and tolerant in their dealing with different ethnic, religious, and language groups throughout the empire. For instance, when Muslim groups began to pose serious military threats, the Mongol rulers proposed to establish alliances with some European kings and the Pope.[1]

The Age of Exploration and Discovery in the fifteenth and sixteenth centuries, ushered in mainly by Spain and Portugal, made the land-based Silk Road less vital for trade between Europe and Asia.

When Christopher Columbus landed on the West Indies in 1492 and Vasco da Gama reached India (East India) in 1498, Europeans shifted their interests to the New World and the Indian subcontinent and beyond. Unlike the old Silk Road, where trade depended on human and animal-born cargo, the ocean-going maritime transportation system was faster, cheaper, and more efficient. The cargo-carrying capacity of the ships was much higher than that of the slow-moving caravans. The risk was high, but the return on investment was worth the risk.

The early maritime European traders to China and Japan were Portuguese by designation. To avoid competition and even conflict between the two neighboring Iberian nations, Spain and Portugal signed the Treaty of Todesillas[2] in June 1494, only two years after the discovery of the West Indies by Columbus. According to the treaty, Spain would concentrate on exploiting the Americas while Portugal would monopolize its trade with Asia, namely India, China, and surrounding areas. That was how the Portuguese started a maritime trading post in Macao before anyone else. Then a group of shipwrecked Portuguese sailors happened to discover Japan in 1543 by accident. Among other things, their introduction of the match-lock long rifle to the Japanese changed the political and military dynamics among China, Japan, and Korea. Equipped with the new western weapon system, Japan invaded Korea on the pretext of conquering China (Ming Dynasty) in 1592. A few European Catholic priests in Japan followed the invading army into Korea.[3]

About two and a half centuries later, Western gun boats began to appear on the horizon of East Asian nations. Some demanded for open trade and

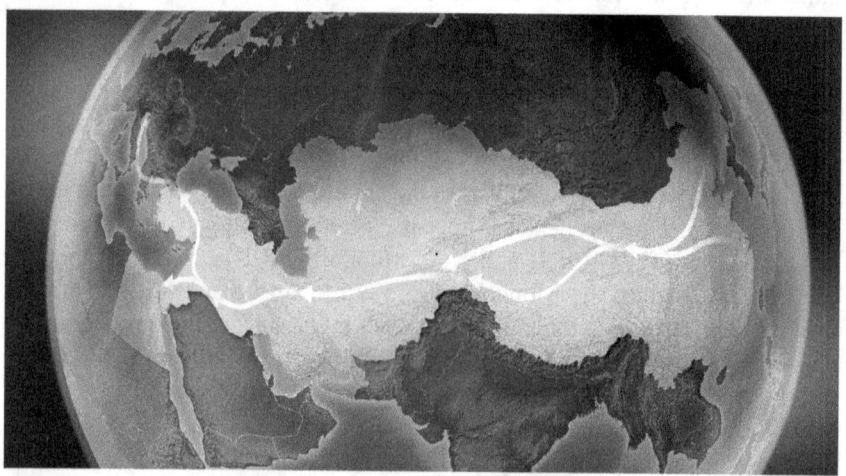

Figure 1.1.   Map of Silk Road. *Maxiphoto* © *iStock*

others defended the commercial interest of their merchants. Eventually, Western imperialistic ambitions materialized in Asia through unequal treaties and trade. As a result, Chinese laborers were first transported to either the Atlantic or Pacific Coast of the Americas. China, Japan, and Korea reluctantly came into contact with the Americas at the government level during the second half of the nineteenth century.

In comparison with European maritime nations, the United States was a latecomer to Pacific Asia. America started showing interest in East Asia only after it had reached the Pacific Coast. Before the nineteenth century, US territory was limited mainly to the area east of the Mississippi River. Over time, the new nation steadily expanded its territory westward. Finally, it became a nation stretching between two oceans, the Atlantic and the Pacific. Before it annexed the Pacific West, the US government conquered the Indian nations (or tribes) in the East and Midwest, purchased the Louisiana Territory[4] from France in 1803, and obtained the vast region of the Southwest[5] from Mexico in 1848 following the American-Mexican war (1844–1848). These territorial acquisitions completed Continental America to what it is today. Only afterwards did American gunboat diplomacy begin in East Asia in 1853 when Commodore Matthew Perry led his black fleet to Japan. From that time onwards, both American navy and merchant ships began to frequent the coasts of China, Japan, and Korea.

CHANGES BROUGHT BY THE WEST

Until the eighteenth century, China was the envy of Europe. Its sociocultural sophistication and economic scale surpassed any European country. Even in scientific and technological advancements, China had demonstrated impressive achievements. Major Chinese inventions included cast-iron, paper, the magnetic compass, gunpowder, suspension bridges, and clockwork, among others. In literature and philosophy, China had produced world-class thinkers like Laozu, Confucius, Mencius, and their disciples. Their writings on human nature and social ethics would turn out to be timeless. Learning was highly sought after and valued as Chinese and Korean governments selected high-ranking officers by imperial examinations regardless of one's social background. The open system of selecting government officers through the central test system provided equal opportunity and meritocracy.

China's material and non-material culture was conveyed to Europe mainly by merchants and Christian missionaries, especially Catholic priests who immersed themselves in the learning of Chinese classics. Stories related to China caught the imagination of many European elites. Those who were disenchanted with the intolerance and conflict of European Christendom were charmed by the humanistic, practical philosophies of East Asia. Some

European thinkers attracted to the teachings of the East included Gottfried Wilhelm Leibniz of Germany (1646–1716), Voltaire–pen name of Francois-Marie Arouet–of France (1694–1778), David Hume of Scotland (1711–1776), and Adam Smith of Scotland (1723–1778). They embraced the humanistic approach of Chinese philosophies to life in general, and Leibniz even suggested that Europe might need Confucian missionaries from China.[6] European Sinophiles (love of China) applied the teachings and practices of China to the Enlightenment to counter the influence of Medieval Christianity.

Not all European thinkers, however, were enthusiastic about Eastern philosophy. Many were uneasy about a Chinese philosophy that was presented as counter to rational Greek philosophy and Christian theology. As Europe progressed as a result of technological advancement, Sinophilia gave way to Sinophobia (fear of China).[7] This shift reflected a growing confidence in Europe stemming from its Scientific and Industrial revolutions. With the benefits of technological advancement, Europeans were able to reach the far corners of the world, including the eastern end of the Asian continent. Eventually, they colonized many Asian countries, including India and Indochina. To rationalize and justify European imperial activity in Africa, Asia, and Latin America, racist ideas were pushed.

The publication of *An Essay on the Inequality of Human Races* (1853–1855), by Joseph Arthur Comte de Gobineau (1816–1882), a French aristocrat, laid the foundation for modern racism. In it, the human race is classified into three categories: white, yellow, and black. De Gobineau's main point was that the white race was superior to the other two. In overall mental and physical capacity, the white race was placed above the colored race. The yellow (Mongoloid) race was placed lower than the white but higher than the black race. In nineteenth-century Europe, such an idea gained popularity and helped to rationalize the colonization of many parts of Africa and Asia. European racial perceptions and attitudes were reflected in the mistreatment of black people, and much of the suffering of East Asian immigrants in the Americas should be understood against the twin backdrops of Western imperialism and racism that were prevalent in the nineteenth and twentieth centuries.

In addition, the idea of Social Darwinism[8] was another intellectual product of the nineteenth century. It was derived from the biological evolutionary theory that was advocated by Charles Darwin. Social Darwinism affected Europeans in their dealing with continents inhabited by colored people. According to this new perspective, people from a more advanced society had a better capacity to adjust to a given environment. The implication was that the more advanced West should guide the less civilized Asia and Africa. Namely, the better fit should lead the less fit in the struggle for existence. The obvious scientific and technological advancement of the West were seen as proof of the white race's superior ability, justifying the dominance of less advanced people. These perspectives manifested in explicit or subtle ways when Westerners dealt with Asians both in Asia and in the Americas.

EAST ASIAN IMMIGRATION TO THE AMERICAS

Asian immigration to the Americas began in the middle part of the nineteenth century. In 1847, the Qing government of China approved a first immigrant group of 612 laborers to Cuba.[9] The first transport of Chinese laborers took place within five years of the end of the First Opium War (1839–1842). From China, Cuba lay on the other side of the earth, and the voyage required the navigation of more than half of the earth's circumference. Not long after this first shipment of Chinese labor recruits, hundreds of Chinese workers went to the United States, especially to the newly annexed, former Mexican territory of California, when the Gold Rush hit the region. America's construction of its transcontinental railroad was another major project that had started in 1863. Both mining and railroad work demanded a huge labor force. At that time, it was cheaper and faster to bring laborers from Asia by ship than to bring laborers from the East using horse-driven wagons.

Besides Cuba and the United States, other countries in the Americas, such as Brazil, Canada, Peru, Panama, and some Caribbean islands, received a considerable number of Chinese migrant workers in the ensuing years. China responded to the desperate labor needs of the Americas by sending thousands of men. The three nations that received the highest number of Chinese laborers were the United States, Cuba, and Peru.[10] The two Latin American countries were Spanish colonies, although Peru declared independence in 1821 while Cuba lasted as a Spanish colony until the end of the Spanish-American War in 1898. For somewhat different domestic and international circumstances, the Japanese government sent its first immigrant group of 153 to work on the booming sugarcane plantations of Hawaii in 1885.[11] In the preceding years, Japan wanted to learn from the West and transform itself through Westernization. This was known as the watershed Meiji Reform that was launched in 1868, not long after the entry of the US Naval fleet into Tokyo Bay. The United States demanded that Japan open up its country for trade, and the leadership yielded to this demand without much resistance. Japan saw what had happened to China in its conflict with Great Britain during the Opium War.

The Japanese government, however, did not allow its people to immigrate to the Americas until 1885. The government was against sending its people mainly because Chinese laborers were mistreated in the Americas, especially in Cuba and Peru. The government officials did not want to degrade the reputation of the rising-sun nation by subjecting its people to humiliation in foreign countries. The anti-Chinese sentiments culminated in the United States when the US Congress passed the Chinese Exclusion Act of 1882. This affirmed the judgment of the Japanese government in not allowing its people to immigrate. Japan's ban on emigration came to an end when the Hawaiian King, David Kalakaua, visited Japan in 1885. King Kalakaua felt an affinity with Japan as an island nation in the Pacific Ocean, much like his Hawaiian kingdom. He asked his counterpart to let Japanese people immigrate to Hawaii and work on the booming sugarcane plantations. Japan reciprocated the good-will gesture by ending its emigration ban.[12]

In 1885, a total of 943 Japanese nationals (676 men, 159 women, and 108 children) left for Hawaii.[13] When Hawaii was annexed to the United States in 1900, many Japanese continued to immigrate to the islands and the mainland. At the same time, the Japanese government looked for other countries in the Americas that were open to Japanese immigrants. Among Latin American countries, Mexico was the first nation to receive Japanese immigrants in 1897. In the ensuing years, Argentina, Bolivia, Brazil, Paraguay, and Peru opened their doors to Japanese immigration, mainly for agricultural workers. Among these nations, the United States, Brazil, and Peru allowed in the largest number of Japanese immigrants in order to support their agriculture. As a result, Japanese immigrants established the largest overseas community in Brazil, and the people of Peru elected a second-generation Japanese (Nisei) Peruvian president, Alberto Fujimori, in 1990.

Not long after Japan witnessed its first overseas immigration, Korea's last Yi Dynasty government sent its first immigrants to the then new American territory of Hawaii, in 1903. Korean immigration to the islands, however, lasted only three years. The Korean king received a report on the appalling mistreatment of Korean immigrants in Yucatan, Mexico. Deeply disturbed, the king banned overseas immigration altogether. By then, Korea had become a Japanese protectorate in 1905 and lost its diplomatic autonomy to negotiate with foreign governments. Eventually, Japan colonized Korea in 1910 and ruled the small peninsula until the end of the Second World War. Korea had to wait until the middle part of the 1960s when the fledgling republic was able to send its first immigrants to Brazil in 1963, Bolivia in 1964, and Argentina in 1965.

Then, unexpectedly, both Canada and the United States began to accept Korean immigrants in large numbers, beginning in the second half of the 1960s as the two North American countries changed their immigration laws in favor of Asians. These changes were an apparent reflection of the spirit of the Civil Rights Movement in the 1960s and a major turnabout on Asian immigration to the United States. It was a far cry from the past when the US Congress had passed the Oriental Exclusion Act of 1924. Because of this act, no more than 105 people could annually immigrate to the United States from each Asian country. During the post-Second World War years, from 1946 to

1965, only the Asian wives of American soldiers stationed in East Asia and orphaned children adopted by American families could come to the United States for permanent residence. This shift in US immigration policy in the 1960s changed the picture of Asian immigration drastically. According to the 2010 US census, for instance, about fifteen million respondents identified themselves as having Asian ancestry. They comprised almost 5 percent of the total US population.

Outside the United States, around two million people of East Asian ancestry reside in Canada and approximately three million in Latin America. Today, nearly twelve million people identify themselves with East Asian ancestry throughout the Americas.[14] Until the nineteenth century, the rulers of the East Asian kingdoms had prohibited the emigration of their subjects. These insular rulers were quite xenophobic toward the outside world. When Westerners arrived, these rulers were either resistant or reluctant in their contact with foreigners. Traditionally, maintaining internal harmony and order was the mandate of East Asian rulers. For this reason, any foreign element, whether it was a different belief, people, or social system, was considered disruptive and disturbing. Until the middle part of the nineteenth century, both Japan and Korea insisted on a strict closed-door policy to keep the West from unsettling their domestic tranquility. However, they could not stop the encroachment of Europe and the United States as it was like a surging tide that no force could stop. While the tradition-bound Asian kingdoms, especially China and Korea, were waning, European countries bolstered by the Enlightenment and the Industrial Revolution were progressive and aggressive.

CHINA AND THE WEST

China's first encounter with Europe dates back to the second century AD when the Roman emperor, Marcus Aurelius Antonius (121–180), dispatched an envoy to the court of the Han Dynasty (206 BC–220 AD) in 166 AD.[15] After him, other emperors of Rome (Western Rome) and Byzantium (Eastern Rome) sent embassies to their counterparts in China, namely the Tang, Song, and Yuan dynasties. For centuries, knowledgeable Europeans had been aware of the Middle Kingdom through the stories of intermediary travelers and traders, mostly Arabs, Persians, and Central Asians. Among the three East Asian countries, however, the better-known China was the main focus of European curiosity and interest in the Orient. As a kingdom, China was many times larger in terms of territory and population than either Japan or Korea. From Europe, the Western frontier of China was the end of the overland Silk Road.

Informed Europeans knew that China lay at the other end of the long Silk Road, which conveyed impressive Chinese products but only a few individuals had the will to set out on such a long, risky expedition. The journey was unpredictable and could take many months or years, depending on unforeseen conditions along the way. In addition, the birth of Islam in the seventh century and its rapid expansion throughout the Middle East and Central Asia sometimes imposed a formidable roadblock to would-be European travelers to China.

While East Asia was revolving around the Middle Kingdom, the West was evolving around the Roman Empire. Following the demise of the Western Roman Empire in the fifth century, the celestial empire of the papacy continued to exert its influence beyond the boundaries of the old empire. The Roman Catholic Church took its mission to reach out to the ends of the world very seriously, and its missionaries were determined to carry out missions to China.

At the same time, the commercial interests of European merchants proved to be as tenacious and intense as the proselytizing interests of Catholic missionaries. Thus, as early as the thirteenth century, the Great Court of Khan of the Yuan Dynasty (1260–1368) received a Franciscan priest from Italy by the name of John de Plano Carpini (1185–1252). Not long after Carpini's visit, the Polo brothers of Venice traveled to China in 1264. In their second visit, Marco Polo, one of the brother's son, accompanied them in 1275. Soon, China became widely known to the West through a book originated from Marco Polo, who claimed to have spent sixteen years in China. It was the first introduction of China to Europeans based on a first-hand eyewitness. Rusticello de Pisa published *The Travels of Marco Polo* around 1300 based on what he had heard from the Venetian merchant while the two were imprisoned together. Christopher Columbus kept the book in his first voyage across the Atlantic Ocean.

Portugal produced many ocean-faring explorers such as Jorge Alvares, who sailed to China in 1513. Only fifteen years before, Vasco da Gama had reached the west coast of India and only twenty-one years before, Columbus reached the West Indies. Alvares' arrival in China occurred about twenty years before the first Portuguese settlement in Brazil in 1532. Following Alvares, Portuguese merchants and sailors used Macao as their base for trade with China.

Around this time, the Spanish colonial administration began annual trade voyages between Acapulco, Mexico, and Manila in the Philippine Islands. This route was known as the Manila Galleon Trade or La Nao de la China. Annual cross-Pacific voyages continued for 250 years, from 1565 to 1815. Such voyages took about four months with a stop in Guam. Each time, the galleon fleet, usually two ships in tandem, transported about four hundred people and cargo. Because of the volume and content of trade between New

Spain (Mexico) and the Spanish East Indies (Philippines), this trade route came to be known as "the Silk Road of the Sea." The galleon ships brought silver from Mexico in exchange for Chinese goods, including porcelain wares, silk, and spice.[16] According to one estimate, about one-third of the silver mined in the Spanish American colonies was taken to Far East Asia during this time.[17] Since the galleon trade was a part of the triangle linking Manila to the Americas, Filipinos, Chinese, and Japanese served as crew members during voyages, and some settled in New Spain.[18] By 1635, an area inhabited by Chinese began to emerge in Mexico.[19]

The most dedicated European to China was an Italian Jesuit priest, Matteo Ricci (1552–1610). He tried to impress Chinese high officials and Confucian scholars with European mathematics and scientific knowledge. The response of Chinese authorities to the introduction of Western knowledge by this priest ranged from being indifferent to lukewarm. "The Chinese *literati*, fixed in their own conceit, evinced no interest in the West.... Matteo Ricci's great map of the world, which ought to have been known to every educated Chinese, went completely disregarded simply because its origins were Western and therefore despicable."[20] Such a conceited attitude resulted in grave military consequences a few centuries later. "In short then, China, even as late as the mid-nineteenth century had no idea of the power or extent of the forces which were threatening her. Despising her enemies and convinced of her own invulnerability, she took no steps to defend herself."[21] At the same time, Matteo Ricci learned the Chinese language and culture to the extent that he could engage in profound conversations with Confucian scholars. As a result, Ricci was able to translate major Chinese classics into Latin. He eventually died in his adoptive country, and the Chinese emperor allowed his body to be buried in Beijing.

Matteo Ricci was a one-way missionary to China where he served twenty-eight years; however, he was not the first Christian missionary to the Middle Kingdom. He found out that other Western Christians, such as Franciscans, had attempted to proselytize the Chinese before him. To his surprise, he came to know the history of much earlier Christian activities by Nestorians belonging to the Church of the East as early as the Tang Dynasty (618–907).[22] Both Catholic and Eastern Orthodox churches regarded the Nestorians as heretic for their differing views on the nature of Christ, among others. Nestorian Christians based their centers in Syria and Persia. From there, the self-supporting Nestorians followed the east-bound Silk Road propagating their teachings to the people of Central Asia and East Asia.

THE SHADOW OF A DECLINING CHINA

China's submission to Europe came at the conclusion of the First Opium War (1839–1842). The Chinese government opposed the supply of opium, an item of imperial prohibition, to the Chinese people by British traders. Through the East India Company, British merchants began promoting Indian opium in China beginning in 1773. When opium supplies began to increase to match the increasing domestic opium addiction, Chinese officials grew alarmed. British traders brought one thousand chests (140,000 pounds or 64 tons) of opium to China in 1773, later forty thousand chests (5,600,000 pounds or 2,553 tons) on the eve of the First Opium War. Each chest was about 140 pounds. In less than seventy years, the British opium supply had increased forty times. It was estimated that about ten million Chinese were addicted to opium at this time.[23] Besides the British, merchants of other countries, including the United States, were involved in the lucrative opium trade. US merchants, for example, supplied about ten thousand chests (1,400,000 pounds or 637 tons) of opium between 1800 and 1839.[24] Realizing the harmful effects of opium addiction and the outflow of silver, the Chinese government confiscated around twenty thousand chests of opium (about 2.66 million pounds or 1,210 tons). Also, Chinese authorities arrested British merchants and sailors who resisted.

The British government took these wholescale confiscations of property as a violation of their sovereignty and dispatched the Royal navy to South China. Equipped with advanced weapon systems, the British navy crushed Chinese forces. At the conclusion of the First Opium War, the two nations signed the Treaty of Nanjing in 1842. China was forced to establish five treaty ports along the South China coast, and Hong Kong was ceded to Great Britain. Robert Trout accuses the British of the opium epidemic in China in connection with their colony of India. "The British seizure of Hong Kong was an aspect of one of the most ugly crimes of the British Empire: the takeover and destruction of India, and the use of India to flood China with opium."[25]

When Qing China was decisively defeated by Great Britain, the Chinese people became angry at their government. They could not believe that the great Middle Kingdom had lost to the navy of a distant country in their own backyard. The defeat magnified the Han-Chinese resentment and distrust of the Qing government that had been established by the Manchurians. As the Han people began to sense a weakening of Qing rule, they began to rebel against the central government in Beijing. A variety of domestic instabilities began to set in, especially in the southern region of China where European presence was more prevalent.

The Taiping Rebellion was one such upheaval. Not long after the First Opium War, the rebellion started in 1850 in the southern region of China.

Figure 1.2. Western Powers over China. *Campwillowlake © iStock*

Hong Xiuquan, the leader, conceived of a new kingdom he called the Taiping Heavenly Kingdom. He claimed to be the younger brother of Jesus. Inspired by Christianity, Hong's policies were quite radical by the standards of nineteenth-century China. He called for an equal share of wealth and rights for women, among others. His followers refused to wear the long queue (or pig tail), a sign of loyalty to Qing rule. The many battles between rebel soldiers and Qing troops claimed up to twenty million lives.[26] The destructive effects of the rebellion were widely felt beyond the southern region of China. Many warlords and marauding thieves plundered villages and towns while the struggling Qing government in Beijing tried for over a decade to quell the Taiping rebellion. The state of politics and the economy were in disarray, and many Chinese were uprooted and displaced. Desperate Chinese looked for an outlet to escape from poverty and domestic instability.

The Second Opium War (1856–1860) broke out fifteen years after the first. It was often called the Arrow War because Chinese authorities had removed the British flag from the ship *Arrow* for its alleged acts of piracy. This seemingly minor incident triggered the Second Opium War. In fact, it was merely an excuse for Great Britain to go to war as it had a hidden agenda: the renegotiation of the Nanjing Treaty that had been signed in 1842 at the end of the First Opium War. Among other concessions, the British government demanded more Chinese ports to be opened to Western trade. Other demands included the legalization of the opium trade, an exemption of tariffs, the establishment of a British embassy in Beijing, and so on. In the Second Opium War, Great Britain was allied with France and the United States. Once again defeated, China was forced to legalize the opium trade, to open more ports to the West, to permit residences of Western ambassadors in Beijing, to allow Westerners to travel throughout China, and to grant Christians full civil rights and the freedom to evangelize.[27]

In particular, the British demanded that China allow British ships to carry Chinese laborers to the Americas as they wanted to join the lucrative transportation business of Chinese migrants. In this regard, they were more than ten years behind their Spanish counterparts. The British colony of Hong Kong would soon become one of the major ports of embarking Chinese workers to the Americas and other regions of the world for many decades to come. Under the pressure, the Chinese government opened up twelve major treaty ports along the south coast. These ports were used to send Chinese laborers to various destinations in North and South America.

At the same time, Chinese emigration laws were changed in favor of Western recruitment efforts for overseas labor needs. Easy access to numerous treaty ports and an abundant Chinese labor pool set the stage for massive laborer flows out of China. The logistics and financing of such a large-scale international operation were coordinated by recruitment firms, ship owners, banks, and insurance companies in New York, Boston, London, Paris, Amsterdam, Liverpool, and other major European cities.

The British also included certain trivial demands in the Tianjin Treaty at the conclusion of the Second Opium War. They insisted that the Chinese should stop two humiliating practices. The first demand was for Chinese officials not to use the word "barbarian" when referring to Westerners. In a similar vein, ordinary Chinese commonly called Westerners "foreign devils." Such verbal expressions reflected Chinese disdain and resentment toward Western invaders. Another demand made of the Qing government was to waive the requirement of kowtowing at the emperor's court in Beijing. For centuries, Kings or their envoys from tributary states in Asia kowtowed to the Chinese emperor as a sign of reverence and loyalty to their suzerain state. Yet the Qing court required European envoys to perform the strange ritual when they had an audience with the Chinese emperor. These foreign emissaries prostrated themselves by kneeling down and touching the court floor three times with their foreheads. After the first set, they would stand up only to repeat this procedure a second and a third time. At the end of this ritual performance, it became very clear who was dominant and who was submissive. A reluctant Chinese concession to the Europeans regarding the kowtow ritual[28] symbolized a change in power positions after the two Opium Wars.

Defeat in these two wars and widespread rebellion and lawlessness devastated the region of South China. On top of domestic and international political disturbance and economic woes, the region experienced frequent famines. Many unemployed and displaced Chinese were desperate and looking for opportunities to work. The majority of them were rural tenant peasants and urban day laborers. Taking advantage of the chaotic domestic situation in China, a triumphant West was able to extract cheap and abundant Chinese labor for agriculture, mining, and construction in the Americas.

Following defeats in the two Opium Wars and later in the Sino-Japan War (1894–1895), China faced another humiliation by the Western powers during the Boxer Rebellion (1899–1901). This was an anti-foreign and anti-Christian movement started in the Shandong region in northern China. When the rebels and some Chinese troops sieged the foreign legation zone in Beijing for almost two months, eight nations formed an alliance. They were America, Austro-Hungary, Great Britain, France, Germany, Italy, Japan, and Russia. The allied army of around twenty thousand broke the siege and rescued foreigners and Chinese Christians who sought refuge in the legation quarter. After 120,000 deaths, of which 250 were foreigners, and a huge sum of indemnity (the equivalent of about one billion dollars in 2020) to the eight nations,[29] China could not overcome the devastating effects of the defeats. China's repeated defeats by the foreign powers had a domino effect upon the much smaller neighboring nations of Japan and Korea. While Western nations gained confidence in dealing with China, other Asian rulers developed a strong suspicion and fear of the West. Both Japan and Korea had tried to resist Western demands for trade and other interactions, but they could withstand Western pressure only for so long.

Superior Western military power broke the will of Japanese and Korean rulers and their countries were forcibly opened. Another long-term effect of the defeats in the hands of foreign nations was the eventual demise of the Qing Dynasty. The last Chinese emperor, Puyi, was dethroned in 1911. He was only three years old when he became emperor in 1908 and six when the dynasty was abolished.

JAPAN AND THE WEST

A few Europeans were vaguely aware of the existence of Japan through Marco Polo. The Italian traveler had mentioned a country named Zipangu (the land of gold) in the book penned by his prison mate in Genoa, which had been circulating since the fourteenth century. Other than this brief reference, the archipelago country had remained obscure and overshadowed by China for centuries. In fact, no European had set out solely to explore Japan. Unlike China, which was accessible from both land and sea, Japan was accessible

Figure 1.3. Map of East Asia. *PeterHermesFurian © iStock*

only by sea. Most early European merchant ships sailed to Macao or Hong Kong, and Japan was still quite far from there. The straight-line distance from Hong Kong to Tokyo is about 1,800 miles (2,900 km), and from Hong Kong to Fukuoka, the first major Japanese harbor in the south, is still 1,300 miles (2,030 km). In the days of voyage by sail, it was a considerable distance.

When Europeans discovered Japan, it was by accident. In 1543, a few Portuguese shipwrecked crews stepped onto a Japanese island without knowing where they were.[30] More than anything else, the Portuguese sailors introduced the crude long rifle, the arquebus, to Japan. It was operated by a matchlock, and this new military technology, copied by the Japanese, changed the military dynamic of the region. Not long after this accidental contact, a Portuguese Jesuit missionary, Francis Xavier, arrived in Kyushu Island in 1549. His followers began to propagate the teachings of Christianity. Many Japanese thought that the Catholic version of Christianity was quite similar to Buddhism, at least in outward appearance. A considerable number of Japanese converted to the new Western religion.

The increasing presence of foreigners and their popularity made the then Shogun (the military ruler of Japan), Toyotomi Hideyoshi,[31] uneasy. In 1587, he decided to expel foreign missionaries and to persecute Japanese Christians. Thousands of Japanese Catholics who refused to repudiate their new religion were martyred. In spite of his determination to eradicate Catholicism in the land of Buddhism, Toyotomi Hideyoshi permitted European traders to remain in Japan and left the southern port of Nagasaki open. Eventually, all European traders were expelled by 1640, with one exception: Dutch traders who could carry on limited trade in Nagasaki harbor.[32] During an isolation of more than two hundred years, the Tokugawa military rulers allowed the import of non-religious books and their translation into Japanese. The major source of Western knowledge was the Netherlands to the point that Western learning in Japan was synonymous with Dutch learning at one time.

America's access to Japan took place toward the end of the eighteenth century. According to an unofficial claim, in 1791 the American explorer John Kendrick sailed to Japan with two ships and stayed on Kii Oshima island for eleven days.[33] Many years later, the US government sent Commander James Biddle with two ships to Japan in 1846 to open trade with the island nation, but the Japanese government refused to negotiate. Two years later, Captain James Glynn sailed to Nagasaki for the same purpose, and this time Japan was open to a trade negotiation. The encouraged Glynn suggested that the US Congress use a show of force to encourage a trade treaty with Japan.[34] Commodore Matthew Perry subsequently led his American black fleet into Edo (Tokyo) Bay in 1853. After this show of American naval power, he left with a warning that he would return. When Perry returned in March of the following year, Japan agreed to comply with the American trade demands. Japanese leaders realized the futility of resisting America as they had learned the might of Western military power in the Chinese Opium Wars. Commodore Perry signed the first US-Japan treaty, the Kanagawa Treaty, on March 31, 1854. The treaty assured mutual peace between the two nations and opening of Shimoda and Hakodate for trade. Japan would provide any assistance to shipwrecked American sailors and services to

American ships. The first American consulate in Japan would be established in Shimoda.[35]

In return, the shogun dispatched a special Japanese delegation to the United States in January 1860 aboard Kanrin Maru, Japan's first screw-driven steam warship. Japan established the first embassy in the United States and ended the long isolation of the Tokugawa rule. Eventually, this transition led to the Meiji Reform in 1868. Japan began to modernize itself by Westernizing almost every aspect of its society. Unlike China, Japan aggressively transformed its institutions and strove to emulate the West. Not long after, the Japanese government responded to the labor needs of countries in the Americas. After some time had passed, the government even actively promoted overseas immigration to establish agricultural colonies in some Latin American countries. Under tremendous population pressure, the Japanese government decided to reduce its population through emigration. The United States was thus indirectly responsible for ending the military rule of the Shogunate that had lasted about seven hundred years. This resulted in the dissolution of the Samurai (warrior) class and the reinstatement of the emperor as a central figure in the Japanese power structure.

When Japan defeated China in Sino-Japan War in 1895, then Russia in Russo-Japan War in 1905, the latter became Japan's first Western victim. The defeat of Russia made Western nations uneasy about the rapidly advancing nation. Japan then inflicted a serious wound upon the United States when it attacked Pearl Harbor in 1941. Much of the Japanese tragedies in the Americas retold in this book stemmed from this provocation.

KOREA AND THE WEST

On a map of Asia, the small Korean peninsula looks like a dangling rabbit at the bottom of the east end of China. This eastern part of China used to be Manchuria, an outlying region of northeast China. In the seventeenth century, the Manchurians conquered China (Ming Dynasty) and established the Qing Dynasty in 1644. Korea shares its northern border with China and Russia, and Japan lies to Korea's east and south across a narrow sea. The tiny peninsular nation appears to be besieged by larger and more powerful neighboring countries: China, Japan, and Russia. The destiny of modern Korean has been affected by its geography.

Instead of using China and Japan as windows to the outside world, the hermit kingdom used its neighbors as shields from the West. Korea's last Yi Dynasty, founded on Confucianism, was quite content with being left alone. The hermit kingdom's name, Chosun, means "morning calm," and domestic tranquility was sought by all means. The tributary state of Korea was considerably removed from the center of action in the suzerain state of China.

Western visitors to China hardly paid any attention to the small, obscure hermit kingdom on China's eastern edge.

The first European stepped on the soil of Korea in the midst of the Japanese invasion of that country in 1593. He was a Spanish Jesuit priest by the name of Gregorio de Cespedes[36] who followed the Japanese forces commanded by the Christian Daimyo, General Konishi Yukinaga. There is no record of his missionary work among civilian Koreans let alone any conversions. Cespedes, however, did have contacts with Koreans captured by the Japanese forces. After the Jesuit priest, other Europeans discovered Korea by accident under unusual circumstances.

Less than forty years later, a Chinese junk carrying Dutch privateers working for Dutch East India Company based in Jakarta, Indonesia, was severely battered by a storm, and the sailors drifted to Korea's southernmost inhabited island, Jeju. The Chinese crew overpowered the outnumbered Dutch privateers and handed them over to Korean authorities. It was in 1627. Of the known three Dutch survivors, Jan Weltvree, Dirk Gijsbertsj, and Jan Verbaest, only Jan Weltvree etched his name into Korean history. He married a Korean woman and had two children. Years later, he helped other Dutch compatriots who encountered a similar situation at sea. In 1653, a group of 36 Dutch sailors was shipwrecked and managed to land on the same island. The survivors were immediately taken to the capital city, Seoul. After thirteen years in Korea, eight of them managed to escape to Japan. From there, they returned to the Netherlands. One of them, Handrik Hamel, introduced the hermit kingdom to the West through his book, *Hamel's Journal and a Description of the Kingdom of Korea, 1653–1666*.[37] By the middle of the nineteenth century, more Western ships had begun to appear on the horizon, in Korean seas to the east, south, and west. The first Western official to visit Korea was Russian Vice Admiral Evfimi V. Putiatin in 1854. At that time, Russia was expanding its control over Siberia, which bordered a tiny portion of the northeastern end of Korea.

Early on, some Koreans were exposed to the teachings of the Catholic faith. A number of learned Koreans were able to contact Catholic priests in Beijing and accept their message. These converted Korean Catholics, including some prominent figures, began to share their Western learning with enthusiasm. Thousands of Koreans responded to the appeal of the new religion. As a result, the first Korean Catholic church was established in 1784. Fearing the spread of foreign ideas, the Korean king declared an anti-Catholic edict the following year. To help Korean Catholics in distress, a handful of European Catholic priests managed to enter Korea. Unlike the shipwrecked Dutch sailors, these priests were the first Westerners who came to Korea with a clearly defined mission. Eventually, Korea became a Catholic diocese in 1836, and three French missionaries arrived in Korea in the same year.[38] By

1850, there were 11,000 Korean Catholics, and the number of Catholics had more than doubled to 23,000 in fifteen years.[39]

Around this time, the Russian Czar demanded that Korea should open itself up for trade. Korean Catholics, who were being persecuted, suggested that the Korean government should seek French aid in countering this Russian threat. The Catholics hoped to receive help from the French government by using a political pretext. However, the French government failed to meet the expectations of the Korean Catholics. In the meantime, the Korean government feared the increasing popularity of Catholicism in a staunch Confucian country. In 1866, the government massacred about eight thousand Korean Catholics,[40] including nine French priests. Other priests in hiding fled and reported the massacre to the French Minister in China. In response, the French dispatched a fleet of gunboats to the Western coast, near the Korean capital of Seoul. For two months, French troops inflicted heavy losses on Korean lives and destroyed many coastal defensive structures. Nonetheless, they could not advance to the capital. This stalemate gave confidence to the Korean government in dealing with a Western military.

In the same year, 1866, a heavily armed American merchant ship, the General Sherman, sailed to Korea for trade. Its destiny was Chemulpo (today's Inchon) not far from Seoul, but the wind and sea currents pushed the ship to the north, near Pyongyang (today's capital of North Korea). Then the merchant ship ran into a sandbank and became immobilized. The American crew angered the local people by stealing food and kidnapping women. Also, a Scottish missionary on board tried to convert the local people. Angry Koreans attacked the ship and killed everyone aboard.[41] The American Minister to China, Frederick F. Low, demanded an apology and compensation from the Korean government, but the latter refused to comply with American demands. Perhaps they figured that America would be the same as the French, who had failed to advance to the capital. In June 1871, an American expeditionary force was sent to Korea under Asiatic Fleet Commander Admiral John Rodgers. The US marines launched an attack on Korean military bases in Kangwha Island, about thirty miles (50 km) to the west of Seoul. The Korean soldiers fought the US marines, but they could not overcome the latter's superior military power. In the end, all but twenty wounded Korean soldiers died in the battle. The Americans suffered minimal losses: three dead and ten injured.[42] The Americans then tried to reach Seoul by sailing up the Han River, but they met fierce resistance from Korean soldiers. When the Korean government refused to negotiate, the American fleet left for China. The United States continued to pursue both trade and diplomatic relations with Korea.

To change the mind of the stubborn Korean government, the US used both Japanese and Chinese mediators, but these initial diplomatic efforts failed to change the situation. Eventually, through the mediation of Li Hung-

Chang of China, Commodore Shufeldt succeeded in signing the Treaty of Chemulpo in May 1882. This Treaty of Amity and Commerce between Korea and the United States gave America the advantages of low tariffs and extraterritoriality. It was ironic that the US Congress passed the Chinese Exclusion Act in the same year. The American government tried to exclude Chinese workers while pursuing diplomatic relations with China's neighbor, the small hermit kingdom. The first American Minister to Korea, Lucius H. Foote, arrived in Seoul in May 1883.[43] In less than two years, Great Britain and Germany signed a similar treaty with Korea in November 1883. In the following year, Italy and Russia reached similar agreements. France was the last major European power to sign a treaty with Korea, in June 1886.

The first American missionary to Korea, Horace Allen, arrived in 1884, and many more followed. Slowly and steadily, the one-time insulated hermit kingdom opened to the West. Within twenty years of the treaty between Korea and the United States, the Korean government had sent its first immigrant group to the American territory of Hawaii in 1903. In order to provide a historical backdrop of East Asian immigration to the Americas, this brief sketch of Western encroachment into China, Japan, and Korea has been presented. The tragic stories of early East Asian immigrants to the Americas can be better understood in the context of international power dynamics in the modern age. In short, it was a time of Western dominance and Eastern submission.

FIRST EAST ASIANS TO THE WEST

For a long time, the Chinese believed that they were the center of the world. The people of the Middle Kingdom thought that they knew about everything and had everything they needed. Their worldview was concentric: the further from the center (Beijing), the less civilized. Thus, they regarded Europeans as barbarians or worse. Such a Sinocentric perspective resulted in no interest or curiosity about the barbaric West. Moreover, they wanted to preserve internal harmony and equilibrium by all means necessary by rejecting any foreign ideas or practices that might disturb the stability of their society. The first European encounters with East Asians in their own lands led to a scary view of Asians. The invading Mongolian armies in the thirteenth century had frightened many in Eastern Europe. Memories of the ruthless and destructive Mongols lingered a long time in the minds of Europeans.

Efforts to make diplomatic contacts came much earlier when Chinese attempted to send an envoy to Europe in the first century AD during the Han Dynasty. The Chinese general, Ban Chao, sent his envoy, Gan Ying,[44] to Rome, which they called Da Qin. Gan Ying succeeded in reaching the region of Persian Gulf and Mesopotamia in 97 AD, but he was dissuaded to change his plan to sail to Rome for the reason of danger and travel time. More than a thousand years later, Arghun,[45] the Mongolian ruler of the Ilkhanate, a sector of the Mongol empire that covered the wider region of Middle East including Iran and Turkey sent an envoy to Western Europe during the seventh campaign of Christian Crusade (1248–1254) led by Louis IX of France. Arghun wanted to form an alliance with some European kingdoms against the threat of Muslims in the region. The appointed envoy, Rabban Bar Sauma, had an audience with the rulers of Byzantium, a few Italian republics, France, England, and the Pope in 1287 and 1288.[46] The ambassador, however, was a Turkic Chinese belonging to a Nestorian Christian community in China. Until much later time, Europeans had not seen a Han Chinese from China proper.

When Catholic converts from Japan and China began to tour Spain, Portugal, Italy, England, and France, it was the first time in more than three hundred years that Europeans encountered East Asians other than Mongols. The Catholic missionaries in Japan and China played key roles in arranging for European tours for their Asian converts. With accompanying priests, these Asian Christians were introduced to European kings, aristocrats, scholars, church leaders, and congregations. A few even had an audience with the Pope in Rome. The first East Asian visitors to Europe were Japanese, a group consisting of four noblemen[47] who arrived in Spain in August 1584. They were chosen for this trip by Japanese Christian daimyos, local feudal lords under the authority of the shogun. After seven years of touring in Europe, they returned to Japan in July 1590. The four noblemen were ordained into the Jesuit priesthood upon their arrival home. The Chinese visited Europe about one hundred years later than the Japanese. In 1682, two converted Chinese Catholics arrived in Portugal. The Chinese visitors were under the guidance of a Jesuit priest, Philippe Couplet, who had worked in China for almost thirty years. Couplet was sent back to Rome to obtain papal permission for the liturgy to be performed in Chinese during mass. Only one of the two visiting Chinese Catholics is known, Michael Shen Fu-Tsung.[48] According to records, he died in today's Mozambique in 1691 on his way back to China.

Records show that the Portuguese merchants in Japan engaged in slave trade during the sixteenth and seventeenth centuries. They took Japanese men and women to Macao, where they were resold to India and Portugal, among other locations. Women were sold as sex slaves or concubines. The Asian slave group included Chinese and some former Korean prisoners-of-war captured during the Japanese invasion of Korea (1592–1598). Apparently the Portuguese in Lisbon preferred Asian slaves to African slaves for their perceived intelligence and diligence.[49] The slave trade angered the Japanese rulers, who were already disturbed by the rebellion of some Japanese Christians backed by Western missionaries. They had expelled the Westerners and implemented the lock-down policy (sakogu) for more than two hundred years (1641–1854), until the US navy ships appeared.

Another incidental story took place during the Spanish trade between Manila and the New World. A British explorer and privateer, Thomas Cavendish, seized a Spanish galleon ship and took two Japanese crewmen in 1587. In the following year, Cavendish arrived in London with these two Japanese men,[50] during a time when the four Japanese nobles were in the midst of their Europe tour under the guidance of a Jesuit priest.

Formal diplomatic contacts between Asian and Western governments came much later than religious exchanges. The first Chinese Foreign Office, Zongli Yamen, was established in 1861. Zongli Yamen in Chinese meant the Office in Charge of Affairs of All Nations. It came into existence as a governmental office only after the Second Opium War, which ended in 1860. The establishment of the foreign office was a forced response to the increased complexity of international relations for China. "[T]he Chinese regarded the sending of diplomatic representatives abroad as an act of degradation, weakness, and submission, to be undertaken only as a last resort."[51] Having regarded itself as the center of the world, the Middle Kingdom had no interest in paying attention to the "barbarian" affairs of foreign nations in the West. Reluctantly, the Chinese government dispatched the first resident minister abroad in 1876, "as a result of considerable pressure from the British government."[52] Any Chinese who had to deal with foreigners risked being labeled as "a devil's slave." Therefore, assignments to Zongli Yamen were considered a "disgrace and insult"[53] by most Chinese government officials.

The first Korean visit to the West did not take place until the late nineteenth century, almost three hundred years after the Japanese and two hundred years after the Chinese. The small, obscure hermit kingdom as a tributary state to China did not get much attention from Europeans until the Americans arrived on the scene. The first Korean visit to the West was for a political purpose. The Korean government initiated the first overseas trip to the United States for ten high-ranking government officials, arriving in America in 1883 following the first treaty between Korea and the United States in the previous year. The trip was an attempt to counterbalance the growing influence of China, Japan, and Russia upon the strategically important Korean peninsula. In the nineteenth century, the United States was an emerging Pacific power without an expressed interest in territorial gains in the region of East Asia. Hence, Korea turned to the United States as a neutral party. When the US president, Chester Arthur, received the Korean mission, he did not know how to react to the kowtowing performed by the Korean delegates,[54] who were simply repeating what they had done to the Chinese emperors for centuries. Some of these delegates extended their tour of the West by sailing to Europe, so it is safe to assume that a few Koreans traveled around the world in the mid-1880s. An official Korean presence was arranged in Europe in July 1901 when the first Korean Consul opened in London.

The initial East Asian visits to Europe in the sixteenth and seventeenth centuries might never have happened without the help of Catholic missionaries. In contrast, early European visits to China occurred without any help from Asia. Only the political and commercial interests, sense of religious mission, or cultural curiosity had impelled these early European travelers to venture into East Asia. The mutual discovery of the East and the West might be characterized by an active search for Asia by Europeans and a passive Asian response to Europe.

YELLOW PERIL

Since the thirteenth-century Mongolian invasions of Central Asia and much of Eastern Europe, including Poland, Hungary, Russia, and the Ukraine, Europeans had developed a dreadful fear of East Asians. The highly disciplined Mongol armies were swift and merciless in conquering many European principalities. The loss of human life and the physical destruction of cities and towns by the invading Mongols were overwhelming. The Europeans were traumatized by these strange people from a faraway land in the East, and the invasions had left indelible nightmarish memories among Europeans for many generations. Six centuries later, the latent fear of the conquering Mongolians surfaced in the form of "yellow peril," "yellow terror," or "Asiatic threat" in the United States and other Western nations. This fear had happened when East Asians, especially Chinese, began to immigrate in large numbers to newly established nations, including the United States, Canada, Australia, and New Zealand.

The term "yellow peril" was used by Kaiser Wilhelm II of Germany in 1895.[55] It was the year when Imperial Japan defeated China in the Sino-Japan War (August 1, 1894–April 17, 1895), one that lasted less than ten months. Ten years later, Japan defeated another great power, Russia, in the Russo-Japan War (February 8, 1904–September 5, 1905). All of a sudden, Japan appeared to pose a threat to the West as a strong military power. In particular, Japan's defeat of Russia, one of the major European nations, sent chills throughout the West. Japan's defeat of China had serious political implications mainly in Asia, but its military victory over Russia had far wider repercussions in the West.

Between these two wars, the region was in continual turmoil. China experienced the Boxer Rebellion (Yihetuan Movement). This anti-Western movement was focused against foreign occupation, colonialism, and Christianity. Many Chinese resented a Western presence in the form of extraterritorialities, leased territories, and the propagation of Christianity. Angry Chinese mobs targeted not only foreigners but also fellow Christian countrymen whom the rioters regarded as products of Westernization. Angry Chinese killed thousands of Chinese Christians. Only the allied armies of eight Western nations, including the United States and Great Britain, eventually quelled the rebellion. People in the West, who followed the tense situation in the capital of China, developed a fear of the Chinese.

When increasing numbers of Chinese and other Asian immigrants competed for jobs in their resident countries in the Americas, especially in the United States, old memories of the Mongolian invasions of Europe centuries ago were triggered. Unlike the invading Mongolian soldiers in Europe, the nineteenth-century Chinese came as humble laborers. However, xenophobia resulted in an intense resentment toward these Asian migrant workers. In addition, the fear of "yellow peril" had a sexual connotation. As most Chinese came as single sojourners, the gender ratio was extremely skewed, with twenty or thirty men to one female[56] in many Chinese communities in the Americas. This gender imbalance roused the fear of many white men and women. Newspaper cartoons of the nineteenth and early twentieth centuries depicted such fears by portraying Chinese men as rapists of white women. And many white men saw themselves as defenders of white women from filthy, heathen Asian men. The legal prohibition of intermarriage between Asian men and Caucasian women in some states of America reflected this prevailing white fear.[57] Whether the manifestation of "yellow peril" was explicit or implicit, public or private, it affected relationships between Asian immigrants and the residents of host countries. It ranged from passive fear to open hostility directed toward East Asian immigrants.

REFLECTIONS

Over time, European perceptions of China had changed as the West's economic and military power grew. "In sixteenth and seventeenth-century European writings, references to Chinese as white predominated, but as the eighteenth century progressed, there was an increase in the description of Chinese as nonwhite or yellow. . . . Europeans' military and economic ascendancy over other people, an ascendancy that became more pronounced during the seventeenth and eighteenth centuries."[58] Napoleon Bonaparte (1769–1821), the nineteenth-century French Emperor, compared China to a sleeping lion in his time and warned not to wake her up lest the world be unsettled by an alert China. If he had lived long enough to witness the outcomes of the Opium Wars in 1842 and 1860, however, he might have called China a seriously wounded lion, as the country was thoroughly humiliated by her European enemies. In less than thirty years following the Second Opium War, China was defeated by Japan in the Sino-Japan War in 1895, which led to the eventual demise of its last Qing Dynasty in 1911.

During the first half of the twentieth century, other external forces reshaped China: Japanese Imperialism and Marxism, the latter rooted in China's neighbor, Russia. As a result, China was broken into different political entities: Republic of China on the mainland, the short-lived Manchukuo (1932–1945) in Manchuria, and finally People's Republic of China on the mainland (1949–present). In the twenty-first century, however, China has transformed into a different nation, to say the least. As a superpower, it is almost on par with the United States in many areas. The most populous country with the second largest economy in the world may become again a Middle (or Center) Kingdom of the world in the not so distant future. Its share of the global economy is around 15 percent and growing. This mark is a far cry from the mere 3 percent when it opened up to the outside world in the early part of the 1980s. By the 2030s, the Chinese economy might be the largest in the world, according to some projections.

The other East Asian nations, Japan and Korea, have also advanced in spite of the devastating effects of the wars of the twentieth century: the Pacific War (or World War II, 1941–1945) and the Korean War (1950–1953). One tangible indicator of a nation's political and economic advancement is its ability to host Olympic games. In the vast continent of Asia, with more than fifty nations, only three have hosted Olympics games: Japan, four times, including the summer games postponed to 2021 due to COVID-19; Korea, twice; and China, twice, including the winter games scheduled for 2022. Moreover, all three nations have hosted both summer and winter games. The twenty-first century has been called the Asian century or the Pacific century. The center of global power has been steadily shifting in the direction of Asia, reaching East Asia first. The region's impressive progress so far can be attributed to a modernization process that has often been equated with Westernization. Because of America's dominance in the twentieth century, especially in science and technology, the Westernization of Asia has been largely through interactions with America.

This may change, however. There is an emerging counter-trend in some developing countries in Africa, Asia, and other less developed regions. Many developing countries are searching for a different socioeconomic developmental model. The West in general, and America in particular, are not the models that these countries want to emulate. Instead, some of them turn to China, Japan, or Korea for their future development. Malaysia's Look East Policy is one such example.[59] In 1981, the Malaysian government decided to study Japan and Korea as models for its own socioeconomic progress. Malaysian students and officials sponsored by the government went to these two nations to learn how they had advanced so rapidly. At the same time, the Malaysian government adopted the Buy British Last policy. Although this negative policy may have reflected a lingering anti-British sentiment by a former colony, the Malaysian government assumed that goods and services provided by advanced Asian countries would be as good as any of those from Western countries, including the United Kingdom.

Having joined the World Trade Organization (WTO) in 2001, China, with its growing economic power, has initiated a number of major international projects. The first is the One Road, One Belt project. It is often called the Silk Road of the twenty-first century, connecting countries, regions, oceans, and continents. Another is the Asian Infrastructure Investment Bank (AIIB), headquartered in Beijing. Almost all major countries of the world have joined the AIIB, including Australia, Brazil, Germany, France, United Kingdom, and Canada among other Western nations. It should be noted that both Japan and the United States have not joined the AIIB yet. China's one hundred years of humiliation and defeat by the West has turned out to be a mere dent in the long history of China in particular and East Asia in general. Since 2012, the new political leadership of China has called for the Great Rejuvenation of the Chinese Nation and the Great Revival of the Chinese People. Here both "rejuvenation" and "revival" refer to a glorious old China before the encroachment of the West. China's target dates in achieving its national goals are 2021 and 2049, respectively. The former is the one hundredth anniversary of the establishment of the Chinese Communist Party in 1921 and the latter is the centennial of the establishment of the People's Republic of China in 1949. The Chinese leadership wants to see the year 2050 as a turning-point for its leadership role in the world community. It is the first

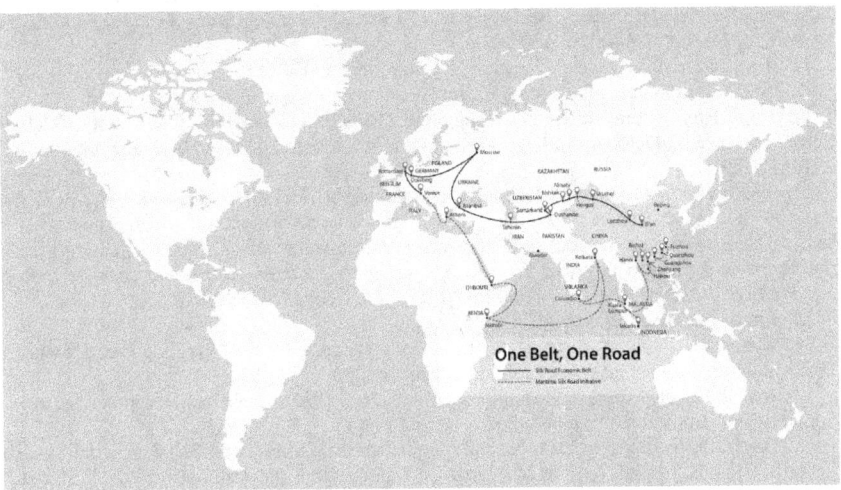

Figure 1.4. New Silk Road: One Belt, One Road. *hakule © iStock*

year of the People's Republic of China's second century. It remains to be seen whether the world is once again going to evolve around a rejuvenated and revived Middle Kingdom. Such a national ambition to be the greatest power in the world, however, has been challenged in all fronts by the United States and its allies. In response to China's aggressive military build-up in South China Sea, India, Australia, Japan, and the United States have formed a new military alliance.

NOTES

1. Peter Frankopan, *The Silk Road: A New History of the World* (New York: Vantage Books, 2015), 168–70.
2. Ibid., 217.
3. The Samurai Archives, "Gregorio de Cespedes," accessed February 2, 2020, https://wiki.samurai-archieves.com/index.phd?title=Gregorious_de_Cespedes.
4. The United States paid about fifteen million dollars for the purchase of the Louisiana Territory. The size of the territory was 828,000 square miles that included present-day fifteen states in the middle part of America, west of the Mississippi River.
5. At the conclusion of the Mexican-American War in 1848, the United States paid fifteen million dollars to Mexico in exchange for Arizona, California, a part of Colorado, a half of New Mexico, Utah, and a part of Wyoming. It was according to the Treaty of Guadalupe Hidalgo signed by the United States and Mexico on February 2, 1848.
6. D. E. Mungello, *The Great Encounter of China and the West, 1500–1800* (New York: Rowman & Littlefield, 2009), 98.
7. Ibid., 113–18.
8. Social Darwinism was proposed by Herbert Spencer (1820–1903), a British sociologist who was a contemporary of Charles Darwin (1809–1882).
9. Kathleen Lopez, *Chinese Cubans: A Transnational History* (Chapel Hill: The University of North Carolina Press, 2013), 21–23.
10. From Hong Kong (1854–1880) and Macao (1851–1874), 177,426 Chinese labor recruits went to the United States, 127,445 to Cuba, and 82,715 to Peru, respectively. See Arnold J. Meagher, *The Coolie Trade: The Traffic of Chinese Laborers to Latin America 1847–1874* (Arnold J. Meagher: 2008), 103 and 121.
11. The Samurai Archives, "Japanese Immigration to Hawaii," accessed May 20, 2020, https://wiki.samurai-archives.com/index.php?title=Japanese_immigration_to_Hawaii.
12. Consulate General of Japan in Honolulu, "King Kalakaua's 180th Birthday Celebration," accessed October 19, 2020, https://www.honolulu.us.emb-japan.go.jp/itpr_en/20161116.html.
13. The Samurai Archives, "Japanese Immigration to Hawaii," accessed May 20 2020, https://wiki.samurai-archives.com/index.php?title=Japanese_immigration_to_Hawaii.
14. The approximate figure is based on American, Canadian, and Latin American residents. See for Latin American figure in Won K. Yoon, *Global Pulls on the Korean Communities in Sao Paulo and Buenos Aires* (Lanham, MD: Lexington Books, 2015), 24.
15. Frankopan, *The Silk Road*, 21.
16. See Nestor Palugod Enriquez, "Manila Galleon Trade 1573–1811," accessed December 10, 2014. chttp://www.philippines.tripod.com/galleon.html.
17. Johana Hecht, "The Manila Galleon Trade (1565–1815)," accessed December 10, 2014, http://www.metmuseum.org/ toah/hd/mgtr/hd_mgtr.htm.
18. "In 1606, there were 3,000 Japanese colonists in Manila, and 15,000 in Dilao, which included Manila." James L. Tigner, "Japanese Immigration into Latin America: A Survey." *Journal of Interamerican Studies and World Affairs* 23, no. 4 (1981): 457–82.
19. "In 1635, a group of Spanish barbers in Mexico city complained about excessive competition from Chinese barbers in that colonial capital city. They petitioned the viceroy to remove

these bothersome Asian barbers to special quarters on the outskirts of town so that they, the Spaniards, would not have to compete with the chinos de Manila for business." Quoted from Lynn Pan, *The Encyclopedia of the Chinese Overseas* (Singapore: Archipelago Press, 2000), 256.

20. J. D. Frodsham, *The First Chinese Embassy to the West: The Journal of Kuo Sung-Tao, Liu His-Hung, and Chang Te-Yi* (Oxford: Claredon Press, 1974), xx.

21. Ibid., xxiii.

22. Frankopan, *The Silk Road*, 52–53.

23. Peter C. Perdue, "The First Opium War: The Anglo-Chinese War of 1839–1842," accessed July 31, 2017, https://ocw.mit.edu/ans7870/21f/21f.027/opium_wars_01/ow1_essay01.html.

24. Ibid.

25. Robert Trout in *Brainy Quote*, accessed July 19, 2017, https://www.brainyquote.com/quotes/robert_trout_279512.

26. Odd Arne Westad, *Restless Empire: China and the World Since 1750* (New York: Basic Books, 2012), 48.

27. Paul H. Clyde and Burton F. Beers. *The Far East: A History of Western Impacts and Eastern Response, 1830–1975* (Englewood Cliffs, NJ: 1975), 99–100.

28. Ibid., 99.

29. Westad, *Restless Empire*, 126–29.

30. Clyde and Beers. *The Far East*, 63.

31. Ibid., 64.

32. Ibid., 65.

33. RevWarTalk, "John Kendrick," accessed January 27, 2020, https://www.revwartalk.com/john-kendrick.

34. Military Wiki, "James Glynn," accessed January 27, 2020, https://military.wikia.org/wiki/James_Glynn.

35. History, "Treaty of Kanagawa signed with Japan," accessed March 1, 2020, https://www.history.com/this-day-in-hisory/treaty-of-kanagawa-signed-with-japan.

36. The Samurai Archives, "Gregorio de Cespedes," accessed February 2, 2020, https://wiki.samurai-archieves.com/index.phd?title=Gregorious_de_Cespedes.

37. Andrew Nam, *Korea: Tradition and Transformation* (Seoul: Hollym Corp., 1988), 126–27.

38. Ibid., 141–42.

39. Ibid., 147.

40. Ibid.

41. Ibid., 148.

42. Ibid., 149.

43. Ibid., 154.

44. Military Wiki, "Gan Ying," accessed March 5, 2020, https://military.wikia.org/wiki/Gan_Ying.

45. Infogalactic, "Arghun," accessed March 5, 2020, https://infogalactic.cominfo/Arghun.

46. Frankopan, *The Silk Road*, 168.

47. *The Japan Times*, "Christian Heritage of Japan," accessed February 7, 2017, https://www.japantimes.co.jp/opinion/2014/08/04/commentary/world-commentary/christian-heritage-japan/.

48. Frodsham, *The First Chinese Embassy to the West*, xxii.

49. *The Japan Times*, "The Rarely, If Ever, Told Story of Japanese Sold as Slaves by Portuguese Traders," accessed February 11, 2020, https://www.japantimes.co.jp/culture/2013/05/26/books/book-reviews/th...-if-ever-told-story--of-japanese-sold-as -slaves-by-portuguese-traders/

50. Ancient History Encyclopedia, "Thomas Cavendish," accessed April 2, 2020, https://www.ancient.eu/Thomas_Cavendish/.

51. Frodsham, *The First Chinese Embassy to the West*, xxv.

52. Ibid., xxiv.

53. Ibid.

54. "The First Koreans Who Met with the American President," (in Korean) accessed August 3, 2016, http://c056.kkk24.kr/bbs/board.php?bo_table=con33&wr_id=158; Park Yong Suk, "The Tragedy of the First Korean Students in the United States," (in Korean) accessed August 3, 2016, http://mijumunha.net/parkyongsuk/board_6/60014.

55. Erika Lee, *The Making of Asia America: A History* (New York: Simon & Schuster Paperbacks, 2015), 123.

56. Between 1900 and 1905, Chinese women admitted to the United States had comprised 0.7 percent in 1900 and 4.5 percent in 1905. See Madeline Y. Hsu, *Dreaming of Gold, Dreaming of Home* (Stanford: Stanford University Press, 2000), 97.

57. Ibid.

58. Mungello, *The Great Encounter of China and the West*, 131.

59. The Mahathir Years, "Look East Policy," accessed October 2, 2020, https://www.mtholyoke.edu/~teh20v/classweb/worldpolitics/LookEast.html.

Chapter Two

A Floating Hell in Devil's Throat

Iguazu Falls, located between Argentina and Brazil, is one of many natural wonders in the Americas. It is many times larger than Niagara Falls, at least in the number and variety of cataracts. Nicknamed the Devil's Throat, a huge cascade on the Argentinean side is a breathtaking site. Until one hears the roaring sound of the cascade, no one would suspect any danger as the Iguazu River meanders calmly along its course. In the old days, indigenous people who were unaware of the impending danger leisurely rowed their canoes downstream. By the time they heard the thundering sound, it was too late. For its unfailing capacity to swallow unsuspecting victims, the falls became known as the Devil's Throat. Many early Chinese labor recruits bound for the Americas were like the unsuspecting victims floating into the Devil's Throat. They had no idea what awaited them when they stepped onto the Western transport ships that would carry them to a promised land in the New World. When other Chinese at home began to hear about the fate their fellow countrymen suffered while sailing to the Americas, they began calling the transports "devil ships" or "floating hells."

Thousands of desperate Chinese dreamed of making their fortunes in a faraway land beyond the big ocean. Struggling for existence in their own country, they hoped to improve their lives by venturing into the unknown regions of the distant Americas. The odds of making such a modest dream a reality, however, turned out to be far more challenging and difficult than they had ever imagined. Many perished en route, and far more were unable to endure the horrid working and living conditions.

THE RECRUITMENT OF CHINESE LABORERS

Beginning in the mid-nineteenth century, Western merchant ships from Europe and the Americas anchored in the major treaty ports along China's south coast: Hong Kong, Macao, Guangzhou (Canton), Swatow, and Amoy, among others. These ships would anchor for weeks even months at a time until they had enough Chinese labor recruits to justify the long voyage to distant destinations in the Americas. Unfilled ships would stop at other harbors, ensuring their loads were filled to capacity or near capacity. The majority of the early Chinese labor recruits to Latin America were bound for Cuba in the Atlantic and Peru in the Pacific. At that time, the Spanish colony of Cuba was booming due to a high demand for sugar in Europe. Growing and refining sugarcane, however, required intense labor heretofore provided by African slaves. For this purpose, Cuba alone had brought in almost a million slaves from Africa, its slave trade peaking between 1790 and 1817.[1]

For almost three centuries, Cuba's sugar industry had depended on the free labor of African slaves. In 1806, when Great Britain and the United States banned the slave trade between West Africa and the Americas, Cuba found it difficult to replenish its labor needs. The joint British and American blockade of slave ships greatly reduced the numbers of African slaves coming to Cuba. For instance, "slave imports dropped from 10,000 Africans in 1844 to 1,300 in 1845 and 1,000 in 1847."[2] The Cuban sugar plantation owners were desperate, and in the face of this labor shortage, plantation owners, shipping companies, and capital investors turned to Asia to supplant a diminishing labor force of slaves. They realized that both China and India had a vast pool of cheap labor. While Britain looked to its colony, India, to meet its labor needs in the Caribbean region, other European countries were far more interested in China as a source of cheap labor.

In 1844, only two years after the end of the First Opium War, Cuban sugarcane growers initiated a plan to import Chinese laborers. Pedro Zulueta, the most powerful and wealthy man in Cuba at the time, spearheaded the initiative. He had already made his fortune in slave trade and the sugar industry, so he was an ideal candidate for the task. Once an Asian labor recruitment plan was established, Zulueta opened offices in Havana, London, Manila, Macao, and Amoy. This highly organized international venture resulted in the arrival of the first Chinese coolies in 1847.[3] The first transport ship, the Oquendo, arrived in Havana with 212 Chinese labor recruits. The voyage took 131 days from South China, and each coolie was sold for 170 pesos in Cuba.[4] It was much cheaper to import Chinese coolies as the cost of African slaves continued to rise due to the embargo enforced by the British and American navies. In time, Western companies began to operate labor recruitment offices in major Chinese ports along China's south coast, a joint effort by Western representatives and Chinese brokers and local recruiters.

Westerners provided funds while local Chinese agents did the legwork of recruiting prospective Chinese laborers. These recruiters advertised employment opportunities in the Americas. Their promotional materials described a variety of overseas employment opportunities, ranging from carpentry and masonry to physical labor, thus giving chances to anyone who wished to work. Interested Chinese applicants would sign eight-year labor contracts. Dreaming of returning home with a small fortune, many jobless Chinese were unable to resist the lure of the Americas.

In spite of the prospect of a complete, nearly decade-long uprooting from their native land, many Chinese were willing to bear the pain of leaving loved ones to work in a faraway, strange place. They were desperate enough to ignore the shame and stigma attached to those who would leave their ancestral land. At the time, it was a social taboo for men to leave their parents and ancestral villages to work elsewhere. Emigration was considered a form of banishment. "[T]he Chinese government could hardly expect to find men willing to suffer the humiliation of being sent abroad—a fate considered worse than banishment—without considerable difficulty."[5] Nonetheless, "many . . . had deserted their fatherland in defiance of their government's prohibitory laws and to the neglect of their ancestral tombs, in the sordid pursuit of profit."[6] Although the labor contracts were written in both Chinese and Spanish, many of the recruits were illiterate. Those who could read, however, were often unable to understand the legal implications of the international labor contracts they were signing. As a consequence, these naïve laborers took at face value the promises of the local recruiters, assuming that riches awaited and never guessing the hellish conditions that were in store for them. "Prostrate from opium wars and divided into spheres of European influences, China was unable to protect her citizens from the Occidentals who seduced them to emigrate."[7]

Not all recruits, however, were physical laborers. Some were former army officers, soldiers, civil servants, teachers, craftsmen, and even medical doctors. A few had passed the imperial examination for high government positions,[8] but because of the rapidly deteriorating socioeconomic situation in China, they sought these overseas opportunities. Since Chinese brokers and local recruiters were compensated for the number of laborers recruited, they often employed less than savory tactics to boost their earnings. As a result, some laborers were kidnapped by friends, coworkers, and even relatives. Those residing outside harbor cities were invited, then persuaded, voluntarily or not, to sign labor contracts. Many of the recruits were lured, deceived, or coerced to somewhere in the Americas. Until boarding the transport ships bound for the Americas, Chinese recruits were kept for days or weeks in what they described as prison-like pigpens. To Westerners, these confinement areas were known as "barracoon," the same term used for the temporary confinement of slaves or convicts. As soon as the recruits set foot in these "barracoons," many realized that they were trapped. Cut off from the outside, they were unable to reverse their fate.

The majority of Chinese labor recruits were men in their twenties, thirties, and forties, taken from the lower tiers of Chinese society. Although very small in number, women and children were also recruited, some of the latter being less than ten years of age. At one pigpen, waiting recruits were marked with paint according to their destination. For instance, their bare chests were marked with a C for California, P for Peru, and S for the Sandwich Islands (Hawaii). These markings made it easy to sort and identify the human cargo when boarding different transport ships. Although these paint markings were not as cruel as the iron branding of African slaves, the idea of marking human passengers in this manner revealed the attitude of the recruitment agents toward the Chinese laborers. This particularly inhumane act occurred in the Chinese port of Amoy.[9] Even during a short period of waiting in the "barracoons," some recruits died of disease while others committed suicide. The detention facilities under foreign management, such as those in Macao, were not so different in the mistreatment of Chinese recruits as those under Chinese supervision. "Poor, illiterate Chinese peasants—especially at Macao after the British Passenger Act (1855) drove the "coolie trade" from Hong Kong—were easily duped by foreigners who promised them better lives. . . . Others were simply kidnapped, chained together in the holds of ships that were little different from African slavers."[10]

PERILOUS VOYAGES

Once the captains of the transport ships felt that they had enough human cargo to justify the cost of the long voyage, they lifted anchor and began the perilous journey. In the early years of Chinese labor transport, most ships were bound for Cuba. Some were also headed for countries along the Pacific Coast of the Americas, especially America and Peru.[11] Until the newly invented steam engine was installed on ships, sailings ships, especially clippers, harnessed the wind in their long arduous journeys. The distance between ports in South China and destinations along the Pacific Coast of the Americas was great, and the voyage took many months. Before the Panama Canal bisected the Americas in 1914, ships bound for the Caribbean region and other Atlantic-facing nations, such as Brazil, took the long westward route from China. Instead of risking the treacherous seas and unpredictable weather around Cape Horn on the tip of South America, ships would sail around the southern tip of Africa. Departing from a treaty port in South China, usually Hong Kong or Macao, ships would cross the South China Sea and the Indian Ocean first, then sail around the Cape of Good Hope on the southern tip of Africa. From there, they would sail northward, cutting diagonally across the South Atlantic Ocean. When the Suez Canal opened in October 1869, an alternative route became available. After sailing along the coast of the Asian continent, ships would sail through the narrow Red Sea before reaching the Suez. The one hundred-mile long Canal located in Egypt shortened the duration and the expense of the voyage. After passing through the canal, ships would cross the Mediterranean Sea. From the southern tip of Europe, they then followed the route Columbus had taken to reach the Caribbean.

The route from the coast of Southern China to the Caribbean Sea was approximately fifteen thousand miles (24,300 km), almost two-thirds of the earth's circumference.[12] The voyage took anywhere from four to six months, depending on weather and sea conditions.[13] During the age of sail, deviations in duration and route were quite common. Two ships departing from the same port in China on the same day could reach their final destination in Europe or the Americas many weeks apart. Another factor to be considered was the condition of the transport ships. A major repair en route could delay a ship's arrival by weeks or even months.

On the other hand, the Pacific route was somewhat shorter than the Indian-Atlantic Ocean route, consisting of about 11,400 miles (18,400 km). From Macao to Callao/Lima, Peru, for instance, ships took either the northern route by making a big half circle above the Hawaiian Islands or the southern route by sailing around Australia. The route was determined by season as the direction of wind and ocean currents changed. The ships propelled by steam engines, however, took a relatively straight course from South China to Peru.[14] Typically, ships headed for Peru sailed southward toward Australia, then eastward in the direction of South America. After

Figure 2.1. Coolie Trade Routes. *Fourleaflover* © *iStock*

passing by certain South Pacific islands such as the Cook and Society Islands, they would reach the southern part of South America. From there, they headed for Peru by sailing northward along the Pacific Coast. The whole route resembled a large "U" with a long, flat bottom. During the voyage, stops for unexpected repairs or weather conditions could delay the arrival time considerably. From Hong Kong, for instance, in 1853 it took on average of 100 days to California, 120 days to Peru, and 147 days to the West Indies. The farthest destination from South China was Cuba, which took up to 150 days. The longest voyage to Cuba on record took 226 days when the French ship *Carmelina* left Macao on November 7, 1867, and arrived in Havana on September 12 of the following year.[15] The ship and its passengers had been at sea for seven months and two weeks.

Many ships that transported Chinese labor recruits were originally built for freight transport. As the demand for Chinese laborers surged, cargo ship owners hastened to convert their ships for human transportation as it was far more profitable. Since these old freight ships were hastily converted, space allocated for human cargo was often barely adequate. With no regard for the comfort or safety of the labor recruits, ship owners sought to squeeze as many laborers as possible into their cargo holds. According to regulations, upon embarking from a Chinese treaty port under either Portuguese or British authority, each ship was allowed to carry a maximum number of people equivalent to half its total weight in tons (one ton is 2,205 pounds). Thus, a five hundred-ton ship could take no more than 250 people. Such regulations, however, were often disregarded by captains even though the officially designated space for each passenger was far from adequate.[16] Yet this minimal requirement was often violated: "As it was, two tons of space can be described as fourteen superficial and seventy-two cubic feet, that is to say, a space about the size of a coffin."[17] While cramped conditions were unendurable for any length of time, some violations were extreme. For instance, the *John Calvin* was cleared to transport only eighty-one passengers, yet the ship left Hong Kong in 1855 with 298 Chinese laborers. The overload was almost four times the official limit.[18] Other violations reported were not as egregious as the *John Calvin*, but many ships overloaded well beyond the permitted capacity: "The *Duke of Portland*, in 1856, packed 334 men when its size allowed for only 238; another ship of thirteen hundred tons was cleared for 650 passengers but was fitted with bunks for 800 for its trip to Callao [Lima, Peru]."[19]

A DEATH TRAP

Uprooted from their native land, many Chinese recruits fell into despair early in the journey. Sensing what a terrible life they might face in the New World, some decided to end their misery during the initial phase of the horrifying journey. While still sailing in the southern part of the South China Sea, facing Malaysia and Indonesia, some Chinese recruits committed suicide. According to the captain of the *Duke of Portland*, "The first line of defense of the Asiatic under oppression is suicide. . . . The third day I (Master of the *Duke of Portland*) had the third suicide, and on an average I had three suicides daily between Hong Kong until I passed the Straits of Sonda."[20] The strait lies between the northern tip of Java and the southern tip of Sumatra near Jakarta in Indonesia. These early suicides underscored the terrible conditions to be endured by the Chinese labor recruits. "We were all locked up in the cabin with an entrance that merely allowed one person to go through. And the smell there was terrible. Lots of people died of disease and their bodies were thrown into the sea."[21]

Aboard, the Chinese recruits experienced numerous problems. As a result, the mortality rate was high. For example, between 1847 and 1873, a total of 138,156 Chinese embarked for Cuba aboard 342 ships but 16,346 did not survive the voyage. On average, about twelve out of one hundred Chinese died at sea.[22] The causes of death included sickness, accident, suicide, and homicide. Although conditions were unilaterally terrible for Chinese being transported to the Americas, some had it worse than others. Ships from different nations had different mortality rates. For instance, six Peruvian ships carried 2,609 Chinese bound for Cuba but as many as 610 of them died, a mortality rate of 23.38 percent. Chilean ships were not much better with 19.76 percent mortality rate. European ships were just as bad. The mortality rates of Danish, Norwegian, and British ships were 38, 19.18, and 16.31 percent, respectively.[23] While these mortality rates accentuated the severity of the treacherous voyage and the below-deck conditions for the Chinese recruits, some cases were even more egregious. In two particular voyages, the mortality rate rose above 50 percent: "The highest death rate was 66.6 percent for the *Lady Montague* out of Hong Kong in 1850, followed by 50 percent on the *British Sovereign* out of Amoy in 1852."[24] Less than 50 percent but more than 30 percent mortality rates included "45.3 percent on the *John Calvin* out of Hong Kong in 1856; 44.4 percent on the *Dolores Ugarte* from Macao in 1870, and 40 percent on the *Cora* from Macao in 1870. . . . For the Peru trade, mortality remained high throughout, with an average 30.4 percent during 1860–63."[25]

During the twenty-seven-year period of the Chinese-Cuban coolie trade (1847–1874), an annual average of 5,116 labor recruits left China. Each year, an average of 4,511 disembarked in Cuba and 604 were lost at sea, a mortality rate of 12 percent. A specific year stands out, however, in terms of losses at sea. In 1858, a record number of Chinese recruits left for Cuba, 16,411; 3,027 did not see Havana. The mortality rate for that year was 18.4 percent. The second highest annual departure came in 1867 when 15,661 Chinese left

Figure 2.2. Old Merchant Clipper. *Elenarts © iStock*

for Cuba with a relatively low mortality rate of 8 percent, or 1,247 deaths at sea.[26] Over a ten-year period between 1858 and 1867, both governments attempted to reduce mortality rates at sea. After 1865, the overall annual mortality rate fell to less than 10 percent. During the same period, there was only one exception, in 1869, when the mortality rate rose to 20 percent. Even in the year of lowest emigration, with only 400 Chinese in 1862, the mortality rate was still 14 percent.[27] The decline in mortality rates may have been due to a number of measures taken to reduce the loss of human life during these voyages. Such measures might have included more strict government supervision, improvements in navigation technology, and better treatment of labor recruits by crew members.

The high at-sea mortality rates among the Chinese labor recruits to Cuba could be attributed to a number of underlying causes, such as socialized racial discrimination. Cuba was one of the last nations to ban slavery, and Chinese laborers worked side by side with black slaves. The practice of slavery in Cuba might have affected the treatment of the Chinese by crew during transport. For instance, the captain of a coolie trade ship bound for Havana decided to abandon sick recruits on an uninhabited beach, calculating it would be too expensive and time-consuming to take care of them. Many jettisoned Chinese died of starvation, and the rest were killed by wild animals on the island.[28] Such heartless treatment of sick passengers was indicative of the prevalent attitude toward the Chinese who were regarded as no better than slaves. In the eyes of transport crews, the Chinese labor recruits were dehumanized commodities.

In the nineteenth century, ocean-crossing voyages were a considerable risk to passengers, regardless of a ship's size or condition. The crew's attitude toward the Chinese laborers, however, seemed to have made a significant difference. For instance, the mortality rate of European passengers sailing to New York or South Africa was no more than 1.5 percent.[29] Even considering the much longer distance and duration of the voyages between South China and the Americas, Chinese mortality rates were exceptionally high.

Final destinations also affected the Chinese at-sea mortality rates. Those bound for the British West Indies had a 5.6 percent mortality rate.[30] This figure was approximately half of the mortality rate among Chinese recruits bound for either Cuba or Peru. In spite of the nearly identical distance, this considerable difference can only be explained by the living conditions on board, including daily provisions, sanitary conditions, available medical treatment, ventilation, and crew interaction. In fact, many ship companies had stiff penalties for high mortality rates and incentives for low ones.[31] The loss of life at sea was a loss of investment and profits for both ship owners and investors alike.

Opium was commonly used to numb the pain of Chinese recruits in physical suffering and mental anguish. As a matter of fact, opium use started in the "barracoons" at the ports of departure. Opium addiction was already rampant in China, and some recruits were opium users before they responded to labor recruitment. Some had applied for overseas work to pay for debts they had incurred to support their opium-smoking habits.

MUTINY AT SEA

On transport ships bound for the Americas, Chinese labor recruits had three options in the face of unbearable conditions. The first was to survive the long, painful voyage by any means necessary, and most recruits endured the physical suffering and mental despair. They held onto dreams of making fortunes in the Americas or promises made to family and friends back home. They could not erase the faces of their loved ones at home from their memories or mute their voices; they were determined to survive at any cost. A second option was suicide. Unable to endure the journey any longer, especially the physical suffering caused by constant seasickness and the mental agony of the unknown, many gave up hope of a better life in the New World. Witnessing the frequent deaths of fellow Chinese either by sickness or suicide blurred the boundary between life and death. Suicide became an easy option among those who despaired. The last option was mutiny. Many recruits realized that they had been deceived. Succumbing to anger and frustration, they lashed out, attempting to reverse their fate no matter the outcome. They sought revenge on crew members who they felt were responsible for the terrible conditions below deck and for the harsh treatment they received.

Whether mutinies were out of despair or anger, the rebellious acts were in response to the terrible conditions aboard. Many regarded the frequent deaths of fellow countrymen as a foreboding of their own fate awaiting them in a strange land. Being in such a state of mind led to fatalistic attitudes. They looked for any excuse to protest, often disregarding their own safety. In turn, nervous crew members became more belligerent in dealing with any signs of potential rebellion. The tension between Chinese labor recruits and crews would build up and trigger in the form of emotional explosions. Desperate people resorted to desperate means. The odds of a successful mutiny were not favorable for the Chinese. Although they outnumbered the crew many times over, often more than sixteen to one,[32] the strategic difference between the upper and lower deck was significant. The Chinese recruits were kept below deck, with a tiny exit hole for just one person at a time for access to the main deck. Each time a Chinese came up through the narrow hole, he was under the keen watch of the crew, who were armed with firearms and other weapons. In spite of the strategic arrangement to control labor recruits below deck, mutinies did occur during such voyages. Some were planned carefully and executed at opportune times while others were spontaneous reactions to certain hostile acts by the crew or the continuance of terrible conditions. In either case, a violent clash between the Chinese and the crew in the confines of a ship often had devastating effects. In the event of an all-out clash between crew and recruits, the burning and sinking of the ship was a real possibility. Unless there was a passing ship nearby, the loss would be total for both the ship and its passengers.

Each transport ship maintained a crew of anywhere between thirty and sixty men, depending on size. The crew included cooks, sail-makers, and medical doctors. In addition, a dozen guards were responsible for controlling any Chinese who came up on deck. "Going to Peru and Cuba their ships are fitted as prisons with bars and grates, the same as the slave ships are said to have been fitted, and with much larger crews."[33] While the upper deck was the exclusive domain of the crew, the cabin below the deck was under the control of the Chinese themselves. The narrow hatch for one person at a time was the only connection between the two areas of a transport ship. As a measure to prevent riots or mutinies aboard, the Chinese recruits were organized into smaller cohorts for easier management: "[T]he captain organized his human cargo into a self-policing military-style system of fifty-man platoons subdivided into ten-man squads, with sergeants and corporals selected for each unit, each paid a small sum."[34] Nonetheless, such an arrangement was useless at a time of tension or explosive outburst.

Anticipating the possibilities of mutiny, ship owners implemented the hatch system to keep the Chinese from rushing up and swarming the upper deck. If the crew sensed any sign of agitation below deck, they would close the hatch. During one riot, the scared crew members shut the hatch which was normal protocol. Below deck, the Chinese screamed and pounded on the hatch with their fists. When the crew opened the hatch a few hours later, the holding area below was deadly silent. Every Chinese recruit had died of suffocation. If a mutiny failed, punishments were severe. After being whipped, the mutineers would be shackled below deck, severely limiting their mobility. Often, captains executed some of those perceived as ringleaders. Between 1847 to 1874, there were altogether 736 transport voyages from China to Cuba. In the course of these twenty-seven years, the Chinese mutinied sixty-eight times, roughly one mutiny in every ten voyages. Mutinies seemed to be more common in the ships flying the French, British, and American flags. For instance, French ships reported 23 mutinies (16.3%) in 141 voyages, British ships 13 mutinies (12.4%) in 105 voyages, and American ships 11 mutinies (17.2%) in 64 voyages. On the other hand, German (17 voyages), Russian (14 voyages), Austrian (5 voyages), Norwegian (3 voyages), and Danish (3 voyages) ships were mutiny free.[35]

While the number of mutinies appears to correlate with the number of transport voyages taken by each country, if another perspective is taken, a pattern emerges. The countries with a high number of mutinies had, at one time or another, maintained slaves in their colonies in the Americas. In contrast, European countries with no colonies in the Americas or a history of slavery did not have a single mutiny. Perhaps the mistreatment of the Chinese labor recruits by French, British, and American crews might have manifested their deeply rooted and socialized racism. The likelihood of a mutiny also could have depended on some ancillary factors. Besides the racist discriminatory attitude of the crew and horrid living conditions, if recruits came from the same town or region in China, it would have been much easier to coordinate a mutiny among the Chinese passengers. In any mutiny, communication was key for coordinated action. In nineteenth-century China, regional dialects made communication among Chinese difficult. A Cantonese-speaking Chinese from Hong Kong, for instance, would have a hard time conversing with a Mandarin-speaking Chinese from Beijing. Since the majority of Chinese laborers was recruited from the region surrounding Hong Kong and Macao, they shared a regional identity and spoke the same dialect, thus making mutiny easier.

The port of embarkation also appeared to have an effect on the probability of a mutiny at sea. Among the multiple treaty ports, more than two-thirds (68%) of all coolie trade ships left from Macao, yet proportionally, they had the least number of mutinies at 7 percent. On the other hand, ships originating from Amoy, a port not far from Hong Kong, launched thirty-six voyages for Cuba, and one in five ships (20%) experienced a mutiny. Ships that embarked from Cumsingmoon off the Southern Chinese coast experienced the most mutinies with one in three ships (33.3%).[36] The differing percentages likely reveal a discrepancy in the enforcement of regulations at each port. Different port authorities might have had different enforcement standards. Transport ships out of Macao under Portuguese supervision might have had more rigorous inspections, thus mitigating overcrowding and other ship conditions. It was also the responsibility of port authorities to check the intentions of labor recruits. Before departure, official inspectors were to ask recruits if they had been coerced into leaving their villages and to sign contracts they did not understand. As corruption was common, many inspectors did not ask such questions, thereby robbing recruits of the opportunity to disembark. Some who had been kidnapped or forced to sign contracts hesitated to speak out for fear of vengeance. Others held onto a glimmer of hope that the New World would bring them fortune in spite of their forced recruitment. Thus, they remained silent when the inspector checked with them.

During the twenty-seven years of the Chinese coolie trade (1847–1874), "more than 4,000 Chinese emigrants, 12 captains, and at least 200 sailors were killed during mutinies on the high seas."[37] These victim numbers accounted for about 16 percent of total Chinese deaths at sea from an overall total of 25,755. The breakdown of reported Chinese deaths at sea during this period was: Cuba-bound 16,305, Peru-bound 8,492, and British West Indies-bound 958.[38] The possibility of mutiny was so real that Western labor suppliers in China sometimes could not find ships willing to take Chinese recruits.[39] To many captains, human rage was more frightening than any storm.

A LUCRATIVE BUSINESS

In spite of the potential dangers and risks at sea, the Chinese coolie trade was enticing to many ship owners for its high return. It was a gamble well worth it, and once word spread of its profitability, many clamored for a piece of the pie. Before the coolie trade, most Western merchant ships trading in Asia dealt in tea, spices, ceramics, and other material goods. Transporting Chinese laborers to the Americas, however, turned out to be far more profitable than transporting commodities. Often, the profits of human transportation yielded as much as ten times the profit of transporting tea.[40] A consortium of international financial networks and the revenues generated from the sale of sugar provided most of the capital for the operation of the coolie trade.[41]

According to a detailed statement regarding the shipment of three hundred Chinese laborers to Cuba in 1866, the total cost of transporting a recruit from South China was between 92 and 177 dollars (from 1,486 to 2,860 in 2020).[42] Typically, an operator paid between 3 and 45 dollars (from 49 to

727 in 2020) to a Chinese recruiter per labor recruit and between 4 and 8 dollars (from 65 to 130 in 2020) for the brokerage fee. The Chinese recruit was then paid between 8 and 12 dollars (around 130 to 194 in 2020) as an advance and between 5 and 12 dollars (from 81 to 194 in 2020) for provisions.

In Cuba, each Chinese recruit would be sold for between 122 and 500 dollars (from 1,972 to 8,080 in 2020). Therefore, the net profit for transporting three hundred Chinese laborers could range from 6,150 dollars (from 99,384 in 2020) at the lower end to 81,900 dollars (from 1,323,504 in 2020) at the upper end. Depending on the demands of the labor market, ship owners and investors could anticipate a wide range of profit, from 30 up to 323 dollars (around 485 to 5,220 in 2020) for each Chinese laborer delivered. These projected minimum and maximum profits also took into account a mortality rate of 10 percent during the voyage. The potential loss of thirty Chinese recruits from a load of three hundred would thus result in the loss of 3,660 to 15,000 potential dollars (from 59,146 to 242,400 in 2020). Considering the total outlay of 27,600 to 53,100 dollars (around 446,016 to 858,096 in 2020) for taking three hundred labor recruits to Cuba, the anticipated profit was quite hefty.[43] In the end, ship owners and their investors had the potential to profit 1.3 times (or 130%) their capital outlay and even up to three times (or 300%). In comparison with earnings from the fares of ticketed passengers from South China to California, transporting Chinese laborers either to Cuba or Peru was far more profitable. Indeed, the profit could be as much as four times greater,[44] as the quality and cost of accommodations and services for ticketed passengers was not comparable to the steerage-like conditions for the labor recruits.

When compared to the profit margins of the African slave trade, those of the Chinese coolie trade were comparable or even higher. For instance, in 1845 an African slave trader would spend 11,700 British pounds (around two million dollars in 2020) to bring five hundred African slaves from Angola to Brazil. At that time, each slave cost 23.4 British pounds (around $4,000 in 2020). After taking into account a 10 percent at-sea mortality rate, the trader would sell each slave for about 60 pounds (around $10,200 in 2020) in Brazil, thus making a total revenue of 27,000 pounds (around $4.6 million in 2020). The net profit would be 15,300 pounds (around $2.6 million in 2020), the return of initial investment being 1.3 times (or 130%).[45] It should be noted that the African slave trade route was much shorter than that of the Chinese coolie by nearly a third, so slave traders required far less provisions and spent less time at sea. In addition, slave traders did not have to pay advance money whereas coolie trade operators had to pay a certain amount in advance to Chinese recruits. Even considering the additional cost of bringing laborers from China to Latin America due to the much longer sail distances, voyage time and advance payments, coolie traders enjoyed higher profits.

Over a thirty-year period in Chinese emigration, from 1847 to 1880, Hong Kong and Macao played key roles. Out of these two harbors, Chinese went to the United States (177,415), Cuba (127,445), Australia (93,209), Peru (82,315), and New Zealand (5,191).[46] Besides these two harbors under European administration, other treaty ports along the South China coast were also involved in sending Chinese abroad, some of which went to the British colonies in the Caribbean region. Between 1847 and 1874, almost 17,000 Chinese coolies were transported to British Guiana (13,830), Jamaica (515), and Trinidad (2,643). These colonies, however, met the bulk of their labor needs with almost 150,000 laborers from India during the same time period. Among the three, British Guiana brought the most Indian laborers, almost two-thirds (87,678) of the overall total as opposed to the other two: Trinidad (42,416) and Jamaica (13,887).[47] It is interesting to note that former British colonies such as the United States, some Caribbean islands, Australia, and New Zealand used ships out of Hong Kong, from which more than half a million Chinese (543,097) departed. On the other hand, Spanish colonies such as Cuba and Peru used ships mainly from Macao, from which more than one fifth of a million Chinese (210,054) embarked. The traffickers of Chinese indentured laborers also used other harbors such as Swatow (24,953), Canton (13,262), and Amoy (11,402) during the same period.[48] In the nineteenth century, about one tenth of Chinese overseas migrants went to the Americas while the remainder headed for Southeast Asia, Oceania, and South Africa.

THE SLAVE TRADE AND THE COOLIE TRADE

Many eyewitnesses of the Chinese coolie trade compared it with the African slave trade for its cruelty. Both groups in the Americas were not so different from each other in terms of hardship and suffering. In some cases, Chinese laborers perceived their treatment as worse than those of black slaves. "It is high time that a traffic embodying all the worst features of the African slave trade was put to a stop. The contemptible little Portuguese colony [Macao] which maintains its existence upon the profits derived from the accursed system has long been the disgrace of civilization in the Far East of Asia."[49] Less than ten years into the Chinese coolie trade, the *New York Times* castigated in strong terms both the governments of the United States and Great Britain for their failure to enforce an anti-coolie trade policy. On March 12, 1856, the newspaper questioned the intentions of both governments: "Would our American Consuls have winked at this trade had it the slightest approximation to slavery? Where are all of the British and American ships of war on the East India station if this is modern or new fashioned slave trade?"[50] Then the same paper wondered if both governments deliberately avoided confronting the issue: "They too must be blinded or else they would long ago have seized these coolie-carrying ships and sent them into ports for trial and condemnation."[51] Indeed, the conditions of human trafficking had not changed much. The *New York Times* did not see any difference between the barbaric African slave trade and the Chinese coolie trade: "[I]t is time for the civilized nations of the world to interfere. . . . [I]f the slave trade of Zanzibar is an iniquity and a crime against civilization, then the traffic in coolies is likewise."[52] Seventeen years later, in 1873, the *New York Times* once again called for strong action against the Chinese coolie trade one year before the official end of the trade agreed upon by China and Latin American nations.

As pointed out earlier, the Chinese coolie trade began at the tail end of the African slave trade across the Atlantic Ocean. During the coolie trade period, slave systems were still maintained in Cuba, the United States, and Brazil, and Chinese laborers were used either to supplement or replace the slaves in these countries. In the case of supplementing labor, such as in Cuba, the two systems coexisted. In legal terms, the Chinese were not slaves as they were contract laborers for a fixed amount of time whereas slaves were the lifelong property of their owners. Nevertheless, the two systems of sourcing migrant human labor, one originating in West Africa and the other in South China, bore many resemblances. First of all, both trades were multinational and multi-continental operations involving long ocean voyages. The African slave trade required the interaction and coordination of parties in three continents: Europe, Africa, and either North or South America. The logistics of the slave trade were vast: planning, finance, recruitment, contracts, insurance, transportation, delivery, and so forth. At one time, the slave trade was the largest global economic activity. Likewise, the Chinese coolie trade required transnational coordination among parties in Europe, Asia, and the Americas. In the mid-nineteenth century, the coolie trade, covering almost half of the earth's circumference, was too big and too complex for a single company or country to handle. Second, both trades consisted of triangular transactions. They involved European or American financing and shipping, the raw materials of the Americas, and African or Asian human laborers. The transportation of human cargo occurred in the Middle Passage of the multi-continental transaction: African slaves from the west coast of Africa to the Americas and the Chinese coolies from the south coast of China to the Americas. The inhumane mistreatment of human cargo happened during this Middle Passage phase.

Third, mortality rates were very high during the Middle Passage in both groups. On average, it was about 10 percent for African slaves and 12 percent for Chinese coolies. For more than three hundred years of the African slave trade, about 1.8 million African slaves died while crossing the Atlantic Ocean.[53] Considering the much shorter distance between West Africa and the Atlantic coast of the Americas, the 10-percent mortality rate on slave ships appears to be high in comparison with the average 12 percent mortality of Chinese labor recruits who sailed far longer distances, easily two or three times further.[54] Of course, African slaves were subjected to far crueler treatment by crews. That included the miserable conditions in the holding areas where the slaves were tightly packed, food and sanitation were inadequate, and the navigation technology of the time was much cruder. Shipwrecks were more common in the days of the African slave trade. The mortality rates of both groups during their voyages were very high by modern standards. In 2017, for instance, the mortality rate of the three African nations with the highest rates-Lesotho, Guinea-Bissau, and Chad-was about 1.5 percent.[55] The mortality rate was calculated including those in the most vulnerable segments of the population: infants and seniors. The high mortality rates during the transport of dominantly male slaves or coolies in their prime years is somewhat comparable with the infant mortality rates of the three African nations with the highest rates in 2017. The infant mortality rate among babies in the first year of their lives was near 10 percent. They were Somalia (9.5%), Central African Republic (8.6%), and Guinea-Bissau (8.6%), respectively.[56]

Finally, European settlers and their descendants in the Americas initiated human trafficking to meet labor needs in the Americas, especially for large-scale plantation agriculture. The Western imperial powers who subjugated both Africans and Asians to unbearable conditions on the trade ships reflected a disregard for the human value of African and Chinese life. In the mistreatment of their human cargo, the crews reflected the prevailing racist, Eurocentric attitudes of the time. The miserable conditions inflicted upon the labor migrants included overcrowding, inadequate ventilation under deck, insufficient food and water, and terrible sanitation. All these contributed to high mortality rates during long voyages. Indeed, the coolie trade ships were a floating hell.

REFLECTIONS

Like the dandelion, the Chinese were dispersed by nineteenth-century winds blown from the West. These seeds took root in hostile foreign soils and grew in harsh climates. They were often downtrodden, yet they spread all over the world. The tough and tenacious Chinese overcame many obstacles and challenges. Today, overseas Chinese outside of Greater China (including Hong Kong, Macao, and Taiwan) are one of the largest diaspora communities in the world, with over forty million people in more than seventy countries. Ten countries report more than one million people of Chinese ancestry: Thailand (8.5 million–14% of the total national population), Indonesia (7.3 million–3%), Malaysia (7 million–25%), the United States (3.8 million–1%), Singapore (2.7 million–76%), Vietnam (2.3 million–3%), Philippines (1.5

million–3%), Canada (1.3 million–4%), and Peru (1.3 million–4%), and Myanmar (1.1 million–3%). Two countries, Australia and Russia, are rapidly approaching the one million mark.[57] After the Southeast Asian region, which is close to China both geographically and culturally, the Americas have the second largest number of people of Chinese ancestry. They number near eight million comprising about 20 percent of the entire overseas Chinese.

The total asset value of overseas Chinese is estimated to be anywhere between 1.5 and 2 trillion US dollars, equivalent to almost a quarter of China's annual gross national product or one tenth of the annual US GDP. These overseas Chinese communities and their economic power helped the Chinese economic takeoff in the 1980s and 1990s. When China turned to the outside world for economic development in the early years of its open-door policy, many overseas Chinese responded with investments in their ancestral land. From 1998 to 2009, for instance, overseas Chinese investment resulted in about one-third of Chinese exports. In addition, China has received around fifty billion dollars in annual remittance from overseas Chinese, who have turned out to be a valuable asset in the expansion of China's global economy and cultural influence.

In turn, a prospering China sends millions of tourists and students all over the world every year. In 2018, 149 million outbound Chinese tourists spent 130 billion US dollars abroad.[58] In the same year, more than half a million Chinese students (662,100) left China to study in foreign countries.[59] Almost six million Chinese studied in foreign countries between 1978 and 2018. Also, China has funded many mega-size global projects in developing countries, especially in Africa and Asia. The Chinese government has launched the ambitious One Belt, One Road (OBOR) project, commonly known as the twenty-first-century Silk Road. Its purpose is to increase Chinese global influence and economic activity.

The one-time labor-supplying country has become a money-and-technology providing superpower. Now China enjoys G2 (Group of Two) superpower status, and its economy may outrun that of the United States someday. It has been a surprising turnaround, and not many nations have had such a remarkable transformation over such a short period of time. Chinese leadership under President Xi Jin Ping has rallied its citizens to be proud Chinese, many of whom dream of economic prosperity and a clean environment, among other desires. Now ordinary Chinese citizens may be content with pursuing their dreams without leaving home. China has come a long way from the days of its people chasing after their meager dreams in faraway foreign lands and suffering depravations in the Devil's Throat in order to do so.

NOTES

1. In 1817, Great Britain and Spain signed a treaty to abolish the trans-Atlantic slave trade. See Lisa Yun, *The Coolie Speaks: Chinese Indentured Laborers and African Slaves in Cuba* (Philadelphia: Temple University Press, 2008), 13.
2. Yun, *The Coolie Speaks*, 6.
3. Ibid.,15.
4. Ibid.,16.
5. J. D. Frodsham, *The First Chinese Embassy to the West: The Journal of Kuo Sung-Tao, Liu His-Hung and Chang Te-Yi* (Oxford: Clarendon Press, 1974), xxx.
6. Ibid., xxv.
7. Jimmy M. Skagg, *The Great Guano Rush: Entrepreneurs and American Overseas Expansion* (New York: St. Martin Press, 1994), 162.
8. Yun, *The Coolie Speaks*, 66.
9. Elliott Young, *Alien Nation: Chinese Migration in the Americas from the Coolie Era through World War II* (Chapel Hill: The University of North Carolina Press, 2014), 47.
10. Skagg, *The Great Guano Rush,* 162.
11. See the voyage routes in two different directions. Arnold J. Meagher, *The Coolie Trade: The Traffic of Chinese Laborers to Latin America 1847–1874*. (Arnold J. Meagher: 2008), 151.
12. The earth's circumference is 24,901 miles (40,075 km).
13. Arnold J. Meagher, *The Coolie Trade*, 150.
14. Ibid., 150–51.
15. Ibid.
16. Ibid, 153–57.
17. Evelyn Hu-De Hart, "La Trata Amarilla: The Yellow Trade and the Middle Passage, 1847–1884," in *Many Middle Passages: Forced Migration and the Making of the Modern World*, ed. Emma Christopher, Cassandra Pybus and Marcus Rediker (Berkeley: University of California Press, 2007), 173.
18. Ibid.
19. Ibid.
20. Mario Federico Real De Azua, "Chinese Coolies in Peru: the Chincha Islands," in *Asiatic Migrations in Latin America*. ed. Luz M. Martinez Montiel, 37–52 (Mexico: El Colegio De Mexico, 1981), 43.
21. Yun, *The Coolie Speaks*, 139.
22. Meagher, *The Coolie Trade*, 149.
23. Ibid.
24. Hu-De Hart, "La Trata Amarilla," 178.
25. Ibid.
26. Meagher, *The Coolie Trade*, 169.
27. Ibid.
28. Young, *Alien Nation*, 31.
29. Ibid., 30
30. Ibid.
31. Ibid., 31.
32. Ibid., 27.
33. Hu-De Hart, "La Trata Amarilla," 176.
34. Ibid., 175.
35. Meagher, *The Coolie Trade*, 190.
36. Ibid., 191.
37. Young, *Alien Nation*, 29.
38. Meagher, *The Coolie Trade*, 169–71.
39. Young, *Alien Nation*, 37.
40. Meagher, *The Coolie Trade*, 144.
41. Yun, *The Coolie Speaks*, 6
42. Meagher, *The Coolie Trade*, 142.
43. Ibid.

44. Skagg, *The Great Guano Rush*, 162.
45. Meagher, *The Coolie Trade*, 143.
46. Ibid., 103–21. The figures for Cuba and Peru were based on the number of Chinese laborers left out of Macao from 1851 to 1874.
47. Ibid., 250.
48. Ibid., 99–120.
49. Meagher, *The Coolie Trade*, 288.
50. Young, *Alien Nation*, 21.
51. Ibid.
52. Ibid.
53. Meg Greene and Mark G. Malvasi, "Middle Passage: Did the Treatment of Slaves During the Middle Passage Produce Excessively High Mortality Rates?" in *History in Dispute vol. 13: Slavery in the Western Hemisphere, Circa 1500–1888*, ed. Mark G. Malvasi (Detroit: St. James Press, 2003), 129–37.
54. Young, *Alien Nation*, 30.
55. CIA, Country Comparison: Death Rate, *The World Factbook*, accessed August 6, 2020, https://www.cia.gov/library/publications/the-world-factbook/rankorder/2066rank.html.
56. CIA, Country Comparison: Infant Mortality Rate, *The World Factbook*, accessed August 6, 2020. https://www.cia.gov/library/publications/the-worl-factbook/rankorder/2091rank.html.
57. New World Encyclopedia, "Overseas Chinese," accessed October 2, 2020, https://www.newworlencyclopedia.org/entry/Overseas_Chinese. The years of population reports are varied.
58. *China Daily*, "Chinese Tourists Spend $130 Bln Overseas in 2018: Report," accessed October 2, 2020, https://www.chinadaily.com.cn/a/201908/05/WS5d479988a310cf3e35563e6d.html.
59. Statistica, "Number of Chinese Students Studying Abroad 2008–2018," accessed October 2, 2020, https://www.statistica.com/statistics/227240/number-of-chinese-students-that-study-abroad/.

Chapter Three

The Coolie Mart and Bitter Sugar in Cuba

In the nineteenth century, the Cape of Good Hope was about the halfway point in the long voyage from Hong Kong or Macao to Havana, Cuba. The distance between Hong Kong and the Cape is 7,383 straight miles (11,882 km). From this point to Havana is slightly longer, 7,694 straight miles (12,382 km). By journey's end, the coolie trade ships sailed far more than half of the earth's circumference (24,901 miles; 40,074 km). The actual sail distance was much longer than the straight line distances as these ships hugged the coastlines of Asia, Africa, and the Americas.

In the early years of the coolie trade, the average voyage from Hong Kong or Macao to Havana took anywhere from four to six months. Once the coolie trade ships entered the calm, blue Caribbean Sea, they began passing by tropical islands. The Chinese passengers were relieved that the long, dreary voyage was finally coming to an end. They had been at sea for more than 120 days and survived sickness, storms, mistreatment, and mutiny on some ships. It was, however, a bittersweet moment. The beautiful tropical scenery lifted their spirits, yet their joy was mixed with sadness. They could not forget the fellow countrymen who had been lost along the way. The Chinese recruits did not realize just how transient their joy would be upon nearing their destination and that the paradise of their dreams was a mere illusion. What they found in Havana was even worse than what they had suffered during the arduous voyage, a depravation many had at least viewed as bearable in pursuit of a better future on an imagined island.

The almost four-hundred-year-old Spanish colony of Cuba (1511–1898) imported more Chinese laborers than any other country in Latin America due to its sugar industry. Cuba and sugar were synonymous and Europeans referred to sugarcane as the "grass" of Cuba. Ironically, Cuba's rise as a sugar producer could be directly attributed to its neighboring island Haiti, whose slaves had revolted against the French colonists. When Haitians gained their freedom after a fifteen-year long struggle (1791–1805), European nations banned the import of Haitian sugar to punish the newly independent country for standing up to its colonial masters. As a result, the demand for Cuban sugar increased drastically. In 1830, Cuba produced 105,000 tons (231 million pounds) of sugar. By 1870, sugar production had soared to 703,000 tons (1.547 billion pounds). In comparison, Brazil, many times larger and also a sugar-producing nation, produced only 83,000 tons of sugar in 1830 and 101,500 tons in 1870, respectively. Cuba was the sugar capital of the world, with almost 40 percent of the world's sugar of Cuban origin. In the nineteenth century, the largest sugar-importing nation was Great Britain, consuming about one-third of the world's sugar.[1] This reflected the prosperity enjoyed by the people of the dominant empire of the time.

Growing sugarcane and refining it depended almost exclusively on slave labor. The large-scale slave trade to the Americas continued for almost 150 years beginning in 1700. At its height, around one hundred thousand African slaves were transported each year to the various colonies in the Americas. Then beginning in 1861, slave imports declined sharply as the United States and Great Britain began to enforce an anti-slavery policy. In that same year, the American Civil War began, a contest between the abolitionist North and secessionist South. In 1860, nearly 30 percent of Cuba's population were slaves and about 70 percent of Cuban blacks were slaves. In other words, only three out of ten blacks in Cuba were free.[2] It seemed that in Cuba, blacks produced much of the sugar. As the supply of slaves from Africa began to dwindle due to the enforcement of the anti-slave trade laws by America and Great Britain, Cuban plantation owners turned to the nearby Yucatan Peninsula, home to native Mayans in the southeast region of Mexico, as a new source of labor supply. They preferred Mayans because they spoke Spanish and were Catholic. In addition, they were acclimatized to the tropical weather. Also, bringing Mayan laborers across the narrow channel from Yucatan was cheap and quick. However, not many Mayans were interested in leaving their ancestral homeland to work in Cuban sugarcane fields.

So, Cuban plantation owners had to look elsewhere for laborers, far beyond the Western hemisphere. At that time, the only continent yet untapped for cheap labor was Asia. Initially, plantation owners attempted to contract Polynesians and Filipinos. Since the Philippine Islands were a Spanish colony, the sugarcane growers felt an affinity with this Pacific archipelago. Most Filipinos spoke Spanish, and many of them practiced the Catholic faith. However, the idea of labor sourcing Filipinos never materialized. Consequently, Cuban sugarcane growers turned to China.

In the middle part of the nineteenth century, China was experiencing much instability due to Western interference and domestic turbulence in the milieu of many socioeconomic challenges. After much negotiation and logistical coordination in China, two Western ships left the port of Amoy (Xiamen) for Cuba with Chinese labor recruits aboard. On June 3, 1847, the Spanish ship Oquendo arrived in Havana with 206 Chinese laborers. The voyage had taken more than four months. Nine days later, a second ship, the Duke of Argyle, flying the British flag, disembarked 365 Chinese laborers in Havana harbor.[3] The first ship lost six labor recruits and the second ship lost thirty-five during their respective voyages. In the first year of the coolie trade, the median mortality rate was 6.7 percent,[4] which turned out to be unusually low. Perhaps this low mortality rate can be attributed to the extra care and attention paid to the first wave of Chinese laborers. Also, the captains and the crews would have wanted to make a favorable first impression in order to attract more Chinese recruits. Over the next twenty-six years, nearly 130,000 Chinese were transported to Cuba to work in the sugarcane fields and other economic areas.

When Chinese laborers first viewed Havana from the trade ships, the colonial capital looked impressive. Not long after landing, however, the same city looked quite different. The temporary holding facilities and the way they were treated confirmed their suspicions. The initial joy at the end of their long journey was short lived. After a few days in holding pens, foreign bidders sealed their fate. These Chinese laborers could not have imagined they would be auctioned and sold to plantation owners whose words and customs they could not understand. Although they had signed contracts in China, they were treated like slaves imported from Africa. Their passports and contract papers were just mere documents.

On the day of bidding, Chinese laborers would be displayed almost naked at a coolie market. Prospective buyers would scrutinize each laborer with great attention and care. They inspected each coolie from head to toe with just one thing in mind: physical fitness for the labor task each buyer had in mind. A Chinese recruit recalled the fateful day in Havana. "We were all naked when we were inspected by buyers. We never saw people being humiliated in such a terrible way. We were sold to sugar plantations and treated worse than dogs and oxen."[5] If owners needed laborers for difficult work in sugarcane fields, the would-be buyers squeezed and pinched parts of the body to examine the condition of muscles and bones. Already feeling despair and disorientation, many Chinese were in a state of utter disbelief at the scene unfolding before their eyes. They could not believe that this was the conclusion of the agonizing, long voyage they had born. They were treated like cows and horses, pinched, prodded, and degraded.

Around the time the first Chinese labor recruits arrived in Cuba, the price of African slaves had continued to rise. For instance, African male slaves in excellent physical condition sold for as much as a thousand dollars (around $20,000 in 2020). The economy of supply-and-demand was at work in the

Cuban slave market during the years of anti-slave trade enforcement. In the 1850s, on average, Chinese coolies were sold for 125 pesos (around $2,300 in 2020). This amount was about one-third the price of a typical African slave sold for 335 pesos (around $6,200 in 2020). Since one peso was equivalent to about ninety-two cents, Chinese sold for about 115 dollars on average whereas each African slave went for about 308 dollars. The considerable difference in price between Chinese coolies and African slaves remained almost unchanged as the coolie trade continued. More than twenty years later, Chinese laborers cost 420 pesos (around $7,600 in 2020) while African slaves cost 715 pesos (around $13,000 in 2020).[6]

Not far from Cuba, in America's antebellum South, a black slave sold for an average of about four hundred dollars (around $13,200 in 2020) in 1850.[7] The price of a slave represented "the expected net value of the future labor services a slave would provide. In addition, the price included the cost of maintaining a slave in terms of food, clothing, and shelter."[8] At that time, the US annual per capita income was about 110 dollars (around $3,600 in 2020). Therefore, only financially well-to-do Southerners could afford owning a slave as it would cost almost four times the average annual per capita income. The average price of a house was comparable to the price of a slave. To many, owning a slave was a status symbol.[9] Prior to the Civil War in 1860, only 19 percent of free adult males in the South were slave owners, ranging from owning one to one thousand slaves. Slave owners numbered about 385,000 altogether in the United States. Among them, a little over 5 percent possessed ten or more slaves, and half of the owners owned four or less slaves.[10]

The price of a slave was determined by a variety of factors such as age, gender, physical condition, health, skill, escape history, and so forth. A male slave in his early twenties cost as much as 1,450 dollars (around $28,500 in 2020). On the other hand, a fifty-year-old slave cost 150 dollars (around $3,000 in 2020) and a sixty-year-old slave only fifty dollars (around $1,000 in 2020). The value of a slave during his or her lifetime resembled a curve peaking in the twenties and thirties. Thus, children and old slaves were much cheaper than those in their prime years.[11] The difference in cost between African slaves and Chinese coolies in Cuba also had to do with overall physical strength and adaptability to the tropical climate. On average, African slaves were taller and heavier than Chinese laborers. Because African slaves were stronger, many sugarcane plantation owners felt that black slaves were more suitable for the demanding physical labor of weeding and harvesting sugarcane. It was also common practice for slaves to work more than fifteen hours a day. Slavery had yet to be abolished in Cuba when the Chinese laborers arrived, and this fact affected almost every aspect of Chinese life on the island. Moreover, the sheer physical distance between

Cuba and China made the Chinese coolies vulnerable as a weakened China could not provide any protection or assistance to its citizens.

PLANTATION LIFE

There was no uniform standard that regulated both the living and working conditions of plantation workers. Each plantation owner or administrator set the rules and labor expectations according to his needs. Depending on each owner's character and outlook, some were reasonable and humane while others were harsh and exploitive. Since sugarcane plantations were commercialized agriculture, owners tried to maximize profits by pushing workers as much as possible. Furthermore, the tone of labor relations between white ownership and management on one hand and Chinese coolies and black slaves on the other was highly affected by racial perceptions in nineteenth-century Cuba. In the eyes of colonial community leaders and residents, both slaves and indentured Chinese laborers were a subordinate class, to say the least. Accordingly, they were treated on almost a subhuman level. The sense of superiority that white Cubans felt toward both African slaves and Chinese laborers shaped the nature of their relationships. What white Cubans viewed as the intrinsic superiority of civilized Europeans over the uncivilized Africans and Asians was reflected in their cruel treatment of slaves and indentured laborers. In most cases, African slaves and Chinese coolies were no more than expendable property.

Chinese coolies earned four pesos (around $120 dollars in 2020) a month. From this, the owner deducted the cost of passage from China, clothing, food, and lost wages due to sickness.[12] As a result, many Chinese ended up owing money to plantation owners. Often, Chinese laborers had no choice but to extend their contracts and endure another period of indentured servitude. During the contract period, some owners would sell Chinese workers to other high bidders. Only a small number of Chinese were able to buy their freedom with the money they had saved before the end of the eight-year contract period.

When slaves and Chinese labored on the same plantation, the two groups were kept in separate living quarters. In the field, however, they worked side by side, and their field overseers were usually local mestizos, typically descendants of mixed marriages between Spanish settlers and indigenous people. In some plantations, management used black and Chinese field overseers. In general, black field overseers dealt harshly with Chinese coolies. These two subordinate groups on the plantations were not so cordial with each other. Often, slaves resented Chinese workers because they were contract laborers who would be free after a specified period of time. In short, the Chinese could gain their freedom after fulfilling the contract obligations.

This labor feature was not popular with the slaves, whose fate was to remain the lifetime property of their owners. Some plantation owners used blacks for field supervision on purpose. With strong feelings of resentment, some black field overseers were merciless in dealing with Chinese laborers. "In the twist of contract labor married to slavery, coolies resented slaves for having higher social status, and slaves resented coolies for being not slaves."[13]

The daily work routine on a plantation varied widely, depending on season and type of work required. The majority of laborers worked either in sugarcane fields or in sugar refineries. A few were hired as domestic helpers for plantation owners or managers. In the field, the job of either weeding or cutting sugarcane with machetes was very difficult. The unbearable heat and humidity easily weakened even young workers. Food was inadequate both in quality and quantity, and living quarters were bare. On top of this, the lack of sufficient rest made workers vulnerable to disease and sickness. At some plantations, work started at three o'clock in the morning and ended at eight, ten, or midnight, seven days a week. In extreme cases, work began at one o'clock at night and ended at eleven or midnight.[14] Workers had hardly any time to eat or sleep. In the field, overseers on horses moved around with leather whips. If they detected any laborer beginning to slow down, they would whip them. Armed with pistols and machetes, overseers punished sluggish workers without mercy. Anyone who dared to challenge their authority was met with harsh punishment. It was common for Chinese workers to die of severe beatings and machete injuries.

Some owners and overseers regarded the lives of Chinese laborers as expendable. In order to keep workers in line, overseers did not hesitate to kill a disobedient worker to set an example to others. Even the slightest sign of defiance often resulted in the limitation of a worker's mobility. Iron chains or shackles were commonly used to control an insubordinate worker. One Chinese laborer reported that he was in shackles after working for seven months because he had complained to a government officer about too much work and insufficient food.[15] Neither sickness nor feebleness was a valid excuse for missing work. Even sick workers were forced to labor under the constant threat of whippings and beatings.

Legally speaking, Chinese laborers should have been released after the expiration of their contracts, thus becoming free independent workers. However, plantation owners often attempted to keep them indentured as long as possible. Their inability to free themselves after their contracts had expired was an agonizing issue. Using all kinds of reasons and excuses, plantation owners prolonged contract periods indefinitely. Sometimes, they used tricks to trap the Chinese. In particular, frequent changes in ownership of laborer contracts posed a major legal problem. Contracts for indentured laborers were resold many times among plantation owners. Every time the ownership of a contract laborer changed, its legal content became more complex. In

Cuba, most documents regarding the change of ownership were in Spanish, and thus the Chinese had no way of understanding them, let alone the stipulations and implications of multiple transactions. When Chinese workers turned to local police or colonial government officials for help, their pleas often fell on deaf ears. In most cases, officials of the colonial government sided with the rich, influential plantation owners rather than with the nameless foreign laborers. A Chinese laborer revealed his frustration. "It has been eight years till now, but the owner still refused to issue me the proof, . . . Without freedom paper, we would be arrested and shackled up, . . . If no Cuban bail us out, we will be shackled until the day we die. I have already worn the shackles for years."[16]

Out of desperation, some Chinese workers looked to local parish priests to intercede on their behalf. Most Catholic priests were very reluctant to defend the helpless Chinese. Not many priests were courageous enough to pit themselves against the economic interests of plantation owners who had considerable influence in the colonial communities. Often, at the request of plantation owners, many Chinese were introduced to the Western religion of Christianity, and they were baptized by local priests. When they had lived in China, they had regarded Christianity as an agent of Western imperial dominance. To them, Christian missionaries and European merchants were the same agents in the great scheme of conquering China. However, in Cuba, Chinese coolies tried to please plantation owners by pretending to accept the Catholic faith. Thus, their conversions were, by and large, ruses for survival. The nominal Catholics received baptismal names, such as Peter Mao, John Wong, Paul Chen, and the like. Many plantation owners saw religion as a means of controlling and changing the "heathens" from the East. They were far more interested in keeping workers in line rather than in saving their souls. This was not so different from cotton or tobacco plantations in the American South where slaves were introduced to Christianity. Submissive and grateful slaves more interested in the next world helped safeguard the owners.

Petty local leaders, such as policemen and colonial civil servants, were reluctant to challenge the informal authority of plantation owners on behalf of Chinese laborers. In a typical Spanish colonial town in Latin America, local power elites consisted of three groups: plantation owners, colonial administration officials, and Catholic priests. Of the three, the most influential group was the plantation owners. With wealth and connections, they could easily sway the opinion of other community members. In many ways, these colonial towns resembled the European manor system during the medieval era. A typical medieval rural community was centered around the feudal lord.

Some Cubans engaged in the business of rehabilitating disabled or weakened Chinese laborers. They would purchase sick Chinese at a considerably discounted price, then resell them for a hefty profit when the workers regained their strength. Since the cost of caring for sick Chinese laborers was sufficient rest and good food, it was a worthwhile investment. The reselling of Chinese coolies for a variety of reasons was a common practice among the owners. Because of frequent ownership changes, as many as 40 percent of all Chinese laborers worked for at least three different owners. One in four (25%) served four or more owners, and 4 percent had seven or more owners. In extreme cases, some were resold six times in two years. For example, one Chinese laborer worked for twelve different owners over ten years.[17] Each time, the resold Chinese worker had to readjust to a new owner and a new plantation environment.

A little over half of the Chinese laborers were able to finish their eight-year contract terms with one or two owners. When the original owner wanted to sell a Chinese laborer, the reasons were often negative such as frequent sickness, disobedience, diminished strength, or escape attempts. Knowing these reasons, the new owner would treat his newly purchased Chinese laborer with strict control and watchful eyes. Each time ownership changed, the situation of a resold coolie worsened.

Eventually those who survived the long ordeal of hard labor earned their freedom, but their options as free workers were rather limited. With the little money they had saved, some became small shopkeepers, opening vegetable stands or barber shops. Others continued to work as farm laborers as they had no other skills. The language barrier was a constant impediment for Chinese employment in Cuba. Upon the expiration of their labor contracts, either they renegotiated for better wages and working conditions with the previous plantation owners or they moved to other farms. A few went to other countries, including Louisiana in the United States, which had sizable sugarcane plantations. Returning to China was not an option for the majority of these early Chinese laborers.

BLACK SLAVES, YELLOW SLAVES

From the beginning of the coolie trade, slavery in Cuba overshadowed the life of Chinese laborers. In the mid-nineteenth century, the diminishing slave import from Africa led to the inauguration of the coolie trade. Under pressure from Great Britain and the United States, Spain pledged to end the slave trade by signing related treaties in 1817 and 1835, respectively. The British colonies in the Caribbean region ended slavery altogether by 1834. However, Cuban plantation owners could not overcome the temptation of free slave labor, and many of them continued to smuggle slaves from Africa.

When the slave trade was beginning to phase out, Chinese coolies became an alternative labor source for the Cuban sugar industry. This did not mean that the practice of slavery ended in Cuba. The coexistence of the two labor

Figure 3.1. Sugarcane Cutting in Cuba. *duncan1890 © iStock*

groups side by side affected Cuban perceptions of Chinese laborers as the coolie served as substitutes for the shrinking labor pool of black slaves. The image of Chinese coolies became intertwined with that of the black slaves. This created a unique dynamic between the two subjugated labor groups even though both had originated in different continents and civilizations. It must be noted that the slave trade and slavery were different. The former referred to the transportation of new slaves from Africa while slavery was the use of slave labor in the Americas.

Slavery in Cuba lasted until 1886, more than ten years after the end of the Chinese coolie trade. Cuba was the last Spanish colony to maintain slavery in Latin America. Most other Spanish colonies in the region had officially ended slavery by the beginning of the nineteenth century. The main reason they clung to slavery was sugar production. The maintenance of slavery affected the nature of race relations on the island. Just for comparative purposes, it should be pointed out that President Abraham Lincoln had proclaimed emancipation for American slaves in 1863, during the middle of the Civil War. Thus, there was a twenty-three-year gap between Cuba and the United States when it came to ending slavery. Since Chinese laborers were indentured workers bound by contract, they were not slaves in legal terms. In reality, however, they were treated as slaves and they had no one to protect their rights. As foreigners from the far side of the world, they were easy prey.

Figure 3.2. Chinese Coolies in Cuba. *GeorglosArt* © *iStock*

Their fates were often at the mercy of plantation owners or managers. Unfamiliar with the rules and customs of the Spanish colony, these transplanted migrants from a distant land were extremely vulnerable.

So far removed from home, in Cuba they had no one to turn to for support and assistance. Even if the Chinese government was aware of the suffering of its citizens working abroad, a post–Opium War China was too weak to help. Thus, the situation faced by Chinese coolies was not so different from the slaves from Africa, and in fact, possibly worse. In the social hierarchy of Cuba, the newly arrived Chinese laborers stood below the longtime resident black slaves. Often in the eyes of the Chinese laborers, plantation society consisted of these tiers: whites, blacks, livestock, pets, and Chinese. The Chinese felt that they were worse off than dogs and horses, worth as much as the ants and crickets found in the fields.

In terms of assigned roles, most sizable sugarcane plantations in Cuba had the following layers. Below the white owners at the top were white managers, white field overseers, black overseers, Chinese overseers, black slaves, Chinese foremen, and Chinese laborers.[18] The latter were at the very bottom of the plantation totem pole. Often, the Chinese felt that they were treated less than animals, not only by the whites but also by the blacks. Being numerically smaller, physically slighter and weaker, and linguistically and culturally illiterate, the Chinese were the most vulnerable minority in Cuba. Many Chinese felt disconcerted at finding themselves at the bottom of Cuba's social stratosphere, even below the lifelong black slaves who were larger in number and more familiar with Cuban culture. This feeling created uneasiness and tension between the two racial groups on the plantations. Up until the eighteenth century, China was the dominant country in Asia. Chinese laborers were proud of their long history and glorious civilization, and a few were well educated and enjoyed social standing in China. Thus, the degradation they now felt was difficult to accept. They resented the fact that black slaves were considered more valuable than contract laborers. On the other hand, black slaves resented Chinese for the freedom they would earn after the contract period.

One of the most humiliating punishments meted out to Chinese laborers was to force them to drink the urine of a black female slave. On plantations, black female slaves were often considered the most degraded,[19] constantly subject to the sexual lusts of predatory owners and overseers. Nineteenth-century Chinese males held the traditional view that women were inferior, so to be forced to drink female urine was the ultimate humiliation and psychological punishment. At the same time, plantation owners lived in constant fear of a slave rebellion, and they took all security measures to prevent such a thing from happening. A neighboring independent country, Haiti, was a constant reminder of what a slave rebellion could do to slave owners. When Chinese coolies joined the plantation workforce, owners pitted these two subordinate groups against one another in an attempt to foil any form of solidarity. Although both groups worked side by side in the fields, they were separated during off hours and kept in different living quarters. Moreover, so as not to rouse any shared hostility toward plantation ownership or management, field overseers never punished Chinese workers in front of black slaves.[20] The management tried to prevent slaves from feeling sympathy for the Chinese, which could result in an alliance against the owners.

Chinese workers who violated certain plantation rules preferred to be beaten by their own foremen rather than by whites or blacks. They would rather take the humiliation of corporal punishment by a fellow Chinese. Although the Spanish colonial government had prohibited the corporal punishment of workers in 1854, plantation management continued to beat Chinese laborers with impunity.[21] As a way of maintaining social order in race-conscious Cuba, the colonial administration maintained a European view of racial hierarchy: white, yellow, and black in that order, at least in theory if not in reality. This was according to the European scheme of ranking the three races. In the plantation, the rank reflected the amount of freedom each group had: full freedom for whites, constrained or limited freedom for Chinese contract laborers, and no freedom at all for black slaves. Based on the European belief of an intrinsic racial hierarchical order, even free blacks in Cuba were not allowed to purchase the labor contracts of Chinese coolies. The colonial administration wanted to maintain racial order in order to perpetuate their dominance and maintain slavery. In reality, Chinese were used as a buffer group between Cuban whites and blacks.

THE END OF HOPE

Many Chinese had managed to overcome the hopelessness they felt on the sea journey, but in truth their nightmare was just beginning. The moment they were thrown into the pigpen holding areas at the embarkation harbors, most of them felt deceived and ensnared. With feelings of intense anger and disappointment, their encounters with the crew became increasingly volatile. Sold to strange bidders in Cuba as if they were animals, many experienced being shackled or chained by plantation overseers. Their homeland seemed out of reach and their loved ones at home were oblivious to the deadly toil of plantation labor. With no prospect of realizing their dreams of making small fortunes and no prospect of seeing their loved ones again, many fell into despair. The terrible working and living conditions of the sugarcane plantations wore out many Chinese laborers. In addition, the inhumane mistreatment they received was unbearable for many. Feeling so hopeless and helpless, many did not see a reason to continue with the misery of indentured servitude. They had two options before them: escape or suicide.

Suicide was much easier than escape. In a foreign island of unfamiliar geography and language, it was almost impossible for Chinese laborers to escape and hide. Moreover, any Chinese outside the plantation would stand out. Consequently, many ended their misery by committing suicide. Often, groups of three, six, or ten workers committed suicide by drinking poison together. Others chose deep wells to throw themselves into. In sugar refineries, some jumped into the boiling cauldrons. In these instances, callous owners were more concerned about the monetary loss of having to discard the liquid sugar in the caldron than they were about the loss of a Chinese laborer.

From 1850 to 1860, Cuba had the highest suicide rate in the world. Among the different racial groups on the island, Chinese suicide rates were the highest, with five thousand cases per million. In other words, one in two hundred Chinese committed suicide during this ten-year period. After the Chinese, black and white suicide rates were 350 and 57 per million, respectively.[22] These figures illustrate that the Chinese were fourteen times more likely than blacks and eighty-eight times more likely than whites to commit suicide. The much higher rate among the Chinese in Cuba reflected their prevalent sense of hopelessness. Even if they survived the harsh life of a plantation laborer, the chance of establishing themselves in Cuba seemed impossible. In addition, many Chinese felt socially dead as they continued to labor without the joy of family life or meaningful human connection.

Besides suicide, many others died of disease, exhaustion, and malnutrition, and work-related injuries also claimed hundreds of Chinese lives. Instead of sending the sick to health facilities for proper medical treatment, plantation managers and overseers forced Chinese laborers to continue working in the fields. If they failed to work at a normal pace, overseers punished

Figure 3.3. Sugar Processing Factory. *ilbusca © iStock*

them without mercy. Often the exhausted and injured workers were left uncared for and would die in the fields. During their eight-year contract period, the mortality rate was about 50 percent.[23] As indicated previously, about 12 percent of Chinese perished during the long voyage to Cuba. Therefore, the chance of survival beyond the eight-year labor contract term was not much above 40 percent for the original labor recruits who left China for Cuba. Approximately, six out of ten Chinese laborers died before they had a chance to start a new life in Cuba as free men.

In traditional China, it was a cultural imperative to be buried close to one's ancestral home. It was considered an utter misfortune to die and be buried far from one's ancestors, for there would be no way to be remembered or honored by future descendants. Committing suicide either during the voyage or on the plantations was a last resort. For some laborers, to die and be forgotten rather than to live and work as indentured laborers was a more attractive alternative.

Most Chinese who died on the plantations received not even minimally acceptable funeral rites by Chinese standards. Those who died of sickness on plantations were often buried in mass graves. Burial rituals were neither performed nor tombstones erected. To most plantation owners, the body of a Chinese worker was something to dispose of at their convenience. In particular, the bodies of those who rebelled or committed suicide were given unusual treatment. They were cremated, and the ashes were blown into the air or poured into water. Chinese laborers who witnessed such disrespectful treatment of their deceased fellow countrymen were deeply disturbed. On the other hand, the Chinese noticed that slaves were buried in coffins. Once again, this confirmed their view that their place was at the bottom of the plantation social hierarchy. After so much misery and suffering in a faraway land, deceased Chinese were treated like animals, and the living envisioned their own deaths when they witnessed the heartless treatment of their countrymen.

In a culture known for ancestral worship, funeral rituals are of critical importance. The last rite of passage demonstrates to the community the social status of the deceased and their descendants. Family members and relatives express their respect and honor to the deceased under the watch of the whole community, signifying the worth of both the departed and the survivors in the eyes of community members. In ancient days, mourning lasted from one to three years. Since filial piety was the cornerstone of traditional Chinese society, children treated the death of parents with utmost dignity. Some well-to-do families with only a few offspring or relatives would hire professional mourners to impress funeral guests. They did not want to be pitied for having produced so few children.

FROM CALIFORNIA TO CUBA

Unexpectedly, about five thousand Chinese moved from the United States to Cuba in the post–Civil War years from 1865 to 1875. In Cuba, they were called "Californianos" as they came mainly from California during the last phase of the coolie trade. They moved to Cuba after the Gold Rush in California and the completion of the transcontinental railroad in the West. When the demand for Chinese labor diminished in California and other Western states, anti-Chinese sentiment rose to such a pitch that the Workingmen's Party of California was formed to counter an increasingly visible Chinese population. Initially, these Chinese were invisible, confined to remote mines and railroad construction sites deep in the Sierra Nevada Mountains. Once they competed with whites for jobs, housing, and other necessities in towns and cities, the tide of resentment rose. Eventually this led to the passage of a federal law prohibiting the import of Chinese laborers in 1882.

Having been less subjugated and mistreated in the United States, the Chinese from America were somewhat different, being more self-assured and confident. In Cuba, the Californianos began to organize their compatriots and to start ventures of their own. Some independent business activities among free Chinese were a result of the initiatives taken by the Californianos, who were "largely traders and merchants, some with access to substantial capital in China, Hong Kong, and the United States. With their arrival, Havana's *Barrio Chino* began to be transformed into a center of trade, commerce, and banking . . ."[24] As a result, the Chinatown in Havana became the world's second largest after the one in San Francisco.

The Californianos in Cuba also established their own Chinese association in 1867. They organized free laborers into work gangs and negotiated with employers to improve working conditions and wages. Besides plantations, they supplied laborers to load and unload freight at the harbor and construction sites. It was very different from the early days of indentured labor with no one representing the interests of Chinese workers. As a result of their united effort, some savvy Chinese became rich: "By the end of the 1880s, wealthy Chinese were investing capital in sugar. Two sugar mills in Las Villas, one in Sagua la Grande and another in Santo Domingo, were soon Chinese-owned. The 1899 census recorded forty-two Chinese plantation owners."[25] It was a far cry from the servile indentured coolie laborers. During the Cuban independence movement in later years, some Chinese played key roles.

FROM CUBA TO NEW ORLEANS

At the same time, many plantations in the American South experienced severe labor shortages after the emancipation of slaves in 1863 during the Civil War (1861–1865). To solve its labor shortage problem, some plantation owners in Louisiana and Mississippi managed to bring 145 Chinese laborers from Cuba, workers who had fulfilled the terms of their labor contracts in Cuba. The short distance between Cuba and the Gulf states made the move easy. White plantation owners in the Southern states favored the Chinese for their reputation of being hard workers and their previous experience working on sugarcane plantations in Cuba. Moreover, the fact that Chinese laborers could not become naturalized citizens of the United States made Southern whites feel somewhat safe. According to the Naturalization Act of 1790, immigrants from countries other than Europe could not become naturalized citizens. The whites in the post–Civil War South were nervous as large numbers of former slaves could vote and compete for power with their former masters. In short, former slaves had become a political threat to the white majority.

Enthusiasm for Chinese laborers in the South, however, became lukewarm when the US government required plantation owners to apply proper labor standards. This move was to comply with the spirit of the Burlingame Treaty signed between the United States and China (Qing government) in 1868. The treaty was an amendment to the Tientsin Treaty that had been signed at the end of the Second Opium War in 1858. The Burlingame Treaty guaranteed "the same privilege, immunities, and exemptions in respect to travel or residence as may there be enjoyed by the citizens or the subject of the most favored nation."[26] The treaty designated China as a favored nation of the United States. Accordingly, the US government took measures to prevent any mistreatment or exploitation of Chinese citizens, now from a "most favored nation." This requirement dampened the enthusiasm of Southern plantation owners for bringing Chinese laborers from Cuba. Perhaps they thought that they could take advantage of the submissive Chinese by bending government labor regulations involving the treatment of foreign workers.

It is interesting to note that some Chinese left the United States for Cuba while their compatriots in Cuba were eager to come to America. It was much easier for the Chinese in Cuba to come to Louisiana or Mississippi by crossing the Gulf of Mexico. The distance between New Orleans and Havana, for instance, is only 671 miles (1,080 km), while the distance between San Francisco and Havana is 2,571 straight miles (4,137 km). Nonetheless, Southern plantation owners were reluctant to treat the Chinese from Cuba fairly, and the flow of Chinese labor to America ebbed to a trickle. Former slave owners could not shake off the legacy of slavery imbued in their outlook and attitude.

Finally, the Qing government in Beijing discovered the inhumane mistreatment and exploitation of its citizens in Cuba and other parts of Latin America. Hence, the Chinese government dispatched a fact-finding commission to hold hearings in certain Latin American countries. For the first time, frustrated Chinese laborers revealed their suffering to officials in their own government. Their testimonies were complaints and appeals for help. They cursed the recruitment practices at home, the mistreatment endured at plantations, and the unfair local government practices in their resident countries. In 1874, indentured "coolie" trade ended with the Treaty of Tianjin. No more bonded Chinese laborers would be brought to the Americas. After 1874, the Chinese would come as free immigrant laborers.

RETURNING HOME

No exact figure is available as to how many Chinese who labored in Cuba during the coolie trade period (1847–1874) managed to return home. The statistics are partial and approximate. It is safe to assume, however, that the returning number of plantation laborers was low because of a lack of money. Not many who completed eight-year labor contracts could afford the return passage from Cuba to China. The one-way fare cost six ounces of gold, so only a small percentage of Chinese workers were able to afford the journey home, despite the fact that coolie transport ships did their best to tempt freed Chinese workers to return home as a way of increasing profit. The return journey to China, just like the original one, was long and difficult. Passengers had to cross the South Atlantic Ocean, the Indian Ocean, and the South China Sea. Another route was the Mid-Atlantic Ocean, the Mediterranean Sea, the Red Sea, the Indian Ocean, and the South China Sea, if the return voyage used the Suez Canal. The completion of this canal in 1869 shortened the trip by avoiding the voyage around Africa.

Another return route was opened when the US transcontinental railroad was completed in 1869. The Western section of the railroad was constructed mainly by Chinese laborers. Returning Chinese would cross the Gulf of Mexico between Cuba and New Orleans. From the latter, they would take a train bound for San Francisco where many ships sailed to China. To many Chinese, the high cost of the return fare was only one obstacle. Gifts and money for family members also weighed heavily on their minds. Years before, they had left home with promises to return home having earned a small fortune. No Chinese would dare to return home empty-handed after so many years of work abroad. They would rather bear the pain of missing loved ones at home than of going home poor and losing face. Not knowing the difference between California (which the Chinese called Gold Mountain) and Cuba, most family members at home had high expectations for laborers returning from overseas. Moreover, many Chinese would be conscious of their altered appearance. It would take courage to return home with their worn bodies and souls to family members who remembered them differently. After so much toil and suffering, they felt unfit to return home. In fact, many Chinese in Cuba wished that somebody would relate their hellish experiences to their fellow countrymen lest others should repeat the same tragedy.

About two thousand Chinese are estimated to have returned home between 1865 and 1874.[27] The early labor recruits who arrived in Cuba by 1866 numbered 79,084,[28] and they should have completed their eight-year contracts by 1874. If half survived the eight-year contract period, about forty thousand would have been eligible to return home. If this estimate is reliable, only 5 percent ever returned to China. The percent of return is even more depressing when calculated by the number of arrivals (79,084): only 2.5 percent of Chinese who left home were lucky enough to return.

A Chinese laborer, Mariano Segundo, managed to return to China in 1872. The forty-one-year-old Chinese had worked as a cook, and he was one of the first to return home among the hundreds of Chinese who worked in the Santiago de Cuba region. Luis Abdala Pupo, who discovered the case of Mariano Segundo's return in some provincial archives, summed up the rarity of his return in the following statement: "For the majority, almost absolutely, the trip to Cuba would be a trip with no return."[29] Pupo's observation could be applied to most Chinese in Cuba at that time. In the years following 1874, however, more were able to go home. A Chinese study calculated that from 1880 to 1885, 1,885 Chinese returned home.[30] By then, most Chinese laborers in Cuba were free, and some were business owners. The percentage of returnees among free Chinese was much higher than the percentage of returnees during the coolie trade period that ended in 1874. In addition, the returning figures either before or after 1874 did not take into account the varying conditions that Chinese laborers faced. The greater number of returnees might have been mainly those who served as domestic helpers or tradesmen such as cooks, barbers, carpenters, and the like. These non-agricultural workers did not endure the harsh treatment and physical exhaustion of labor on sugarcane plantations.

Many Chinese buried their bodies and dreams in the faraway Caribbean island of Cuba. If they died as indentured laborers on plantations, their bodies were laid in a foreign soil without anything to mark their existence. As sojourners, they wanted to return home upon completion of their labor contracts in Cuba. Many Chinese could not sustain their lives long enough to see even the expiration of their eight-year labor contracts. Some Chinese believed that the souls of the dead might wander around searching for their final resting place in the afterlife. Such a thought made the Chinese in mourning even sadder. Others wanted to believe that the spirit of the dead could return home to be near their loved ones. Although they could not visit home alive, their spirits freed from their bodies could finally return home uninhibited. They wished for the agonized souls of the dead to rest in their place of birth.

In traditional Chinese culture, staying close to one's family was extremely important. It was more so if an adult son had elderly parents. Looking after them was a solemn responsibility for a filial son. In addition, attending and caring for annual memorial services to remember deceased ancestors was an important aspect of family life. For neglecting such family obligations, overseas Chinese emigrants were often despised and called "deserters." Going as far away as Cuba at the other end of earth for as long as eight years was an ultimate betrayal of one's filial obligations. Moreover, there was no assurance that they would return home while their parents were still alive. Yet family members often understood and accepted the promises that one day they would return home. Many Chinese in Cuba suffered from guilt and regret for not having fulfilled their filial duties. With no prospect of seeing their parents and loved ones again, many chose to end their miseries in Cuba.

REFLECTIONS

New republics were proclaimed in China and Cuba in 1949 and 1959, respectively. They were the People's Republic of China and the Republic of Cuba. The two new governments, established ten years apart, were the result of communist revolutions led by Mao Zedong in China and Fidel Castro in Cuba. China became the second communist nation in Asia after North Korea in 1948, and Cuba the first in the Americas. Cuba was the first Latin American nation to recognize the People's Republic of China in 1960. To this date, the two nations have remained communist countries, and both have been less than friendly toward the United States, the bastion of capitalism. The United States lifted its longtime embargo of Cuba in 2015, and diplomatic relations between the two have been somewhat restored.

The United States officially recognized the People's Republic of China in 1978, a change preceded by President Nixon's visit to China in 1972 and Ping Pong Diplomacy. Among the nations that have been sympathetic toward an isolated Cuba since the fall of communism in Eastern Europe, China has been one of its staunchest supporters. It has been the Cuba's largest creditor, and the impact of China's investments in Cuba and Chinese tourism have been quite significant for the Cuban economy. Since September 2015, the two countries have been connected through regularly scheduled, direct flights. Chinese visitors and tourists to the Caribbean island nation has been on the rise.

Beyond Cuba, China's political and economic influence in Latin America has been growing. To counter American dominance in the Americas through the Organization of American States (OAS), thirty-three Latin American countries formed a new regional association in February 2010: the Community of Latin American and Caribbean States (Communidad de Estados Latinamericanos y Caribenos—CELAC in Spanish). In January 2015, China-CELAC held a joint forum in Beijing. They agreed to expand trade and other programs for the development of Latin America. China promised to increase investment in Latin America by 500 billion dollars, almost doubling its investment. China needs a steady supply of energy and other raw materials for its economic growth and sustenance, and also will benefit from markets that are open to its industrial products. Many third world countries in the global south have identified with China for their own developmental models.

The affinity of China and Cuba, however, is more than a shared communist political ideology. Besides the fact that the island nation of Cuba received the largest number of Chinese immigrants among Latin American countries in the nineteenth century, early Chinese immigrants and their descendants joined the Cuban revolt against Spanish colonial rule and military dictators like Gerardo Machado and Fulgencio Batista. Chinese contributions to Cuba's liberation movements were significant, and the Cuban people have not forgotten them.

Some Chinese freedom fighters in Cuba earned national honors. Lieutenant Colonel Jose Bu Tack and Captain Jose Tolon, for example, were eligible to be president of Cuba even though they were born in China. Such constitutional exceptions of foreign-born Cubans were only made for two others, Maximo Gomez of Dominica and Carlos Roloff of Poland. In the uprising against the Batista dictatorship in the 1950s, three Chinese Cubans became generals of the Revolutionary Armed Forces of Cuba. They were Armando Choy, Gustavo Chui, and Moises Sio Wong.[30] In a monument erected in Havana to commemorate the Chinese sacrifices in Cuba's liberation, the following is inscribed: "There was not one Chinese Cuban deserter, not one Cuban Chinese traitor."

Since early Chinese immigrants came to Cuba as indentured workers, they easily identified themselves with the marginalized and exploited Cubans and their struggles against the powerful ruling elite. Chinese engagement in the liberation movement against the establishment was genuine and sincere. Today there are less than five hundred ethnic Chinese residents in Cuba. It is a far cry from the sizable Chinese community of about sixty thousand reported in 1869.[31] The present Chinatown in Havana, known as *Barrio Chino de La Havana*, is no comparison with the one that was once the oldest and largest Chinatown in Latin America.

The drastic decline may be attributed to the demography of the Chinese immigrant community. As most early Chinese laborers to Cuba were men, many of them had no choice but to marry local black and mestizo women. Because of an anti-miscegenation law, they were prohibited from marrying

Spanish women. Such mixed families, dominated by Spanish-speaking mothers, made the preservation and transmission of Chinese culture almost impossible. Another impediment was the sheer distance between China and Cuba. The opportunity to reinforce Chinese culture on the island proved difficult.

Yet the present-day opportunities to reconnect with China through tourism and business contacts may revive ethnic awareness among Cubans of Chinese ancestry regardless of their numbers. The China of the twenty-first century has become a source of pride and opportunity for many overseas Chinese. The early Chinese indentured laborers who were treated almost like slaves would not have believed their eyes if they saw the increasing influence of their mother country, a present-day superpower. The one-time Middle Kingdom that became a source of cheap labor supply for the Caribbean island colony has now become a big brother patron to a financially struggling Cuba.

NOTES

1. Lisa Yun, *The Coolie Speaks: Chinese Indentured Laborers and African Slaves in Cuba* (Philadelphia: Temple University Press, 2008), 13.
2. Ibid., 61.
3. Arnold J. Meagher, *The Coolie Trade: The Traffic in Chinese Laborers to Latin America 1847–1874* (Xlibris Corporation, 2008), 135.
4. Kathleen Lopez, *Chinese Cubans: A Transnational History* (Chapel Hill: The University of North Carolina Press, 2013), 23.
5. Yun, *The Coolie Speaks,* 120.
6. Ibid., 17.
7. One dollar in 1850 was worth around 33 dollars in 2020.
8. Samuel H. Williamson and Louis P. Cain, "Measuring Slavery in 2011 Dollars," accessed November 29, 2017, https://www.measuringworth.com/slavery.php.
9. Ibid., 6.
10. Ibid., 8.
11. Ibid., 3.
12. Yun, *The Coolie Speaks,* 30.
13. Ibid., 163.
14. Ibid., 179.
15. Ibid., 176.
16. Ibid., 115.
17. Ibid., 134–35.
18. Ibid., 166.
19. Ibid., 154.
20. Elliott Young, *Alien Nation: Chinese Migration in the Americas from the Coolie Era through World War II* (Chapel Hill: The University of North Carolina Press, 2014), 77.
21. Ibid., 80.
22. Yun, *The Coolie Speaks,* 84.
23. Ibid., 29.
24. Mary-Alice Waters, "The Unique History of Chinese in Cuba: From Independence War to Socialist Revolution," *The Militant* 75, no. 30, 1–11, accessed August 2, 2016, http://www.themilitant.com/2011/7530/753050.html.
25. Ibid.

26. Office of the Historian, "The Burlingame-Seward Treaty, 1868," accessed August 17, 2020, https://history.state.gov/milestones/1866-1898/burlingame-seward-treaty.
27. Lopez, *Chinese Cubans*, 45.
28. Ibid., 23.
29. Ibid., 45.
30. Ibid.
31. Waters, "The Unique History of Chinese in Cuba," 7–8.

Chapter Four

A One-Way Passage to a Peruvian Hell

Pisco is a medium-size harbor town located on the Peruvian central Pacific Coast. When one enters the city, it is impossible to miss the statue of a large bird erected at the entrance to the town, a monument to the contribution of seabirds to the growth and development of Pisco. To someone, however, who knows something of the history of the early Chinese laborers brought to Pisco, it is a sad reminder of those who slaved on the obscure, rocky islands just off the mouth of the harbor. Perhaps the most tragic Chinese story in the Americas unfolded on these small rocky islands unbeknownst to most of the world. As is often the case, this tragedy was produced to generate wealth at the expense of great human suffering.

To most immigrants from East Asia in the nineteenth century, the Pacific-coast nation of Peru was the gateway to South America. In the Age of Sail, San Francisco and Callao/Lima served as the two major ports of entry into North and South America, respectively. Chinese laborers flooded into Peru during the early phases of nation building. Declaring independence from Spain in 1821, Peru became sovereign in 1824. This fledgling nation needed laborers, especially in agriculture, mining, and construction. The need for physical laborers was further exacerbated when the Peruvian government emancipated slaves in 1854. As Peru searched for a new source of cheap labor, it eyed China, which had already begun to open up its vast laborer pool to the West. Cuba's sugarcane plantations, with their intensive labor needs, served as the model. Anticipating the emancipation of Peru's slaves and a subsequent labor shortage, Peruvian business representatives went to Canton and its surrounding regions to recruit laborers. In October 1849, the first group of seventy-five Chinese laborers was brought to Peru. In the following decade, thirteen thousand Chinese workers were transported,[1] with numbers continuing to increase significantly. Between 1849 and 1874, nearly one hundred thousand Chinese went to Peru.[2] Chinese immigration to Peru, however, was not a smooth, continuous flow. Widespread mistreatment during the Pacific crossing and terrible working conditions precipitated a pause in migration for several years. For instance, 1862 was the worst year in regards to mortality during the Pacific crossing, at 42 percent. Of the 1,726 Chinese labor recruits that left Macao, only 1,008 arrived in Callao/Lima harbor. The second highest year for mortality at sea occurred in 1850, when one-third of the Chinese recruits perished during transport.[3]

Although plantation owners, mine operators, and railroad construction companies in Peru experienced severe labor shortages, no one was more desperate for laborers than *guano* mine operators on the desolate islands off Pisco. Labor shortages were a chronic problem because the work was so backbreaking, thus resulting in high turnover. Even the limited number of free migrant workers, either highland indigenous peasants or mestizos, did not last long on the rocky, bleak islands. Since they were not bound by any constraints, legal or otherwise, quitting and leaving the islands became an easy option. The solution to a high turnover of domestic workers was to bring foreign laborers bound with legal restrictions in the form of labor contracts. To the *guano* mine operators, Chinese laborers were the most attractive option. Far from home, with nowhere to go and no one to turn to for help, the Chinese could be kept regardless of their wishes.

CHINCHA ISLANDS

The Chincha Islands are a group of three granite islets whose combined area is no more than three square miles (about five square kilometers). They lie about 12 miles (about 20 km) off of Pisco, which is about 170 miles (about 270 km) south of Lima, the capital city of Peru. Not far from the equator, the islands are hot, humid, and devoid of vegetation. These uninhabited islands are renowned for their huge *guano* deposits. Over thousands of years, millions of seabirds covered the surface of the islands with droppings that formed into massive mounds or columns, some as high as one hundred feet (about thirty meters), or the equivalent in height of a twelve-story building. Peruvians called these deposits *guano* after the name of the common seabird found in the area. Three natural conditions had to be met, over a long period of time, in order to form the rock-like columns of *guano*. First, the islands needed to attract hordes of birds. With no natural predators and easy access to fish, the islands were an ideal habitat for thousands of birds. Second, the weather needed to be hot. Only hot weather without rain allowed the continuous buildup of *guano*. Otherwise, the bird droppings would be washed away. Finally, humidity needed to be high as moisture in the air hardened the deposits of *guano*. The Chincha Islands met all three conditions, creating an ideal environment for the massive buildup of *guano* deposits. However, the last two conditions, heat and humidity, were miserable for human habitation.

The *guano* deposits on the Chincha Islands remained relatively unknown beyond the region until the nineteenth century. For centuries before the arrival of European settlers, indigenous people along the Peruvian coast had used *guano* to fertilize their farmlands because they knew of its magical properties: "[O]ne ton of Chincha *guano* has been determined to be equal to 33 tons of farmyard manure."[4] It is no surprise, then, that "Peruvian *guano* was the most complete, most concentrated fertilizer available on the world market for many years."[5] Furthermore, *guano* had one other property that made it more in demand than any other fertilizer. It contained the key ingredient for manufacturing gunpowder: saltpeter or potassium nitrate. For this reason, many countries in Europe and the Americas were interested in obtaining *guano* for both agricultural and military purposes. Efforts were made to control and regulate transactions involving *guano* due to its potential military implications.[6]

In spite of *guano*'s high value, it was very hard to recruit and retain an adequate labor force because locals did not want to leave families behind to labor on these desolate islands. Besides the labor-intensive work, the islands were not fit for normal human habitation. Cut off from family and social connections, not many were able to withstand the isolation for long. With the help of the Peruvian government, *guano* mine operators relied on a limited number of prison convicts and army deserters in the early days of *guano* mining. Other than these coerced workers, a few indigenous and mestizo day laborers, former slaves, and a small number of free laborers from neighboring countries comprised the small, fragile labor force. Most free laborers did not last long. They could not stand the extreme physical environment of the hot, humid islands and the unbearable working conditions of the *guano* mines: "The Indians, genetically adapted to breathing the rarefied, cool air of the High Andes, could not be persuaded . . . to toil on the coastal islands. The urban proletariat . . . these proud descendants of the conquistadors undoubtedly considered such work beneath their dignity."[7]

The high turnover caused mine operators to scramble to find other labor sources. Along with Indians, *guano* mine operators began to look at "the only other group that could be considered . . . the negro slaves . . . army deserters and convicts . . . These were supplemented with a few Negro slaves and some hired laborers. . . . The government had provided the contractors with a limited supply of mainly penal labor . . ."[8] These were the sources of labor supply for Chincha *guano* mining throughout the 1840s. Desperate to meet increasing demand for *guano* but with an inadequate labor pool, lawmakers in Lima began to consider passing legislation as a means of incentivizing labor recruitment. One of the proposed ideas in 1847 was to offer "tax free four tons of *guano* for each colonist recruited,"[9] but the incentive bill did not pass.

Figure 4.1.   Chincha Islands in Peru. *Nastasic © iStock*

Another bill proposed to pay thirty pesos for each Chinese worker recruited "between the ages of ten and forty."[10] The labor shortage problem was so severe that the Peruvian government allowed child labor when even adult laborers could not withstand the heavy work of *guano* mining. To that extent, both the government and *guano* mine operators were desperate for workers.

Such were the circumstances under which Chinese laborers were brought to the Chincha Islands. Like other Chinese laborers transported to the Ameri-

Figure 4.2. *Guano* Mine on Chincha Islands. *Nastasic © iStock*

cas, they went through the inhumane recruitment in China and the trauma of a three- to four-month long Pacific Ocean crossing. When they began their journey, none of them imagined the hell that awaited them on the Chincha Islands. Tricked into promises of making good and easy money, Chinese labor recruits were in for a rude awakening. Almost one thousand Chinese laborers were brought to the Chincha Islands in the 1850s. As indentured laborers, they had no freedom to quit no matter how terrible the working conditions. They found themselves in the same position as slaves, convicts, and army deserters who labored against their will on the bleak islands. China was almost nine thousand miles (around 14,000 km) away, and they had no one to come to their aid. Although many considered escape, there was absolutely no chance of succeeding as the islands sit twelve miles off the coast. So certain were the *guano* mine operators about security, they did not chain or shackle any of the laborers.

HELL ON CHINCHA ISLANDS

While farmers in many nations were eager to import *guano*, a natural wonder fertilizer, many Chinese laborers in the *guano* mines slaved to their death. In spite of the tremendous financial bonanza to Peru, *guano* might have been located in the worst possible place on earth: "Tropical heat, high humidity, and yet virtually no rainfall made the Chincha a hell on earth."[11] For centuries, local people living on the coast had visited the islands to collect seabird eggs and catch fish, but no one had ever settled on them. The Chincha Islands remained uninhabited until demand for *guano* greatly increased in the nineteenth century. At the peak of *guano* mining, about three thousand people lived and worked on the small islands. They were mainly laborers and ancillary staff. The islands' temporary residents were mainly young male laborers in their twenties, thirties, and forties, with no women or children. In 1853, for instance, more than two-thirds (71%) of *guano* mine workers on the Chincha Islands were Chinese laborers. The total of 850 laborers at that time "included about 600 Chinese workers, 50 slaves, and about 200 Chilean or Peruvians, most of them convicts or army deserters, although a mere handful were free workers."[12] Although the weather was ideal for the formation of *guano* into solid mounds or columns, it was the worst possible climate for human habitation. It was intensely hot and humid and often foggy at night: "Thick, seasonal fog that shrouded them mostly at night metamorphosed outer layers of bird droppings into a greasy paste, which baked during the day into hard crust that only picks and shovels could penetrate."[13] Extracting *guano* deposits was difficult, and often Chinese laborers had to use dynamite to blast the rock-like deposits. Whenever this measure was necessary, rock and *guano* needed to be separated manually. Extracted *guano* was then moved in wheelbarrows to launching areas. From there, it was poured through canvas chutes to holding areas on freight ships. At any given time, multiple ships were anchored around the islands waiting to be loaded.

For Chinese laborers, one of the most unbearable aspects was breathing air filled with *guano* dust. Every time a *guano* deposit was disturbed, a thick dust would rise and envelop the area. Moreover, the powder-like dry *guano* dust had an awful stench that was inescapable and penetrated the senses. In addition, "the seabird feces emitted strong ammonia vapor. The laborers at work were constantly exposed to the dust and vapor."[14] By far the worst was when Chinese laborers had to work in an enclosed area with no air circulation such as in the cargo hold of a freight ship: "The worst job was to level the *guano* load in the ship's cargo area as the workers were constantly exposed to the dust and the ammonia vapor. Each time they could stay in the hold area below the deck no more than 20 minutes. When they rushed out of the hold area, they often gasped for air."[15] As a result of constant exposure to *guano* dust, Chinese laborers experienced a wide range of health problems. Since *guano* is biomass, it contained all sorts of bacteria. Yet *guano* mine operators did not take any proper preventive measures to protect vulnerable workers: "Some covered their noses and mouths with a piece of crude fabric, but it was far from being adequate. The common respiratory symptoms . . . included asphyxiation, coughing or blood spitting, embarrassed breathing, and fainting spells."[16] In addition to respiratory problems, laborers developed a variety of gastrointestinal problems that "included stomach cramps, diarrhea, dysentery, nausea, vomiting. The seabird feces carried some parasites and germs, and they entered into the body of workers through mouth, noses, and other channels."[17] Even the crews of freight ships could not stand the dust and stink of *guano*. One deckhand observed the effects of "the evil-smelling dust almost blinding and suffocating the sailors waiting below."[18]

Chinese laborers earned thirteen dollars (about $260 in 2020) for loading one hundred tons of *guano* (about 220,460 pounds), thus earning about thirteen cents (about $2.60 in 2020) per ton. In the hot, enclosed cargo holds of ships, their task was to even out the *guano* pouring into the hold area. The workers inside the cargo holds had to wear iron masks "as the guano dust was more penetrating than coal dust, or steel filings, and stronger than volatile salts."[19] Each Chinese laborer was required to extract five tons of *guano* per day. In addition, they had to move the extracted *guano* by wheelbarrow to a loading chute. The only tools at their disposal were either pickaxes or shovels. If they failed to meet the daily quota, they were severely whipped by their overseers. Many Chinese laborers were sick and broken from the hard labor, but these were not acceptable excuses for failing to meet the daily quota. If they could not physically stand up because of injury or weakness, they were forced to work on hands and knees. One English shipmaster who transported *guano* testified as follows: "Two dozen lashes made them breathless and, when released after thirty-nine lashes, they seemed to slowly to stagger over, reeled and fell, and were carried off to the hospital, in most cases, if they recovered, committing suicide."[20]

In spite of the intensive labor under extremely harsh working conditions, provisions for the most basic physical needs such as food and shelter were barely adequate. A description of the reality of laborers toiling on the Chincha Islands is indeed appalling.

> Provided with no more than two meals daily (usually a cup of maize and four unripe bananas), grass mats for beds, and reed huts for dwellings, men (a few free Peruvian native laborers, but mostly indentured laborers, kidnapped Pacific islanders, convicts, army deserters, and a handful of black slaves) labored twenty or more hours a day, six days a week, to fill quotas of four or five tons each, for which they were paid three reales [about a third of a peso], two of which were withheld for meals.[21]

Clothing was as bad as food and shelter: "Most of them go nearly naked; none have more than enough clothing just to cover themselves; they live and feed like dogs; they are constantly within reach of the thongs of hideous black drivers—the link between men and devils."[22] These hellish conditions were further exacerbated by black foremen who often vented their anger on helpless Chinese laborers. Not daring to challenge their white superiors, black foremen picked on the Chinese who could not retaliate and thus were powerless. To assert that *guano* mine operators exploited laborers is a gross understatement. Every ounce of energy and every second of every day was exploited: "They are condemned to be diggers of *guano*; their labor is much more severe and injurious than railway digging; they have no liberty days, no protecting laws, no power to obtain even the pittance said to be paid them, no proper seasons of rest."[23] Punishments for violating rules or failing to meet daily quotas were swift and severe. *Guano* mine operators often tortured laborers by "hanging [them] in ropes and chains around the waist, and in other ways, from sunrise to sunset, without food during that period, one, two, or more days, in proportion to the magnitude of the offence; and lashing to half tide buoys, subject to exposure to the water, in addition to heat and cold."[24]

Since the majority of laborers had no way of quitting the mines, many fell into despair. Their psychological torment eroded their will to live. On clear days, the town of Pisco on the coast was visible. The green fields in the valley and the snow-capped Andes in the far distance were within sight. On certain clear nights when the thick, damp fog dissipated, the soft, amber lights of Pisco beckoned. "Hundreds of ships coming up and going, filled with men like themselves, only free"[25] filled the laborers with anguish as they compared their hellishly surreal existence with those on the mainland.

Many chose suicide as the only exit option available for them: "Countless numbers of them preferred suicide: overdoses of opium, hanging, slashing their own throats, and even headlong dives off hundred-foot cliffs onto the rocks below became commonplace escapes."[26] Some workers killed themselves during work hours, a form of public protest for the misery they had suffered. Instead of "working on their hands and knees, picking small stones from the *guano* before it was dumped into the chutes that emptied, . . . some laborers ended their lives with headlong plunges down the chutes."[27] As each hour and day passed, many Chinese laborers realized that they would never return home. Many committed suicide as a means of escape, believing their spirits would return to their ancestral homelands. An eyewitness account of a worker named Kossuth, who worked for two years on the Chincha Islands, reported that "almost every week some of them [Chinese] commit suicide by throwing themselves from the cliff. They are said to do this in the belief that their spirits will awaken in their native land. . . . more than sixty had killed themselves this way in the two years he had been there."[28]

Kossuth describes a specific incident where a Chinese laborer commits suicide. "One was driven over the cliff or jumped off, and was dashed to pieces, to escape the lash of a black driver, who chased him to the verge in sight of a captain of an American ship, the week before Peck left. The cliff where he leaped is two hundred feet high, and almost perpendicular."[29] Many eyewitnesses around the islands, mainly the crews of Western freight ships, attested to the horrific working conditions and wondered how such cruel things were allowed to continue. They could not believe that powerful nations like Great Britain and the United States, which had forcefully enforced the anti-slave trade act on the open sea, were passive and silent on the fate of Chinese *guano* miners. This sentiment was common among many eyewitnesses: "Does it not seem strange that the civilized nations, banded together to suppress slavery, cannot, by remonstrance or force, with a trifling power like Peru, put an end to such inhuman practices at these islands?"[30] The sailors saw nothing but slavery in the labor of the *guano* workers: "And if the voluntary slavery entered into by the deluded Chinese cannot be prevented, surely something may be done by those who profit by their labors to alleviate their suffering."[31]

Not only were the Chinese laborers grossly mistreated, they were also considered disposable chattel. Although they were promised return passage home upon completion of labor contracts, there is no sign that any Chinese left the Chincha Islands alive: "[T]here is no evidence to suggest that any saw their native land again. . . . For the Chinese the crossing of the Pacific to the Chincha Islands was rightly described as a one-way passage to hell."[32] Karl Marx, a one-time foreign correspondent, argued that the Chinese situation on the Chincha Islands was worse than slavery. In a *New York Daily Times* article dated January 24, 1854, he described the conditions of Chinese laborers both in Peru and Cuba in harsh terms: "We hear nothing of the wrongs 'even unto death' upon misguided and bonded emigrants sold to worse than slavery on the coast of Peru, and into Cuban bondage."[33] Apparently, he had heard accounts of the miserable existence of Chinese *guano* workers via sailors and other witnesses. With an apocalyptic imagination, one observer provided a vivid description of the Chincha Islands. He believed it was worse than any scene he could recall from the literary descriptions of the biblical underworld in Western literature. "No hell has ever been conceived by the Hebrew, the Irish, the Italian, or even the Scotch mind for appeasing the anger and satisfying the vengeance of their awful gods, that can be equaled to the fierceness of its heat, the horror of its stink, and the damnation of those compelled to labor there, to a deposit of Peruvian *guano* when being shoveled into ships."[34]

The barely covered bodies of dead workers on the Chincha Islands revealed the misery of their lives as *guano* workers. Their graves were "too shallow to protect [their] remains from scavenging dogs,"[35] and human bones were scattered about on the islands.

How was such cruel, inhumane treatment of Chinese laborers possible? One reason could be that *guano* mine operators viewed Chinese laborers as disposable. Migrant workers were cheaply available whereas slaves were valuable assets to their owners. Thus, the needs of slaves were taken care of to a degree. Under certain circumstances, slaves could be freed. For example, if an owner should fail to meet a slave's basic necessities, the state was obligated to free him or her. If a slave saved his master's life under unusual circumstances, the owner would free the slave. In other words, there were opportunities for slave owners to give freedom to slaves in Peru. Chinese laborers did not have such provisions. As contract laborers, they were responsible for their own needs and maintenance. If a Chinese laborer became disabled, his employer could abandon him. Without any value as a laborer, an abandoned Chinese had to beg in order to survive. In a twist of irony, free Chinese laborers, responsible for their own lives, were sometimes more vulnerable than slaves under an owner's protection. Another factor in the mistreatment of Chinese laborers was the timing of their arrival on the South American continent. During the first five years, from 1849 to 1854, Chinese laborers in Peru worked side by side with slaves. Following the emancipation of slaves in 1854, they worked with former slaves. Legally, freed slaves were free men, but the attitude of former slave owners and others was slow to change. In the eyes of many Peruvian employers, former slaves and their coworkers, Chinese, were the same.

A Peruvian farm owner branded the letter C on the faces of forty-eight Chinese laborers in 1868, fifteen years after the official emancipation of slaves in Peru. The farm owner wanted to identify his indentured workers more easily in case they should escape from his farm.[36] Although the branding incident was an isolated, extreme case, it revealed an underlying perception toward Chinese laborers. Some employers did not see these Chinese laborers being different from slaves. Furthermore, they were mistreated by two sides: white owners or managers and black field overseers. In contrast, blacks had one tyrant: the whites. The same tension between blacks and Chinese that had existed in Cuba was also found in Peru. Black field overseers resented the Chinese for their being free and independent when their labor contracts expired. Chinese laborers were useful because they were necessary, but many Peruvians feared the potential degenerative effects of the Chinese upon the Peruvian population through interracial mixing. As a result, both whites and blacks developed a negative view of the Chinese. When an anti-Chinese riot broke out in Peru, blacks and *cholos* (Peruvians with Indian blood) killed up to 1,700 Chinese. Only the intervention of the Chilean army on behalf of the Chinese prevented more killings.[37]

The most vulnerable Chinese population in the Americas were the laborers on the Chincha Islands. As international criticism and pressure was applied on behalf of Chinese laborers, the Peruvian government abruptly halted the import of Chinese coolies for several years. When Chinese labor recruitment resumed in China, contracts clearly stated that newly recruited Chinese laborers would not work on the Chincha Islands.[38] By that point, Chincha had become notorious for its human misery. Unlike the Chinese in Cuba, who left volumes of testimonies of their suffering and mistreatment, Chinese laborers on the Chincha Islands left no such record. As some suspected, perhaps no Chinese left the islands alive. Even if a few had survived the hellish ordeal, they would probably not have been in a state of mind to recall their suffering. Without the reports and protests of Western eyewitnesses, mainly the crews of freight ships, the tragic story of these Chinese laborers might have been buried forever on the islands. A few Western newspaper reporters, including Karl Marx, picked up the reports and stirred both official and public opinion on behalf of the Chinese. The suffering ended altogether when the coolie trade ended in 1874. Chinese workers were no longer forced to work as indentured laborers anywhere in the Americas against their will. Often, the end of one group's tragedy leads to the beginning of another group's misfortune. On the heels of Chinese suffering, another heartbreaking story was enacted upon some South Pacific islands.

BLACKBIRDING

The outcry in Peru as well as abroad led to the abrogation of "the Chinese Law" in 1856. As the number of Chinese nationals available to labor on the Chincha Islands diminished, some opportunists sought an alternative source of cheap labor supply. They were eager to profit by engaging in what was known as "blackbirding," a euphemistic expression for enticing dark-skinned Pacific Islanders to work for European and American entrepreneurs.[39] When slaves were phased out in Peru, Chinese laborers filled in the labor shortage gap. When the import of indentured coolie laborers was legally prohibited, Peruvian *guano* operators once again became desperate. Because of the bad publicity related to the Chinese on Chincha, labor recruitment had become very difficult. With global demand for *guano* continuing to intensify, mine operators were scrambling for a replacement to the Chinese laborers. What they came up with was the inhabitants of the South Pacific islands. Due to the geographical isolation of these distant and scattered islands, the inhabitants were unaware of the cruelty at Chincha. Unscrupulous recruiters took the opportunity to exploit the innocent on the numerous islands that dotted the South and West Pacific Ocean. Many of these labor recruiters were familiar with the geography and customs of these islands as they had engaged in trade with the Polynesians and Melanesians. Some were even former pirates. At the same time, Pacific Islanders, especially adult men with their own families, were looking for gainful employment elsewhere as economic opportunities were limited on the islands. The labor recruiters were able to take advantage of the islanders' desire to work and their ignorance of the outside world. It was not so difficult to deceive and lure Polynesians and Melanesians.[40] In some cases, the recruiters resorted to kidnapping. In fact, blackbirding was not much different from kidnapping Africans to sell into slavery.

The first blackbirding ship, the *Adelante,* sailed for the Polynesian Islands on June 15, 1862. The Irish speculator, J. C. Byrne, delivered 253 Polynesian laborers to Peru. From September 1862 to April 1863, about thirty ships engaged in backbirding over an eight-month period. Considering the small size of these islands and the number of inhabitants on each, it was an intense and excessive recruitment effort. The Peruvian government prohibited the practice of "blackbirding" in 1863 when it came under intense international pressure. Two tragic incidents roused international attention and condemnation. Among the many island raids mounted by the blackbirders, the Easter Island incident was widely publicized for the scale of human tragedy and its devastating effects. Easter Island is located about 2,300 miles (3,737 km) from the Chincha Islands. When blackbirders reached Easter Island in 1862, its total population was about three thousand. The raiders managed to take about one thousand men, roughly one-third of the entire island population, including the crown prince and all the island priests. The Easter Islanders were taken to Chincha to labor in the *guano* mines. Nearly nine hundred died soon after arriving. The desolate physical surroundings of the Chincha Islands and the severe working conditions were simply too harsh for the Pacific Islanders to bear. Moreover, they were susceptible to disease and faced the same fate of the indigenous peoples of the Americas when they had first encountered European diseases. As a result, their population was rapidly decimated. The hard labor of the Chincha *guano* mines was so different from what they had known in their soothing, South Pacific paradise.

When news of this terrible human tragedy became public, the embarrassed Peruvian government hastened to return the remaining Easter Islanders home. On the return voyage, eighty-five died from smallpox, measles, and tuberculosis. The dozens who did return home alive infected the remaining island inhabitants, with tragic results. Nearly the entire population of Easter Island was depleted. Around the same time, 280 inhabitants of Penrhyn Island (Tongareva) were delivered to Lima. Unlike the captured Easter Islanders, this group included women and children. The vehement protest from the French government in response to a French cleric's appeal on behalf of the captured islanders attracted the attention of the Peruvian government. Soon, other Western governments, especially the United Kingdom and the United States, joined the protest. Many of the Tongarevians became ill and died of disease while waiting in the capital. When the blackbirders were ordered to take the islanders back home, the captain of the ship did not bother to return them all the way home. The returning Tongarevians were deposited on the first island in the Pacific that the captain spotted. The Chincha Islands, three barren outcroppings less than three square miles in area, had a devastating effect on the lives of so many people simply because of the global demand for seabird droppings.

A BROWN GOLD RUSH

In the mid-nineteenth century, the Gold Rush in California corresponded with the *guano* rush in Peru. The accumulated *guano* on the Chincha Islands became as valuable as gold in California, and it attracted the interest of many nations. During the peak of *guano* exports, hundreds of freight ships anchored around the islands. Besides Spain, Peru, Chile, Great Britain, and the United States, many other countries were eager to have a piece of the lucrative *guano* business. Great Britain and the United States alone imported a large quantity of *guano* in the early 1850s, 760,000 tons (1.7 billion pounds) and 200,000 tons (440 million pounds), respectively. In 1854 and 1855, for instance, more than 70 percent of Peru's export revenues came from *guano*. International demand for this "brown gold" replaced revenues for silver and other Peruvian products combined, with silver generating more revenue for Peru than *guano* until 1848.[41] *Guano* deposits were found on other islands with similar geographical conditions. The West African islands of Possession and Ichaboe were such places. The extraction of *guano* deposits on these other islands did not last for long, however. The *guano* of Chincha was quite different in terms of quantity and quality. More than anything else, the sheer amount of *guano* deposits on these tiny islands was unmatched elsewhere. From 1840 to 1879, for instance, Peru exported an estimated 12.7 million metric tons (about 28 billion pounds) of *guano*, valued in the range of 100 to 150 million British pounds.[42] Among nations using *guano*, Great Britain had the greatest imports followed by Germany, the United States, and other European countries.

Guano was of vital economic importance to Peru and its people: "It enabled Peru's post-colonial rulers to expend vast sums of money to purchase political order, economic progress, social aggrandizement, and protection from invasion and disease. . . . comparable to some of today's oil-exporting countries. . . ."[43] The Peruvian "government expenditures on public works and services of this sort consumed 29 percent of the total state income from the *guano* trade."[44] In 1854, for instance, the *guano* trade made up three-quarters (74%) of Peru's total exports. The 533,280 tons (about 1.2 billion pounds) generated thirteen million pesos of revenue for the year. In the following year, the price of *guano* increased by 21 percent, thus increasing profits to fifteen million pesos. When compared with another famous Peruvian natural resource, silver, *guano* stands out in terms of its contribution to the national treasury. During the boom years of silver production, the total monetary value of silver in its peak year of 1842 was 5,807,433 pesos. Earnings from *guano* exports were comparable or even better. Between 1846 and 1855, *guano* exports were in excess of five million pesos per year during four different years.[45] In 1860, as many as 433 vessels, with a combined tonnage of about 350,000 (770,000,000 pounds), carried *guano* from the Chincha Islands to farms in Europe, North America and Asia.[46]

During the peak of the *guano* trade, the Chincha islands became the envy of the world. Spain, the former colonial ruler of Peru, occupied the Chincha Islands briefly during its confrontation with Peru over *guano*. The Spanish armada was sent to Peru's coast "under the guise of a scientific expedition to the Pacific—the opening battle of South America's Nitrogen Wars."[47] However, the Spanish attempt to occupy the islands failed as it foolishly "underestimated the military strength that *guano* had purchased for Peru."[48] Peru was determined to defend the Chincha Islands from foreign invasions by any means, at any cost. The *guano* craze was also reflected in the US government's policies related to the discovery of *guano*. In order to not miss out on the *guano* bonanza, the US Congress passed the Guano Islands Act in August 1856. According to the law, the US government could claim ownership on any unclaimed island, rock, or key with *guano* deposits. This bill was to provide protection to any US citizens who might discover *guano* deposits. It reads as follows:

> That when any citizen or citizens of the United States may have discovered, or shall hereafter discover, a deposit of guano on any island, rock, or key not within the lawful jurisdiction of any other government, and not occupied by the citizens of any other government, and shall take peaceable possession thereof, and occupy the same, said island, rock, or key may, at the discretion of the President of the United States, be considered as appertaining to the United States.[49]

The US government would be able to mobilize the military to protect any *guano* deposit discovered by American citizens. It was determined not to lose any opportunity for future *guano*:

> That the said discoverer or discoverers, or his or their assigns, being citizens of the United States, may be allowed, at the pleasure of the Congress, the exclusive right of occupying said island, rocks, or keys, for the purpose of obtaining said guano, and of selling and delivering the same to citizens of the United States, for the purpose of being used therein, . . . That the President of the United States is hereby authorized, at his discretion to employ the land and naval forces of the United States to protect the rights of the said discoverer or discoverers or their assigned, as aforesaid.[50]

As a result, the US government compiled a list of 103 islands, rocks, or keys claimed by US citizens. Later, the American government transferred or conceded some of these claimed territories to countries in the Pacific or Atlantic Oceans. About two dozen sites were listed as "nonexistent" perhaps because of false claims or simply the disappearance in cases of tiny keys or rocks.

This island initiative was a testament to the allure of *guano* and the eagerness to claim deposits.[51]

As Britain was the leading importer of *guano*, many British farmers complained of rising prices. Certain political figures began to agitate for the possibility of claiming uninhabited islands off the coast of Peru. They felt it politically advantageous to provide cheap *guano* to British farmers. Moreover, they were confident in the might of the British navy to protect any *guano* hunting expeditions. British mariners sailing along the Peruvian Pacific Coast spotted two particular islands with *guano* deposits: the Lobos Inner Island (Lobos de Tierra) and the Lobos Outer Island (Lobos de Afuera). The former was only twelve miles off the Peruvian coast and the other forty miles. Informed of the British *guano* expedition, the Peruvian government made sovereignty claims over both the islands. The Peruvian government reminded the British that Peruvians had visited these islands for fishing and egg collection for many generations. The British government was aware of these claims, and to its credit, it backed down from its territorial claim of these two islands, which were under British naval protection at the time.[52] Nonetheless, a British captain by the name of Fielding sailed a merchant ship, *Vitula,* to the coast of Peru for *guano* extraction. Alerted of this unauthorized expedition, the Peruvian government dispatched an army unit to the islands. As the British were about to commence mining the *guano*, the Peruvian army captured the entire crew, including the captain. They were tried in Lima, and the ship was confiscated. After a brief imprisonment, the British were set free, but the ship was not returned.[53]

The Chincha Islands drew the attention of major global powers in the mid-nineteenth century. Amid the international swirl of commerce and political intrigue, most Chinese coolies perished on the islands. Unlike the coerced Peruvian convicts, army deserters, and slaves, Chinese laborers had no emotional ties to Peru, let alone the Chincha Islands. Yet in a tragic twist of fate, most of the Chinese never left these islands of *guano*. "As late as 1920s, a grisly relic of the guano age was visible on almost every island—the Chinese graveyard—where garments, detached bones, and twisted corpses of poor laborers have for many years been exposed to the merciless sun."[54]

THE END OF THE CHINESE COOLIE TRADE

The indentured Chinese labor trade lasted twenty-seven years from 1847 to 1874. Reports of the inhumane mistreatment of Chinese laborers every step of their journey, from recruitment to plantation working conditions, evoked domestic and international criticism and protest. The excessively high mortality rate of Chinese workers during sea transport, the inhumane mistreatment, and indentured servitude put pressure on the host governments to put a stop to it. Journalists, eyewitnesses, politicians, and anti-slavery activists cried out for the end of cruelty upon Chinese laborers. In response to reports of horrible conditions laborers faced and their eventual fates, the Kwangtung Provincial authorities imposed a death penalty on anyone who engaged in kidnapping Chinese nationals for foreign labor recruitment agents. The two major centers for the Chinese labor trade, Hong Kong and Macao, were not under the jurisdiction of Chinese authorities, thus limiting the enforcement power of the Qing government in these territories. Western officials in Hong Kong and Macao, however, did begin to impose stricter rules and regulations for protecting Chinese laborers. Spanish colonial authorities in Cuba and the Peruvian government also proposed regulations to prevent the mistreatment of Chinese laborers, although they did not oppose the coolie trade in principle. From the beginning of the Chinese labor trade, the US government was very clear in opposing Chinese indentured labor contract. In fact, the United States was the only Western nation to officially do so. One year before President Lincoln's 1863 emancipation of slaves during the middle of the Civil War, the US Congress had "prohibited American citizens and ships from any participation whatsoever in the traffic [of Chinese laborers]."[55]

The end of the Chinese coolie trade was furthered by the establishment of formal diplomatic relations between the nations of Asia and Latin America. Peru became the first Latin American country to establish relations with both Japan and China. Ironically, this move came about as a result of the inhumane treatment of Chinese laborers in a single incident aboard a ship bound for Peru in Japanese waters. The Peruvian ship, the *Maria Rutz,* with 238 Chinese laborers, stopped at Yokohama near Tokyo because of bad weather. On the night of July 13, 1872, a Chinese labor recruit jumped overboard only to be picked up by a British ship. The captain of the latter handed him over to Japanese authorities. After hearing his complaints about the mistreatment he had faced at the hands of the crew, the Japanese investigated the case. When other Chinese laborers escaped and corroborated the initial complaint, the captain of the *Maria Rutz,* Ricardo Herrera, was arrested and tried in a Japanese court. The judge ordered one hundred lashes upon the Peruvian captain and all Chinese laborers to be returned to China. The Peruvian government considered the Japanese action unacceptable and offensive, and the president of Peru sent an envoy to Japan to reclaim the Peruvian ship and its crew. Dishonored by the incident in Japan, the Peruvian government wanted to establish diplomatic relations with Japan and China. The Peruvian envoy, Garcia y Garcia, a Peruvian navy captain, managed to negotiate a treaty of friendship and commerce between Japan and Peru. The treaty was signed on August 21, 1873.[56]

The envoy then continued to China. In spite of the Chinese government's initial reluctance and resistance against Peru's desire to establish diplomatic relations, the two countries reached an agreement similar to the Japan-Peru treaty. Representatives from both countries signed an agreement on June 26, 1874, and the treaty was ratified on August 7 of the same year. The Chinese government set two conditions on the treaty: a thorough investigation of the complaints of Chinese workers in Peru by a Chinese commission and the repatriation of any Chinese workers who desired to return home. The two countries also agreed to end the practice of indentured labor contracts or involuntary immigration. Thus, the infamous Chinese coolie trade between China and Latin America ended in 1874. From that year on, Chinese immigration to Latin America was to be free and voluntary, with movement under the rigorous supervision at both ports of departure and arrival.

REFLECTIONS

"Capitalism is the astounding belief that the most wicked of men will do the most wickedest of things for the greatest good of everyone." This quote encapsulates the ambivalent view of the renowned British economist John Maynard Keynes (1883–1946). The wicked *guano* mine operators did the wickedest things to Chinese laborers with absolutely no regard for their well-being, partially for Peru and farmers around the world but really for their profit. Perhaps knowing something about the misery of the Chinese laborers, Winston Churchill disclosed his feelings about them in a personal way: "It is conceivable that I might well be reborn as a Chinese *coolie*. In such a case, I should lodge a protest."[57] If Churchill had known full details of the wretched condition of the Chinese on the Chincha Islands, he might have used much stronger language. Hundreds of freight ships came and left with *guano*, and many witnessed the misery of the Chinese laborers. If some of these witnesses had not reported on the wretched conditions to the outside world, the tragic fate of Chinese laborers slaving on the isolated Chincha Islands might never have been exposed. *Guano* mine operators might have continued their horrible, inhumane mistreatment with impunity.

Around the world today, many are exploited as child laborers, sex workers, and modern-day slaves. In addition, millions of refugees and undocumented foreign residents have become easy prey. These victims are usually citizens of third world countries, and they are hidden underground. Unless national or international governmental or nongovernmental organizations stand up on behalf of these vulnerable people, they may never have a second chance. One cannot help but superimpose the image of Chinese laborers on the Chincha Islands in the nineteenth century with those who are vulnerable in the twenty-first century.

A Chinese movie titled *Wolf Warriors II* was released in 2017, which was about Chinese special forces carrying out a mission for Chinese civilians caught in an African civil war. In the movie, Chinese special forces shout,

"We will find out and punish anyone who hurts our Chinese people, no matter how far they are hiding." These soldiers follow up with the statement, "Overseas Chinese, remember that your fatherland is always behind you." Almost two hundred million Chinese viewers of the movie were touched by the promise of their government. Today, many Chinese around the world are proud that their ancestral home has become powerful and prosperous. They know that they can count on China in times of danger and mistreatment. The fate of Chinese laborers on the Chincha Islands was overlapped with the national fate of China following the Opium Wars. The Chinese government has established a global network for economic and military coordination. Major harbors at strategic points around the world serve as Chinese footholds for its global activities. China aims at being the strongest nation both in economic and military power by 2050, and that year is the first year of the second century of the People's Republic of China. Tragedies such as what transpired on the Chincha Islands will never be repeated against Chinese people under the watch of a strong China in the twenty-first century.

NOTES

1. Watt Stewart, *Chinese Bondage in Peru: A History of the Chinese Coolie in Peru, 1849–1874* (Westport, CT: Greenwood Press, 1951), 16–17.
2. Michael J. Gonzales, "Chinese Plantation Workers and Social Conflict in Peru in the Late Nineteenth Century," in *Journal of Latin American Studies* 21, 385–424 (1989): 391.
3. Stewart, *Chinese Bondage in Peru,* 18.
4. Mario Federico Real De Azua, "Chinese Coolies in Peru: The Chincha Islands," in *Asiatic Migrations in Latin America,* ed. Luz M. Martinez Montiel, 37–52 (Mexico: El Colegio De Mexico, 1981), 44.
5. Gregory T. Cushman, *Guano and the Opening of the Pacific World: A Global Ecological History* (Cambridge: Cambridge University Press, 2013), 45.
6. Ibid., 63.
7. David Hollett, *More Precious than Gold: The Story of the Peruvian Guano Trade* (Madison: Fairleigh Dickinson University Press, 2008), 119.
8. Ibid.
9. Jimmy M. Skagg, *The Great Guano Rush: Entrepreneurs and American Overseas Expansion* (New York: St. Martin Press, 1994), 162.
10. Ibid.
11. Skagg, *The Great Guano Rush,* 159.
12. Hollett, *More Precious than Gold,* 121.
13. Skagg, *The Great Guano Rush,* 159.
14. Ibid., 159–60.
15. Ibid.
16. Ibid.
17. Ibid.
18. Hollett, *More Precious than Gold,* 124.
19. Ibid., 125.
20. De Azua, "Chinese Coolies in Peru," 43.
21. Skagg, *The Great Guano Rush,* 159, 160.
22. Hollett, *More Precious than Gold,* 129.
23. Ibid.
24. Ibid.

25. Ibid.
26. Skagg, *The Great Guano Rush,* 165.
27. Ibid., 161.
28. Hollett, *More Precious than Gold,* 129.
29. Ibid.
30. Ibid., 131.
31. Ibid.
32. Ibid., 121.
33. Karl Marx, "British Philanthropy—The Coolies at the Chincha Islands," in *New York Daily Times,* January 24, 1854.
34. Arnold J. Meagher, *The Coolie Trade: The Traffic in Chinese Laborers to Latin America 1847–1874* (Xlibris Corporation, 2008), 227.
35. Skagg, *The Great Guano Rush,* 161.
36. Elliott Young, *Alien Nation: Chinese Migration in the Americas from the Coolie Era Through World War II* (Chapel Hill: The University of North Carolina Press, 2014), 47.
37. Ibid., 79.
38. Ibid., 65.
39. Skagg, *The Great Guano Rush,* 165.
40. Ibid., 163–64.
41. Paul Gootenberg, *Between Silver and Guano: Commercial Policy and the State in Post-independence Peru* (Princeton: Princeton University Press, 1989), 161–62.
42. Cushman, *Guano and the Opening of the Pacific World,* 45.
43. Ibid., 54.
44. Ibid.
45. Gootenberg, *Between Silver and Guano,* 161–62.
46. Meagher, *The Coolie Trade,* 222–23.
47. Cushman, *Guano and the Opening of the Pacific World,* 53.
48. Ibid., 57.
49. US Congress, "An Act to Authorize Protection to be Given to Citizens of the United States Who May Discover Deposits of Guano." 34th Congress. Chap. CLXIV August 18, 1856, accessed March 19, 2017, www./loc.gov/law/help/Statues-at-large/34th-congress/c34.pdf
50. Ibid.
51. Skagg, *The Great Guano Rush,* 230–36.
52. Hollett, *More Precious than Gold,* 173–92.
53. Ibid.
54. Cushman, *Guano and the Opening of the Pacific World,* 55.
55. Meagher, *The Coolie Trade,* 283.
56. Ibid., 238–39.
57. Winston Churchill, *Quotefancy,* accessed June 24, 2017, https://quotefancy.com/quote/939816/Winston-Churchill.

Chapter Five

Paper Children

The Enticement of Gold Mountain

Unlike their fellow countrymen suffering and perishing in the crucibles of Cuba's sugarcane fields and the Peruvian *guano* mines of the Chincha Islands, Chinese in the United States fascinated their countrymen back at home. Their stories of making a fortune in America, often exaggerated and fabricated, caught the imagination of many Chinese at home who struggled for even the basic necessities of life. The amount of money some Chinese workers sent home and its purchasing power was amazing. From time to time, those who had made their fortunes came home, dazzling with their wealth and worldliness. It was no wonder then that the Chinese called the United States the "Gold Mountain" (*Gam Saan*), although this name referred mainly to California. Such a glorious name used by the Chinese was primarily associated with the discovery of gold in the Sacramento Valley of California, and the name continued to evoke the image of fortunes to be made in that faraway country.

Nicknames other than Gold Mountain included the "Flowery Flag Nation" (*Faa Kei Gwok*), a reference to the stars on America's red, white, and blue flag. The official name of the United States in Chinese was "Beautiful Country" (*Mei Gwok*). The adjectives for America, such as gold, beautiful, and flowery, were enticing. Not having seen America with their own eyes, many Chinese believed it to be a paradise on earth. In contrast, Japan decided to call the United States "Rice Nation" while Korea adopted the Chinese name for America: "Beautiful Country." The Chinese words for "beauty" and "rice" sound similar.

The two Opium Wars and numerous civil disorders had devastated the Chinese, and many began to look for opportunities elsewhere. No matter how exaggerated the Gold Mountain stories might have been, the Chinese obsession with America was unshakable. Once the image of Gold Mountain became etched in their minds, many Chinese were determined to go and seek their fortunes by any means possible. Chinese laborers began to come to America in large numbers during the California Gold Rush of the 1850s. The discovery of gold caught the imagination of millions of people in America and beyond.

The Chinese to the United States were free, voluntary immigrants, not indentured laborers. They were relatively free to move about as they chose, and many of them worked in the Golden State that became a part of the United States in 1848 when America annexed the northwest of Mexico following the Mexican-American War. The United States paid 18 million dollars for much of today's Southwestern region of America. Many poor Chinese could not afford the cost of passage. In 1860, the fare from Hong Kong to San Francisco cost about fifty dollars (around $1,550 in 2020). Nonetheless, more than a quarter million Chinese, 258,210, had managed to arrive in America by 1882.[1] To restrict immigration, the US Congress passed the Chinese Exclusion Act in 1882 prohibiting the admission of Chinese laborers. By and large, it was a response to an anti-Chinese movement launched mainly by white laborers in California and other Western states.

Once the dust of the Gold Rush had settled and employment opportunities in railroad construction dried up, many Chinese were pushed to look for petty jobs in towns and cities. When Chinese laborers had worked in remote mines or railroads in the deep Sierra Nevada, they had been out of sight. Once they moved to cities and encountered white Americans daily, the latter began to resent the presence of these foreign and visible minorities. Moreover, the Chinese competed for jobs and housing with white workers. The fact that they were willing to work for lower wages angered many whites. After a time, white workers in California formed the Workingmen's Party in 1877 to protect their jobs from Chinese laborers. Its founder and leader, Denis Kearney, always ended his hate-filled public speeches with the following phrase: "And whatever happens, the Chinese must go."[2]

The rapid growth of the Chinese population intensified anti-Chinese sentiment. With their foreign appearance and different lifestyle, the Chinese were an easy target. Many whites felt threatened as the number of Chinese continued to increase. It was a visceral reaction as daily encounters with Chinese became more common. A US census following the Gold Rush numbered the Chinese population at about 35,000 in 1860. Twenty years later, in 1880, the Chinese had tripled to about 105,000. In 1870, the Chinese population comprised about 8.3 percent of California, but they made up one quarter of hired laborers in the Golden State.[3] The rapid increase of the Chinese population was the result of the influx of migrant laborers, and white residents were alarmed.

With no enthusiasm for assimilation and integration into the mainstream society, Chinese laborers appeared to be alien invaders in the eyes of whites. Only a few white groups, such as former Christian missionaries to China, domestic missionaries to Chinese workers in the West, and white mine and farm owners, were sympathetic to the Chinese.[4] The laborers stood out for their quaint appearance. It was the custom for Chinese laborers to shave their foreheads and wear waist-length pigtails, physical symbols of loyalty to the Qing rulers in Beijing. In addition, they wore baggy clothes which, along with their long hair, caused further gender confusion. Without wives and children, bored Chinese laborers often engaged in drinking, gambling, and opium smoking in their free time. Prostitution was also an issue.

No matter how diluted America had become by the Wild West of the nineteenth century, it was a country whose vestiges of puritanical morals and norms still lingered. Many Americans viewed the idle pursuits of pleasure by Chinese laborers as immoral. In their eyes, the Chinese were heathen aliens who came from a lower civilization that was incompatible with Judeo-Christian, European civilization. Much Chinese behavior could be explained by their sojourner mindset. Many Chinese laborers, if not all, had come to America with only one thing on their minds: to return home gloriously wealthy. The main concern of these sojourner workers in the United States was to earn and save as much as they could for their eventual return to China. Therefore, learning the American way was not a primary concern for most of them. Confined to their own living quarters and obsessed with the idea of going home, early Chinese immigrants were rarely interested in mixing with others. The early migrant workers had left home without governmental approval as the Qing government regarded Chinese immigrants as traitors, and did not formally legalize the emigration of its subjects until 1868. In time, the government realized the significant financial benefits of overseas Chinese remittance, yet the official approval for returning or visiting China came much later, in 1893.

THE CHINESE EXCLUSION ACT

When the US Congress passed the Chinese Exclusion Act in 1882, its intent was to ban Chinese laborers for the next ten years. The act, however, was repeatedly renewed every ten years until the passage of the Oriental Exclusion Act in 1924. The Chinese Exclusion Act targeted only Chinese working-class people, and the US government exempted Chinese merchants, students, teachers, tourists, diplomats, and their spouses and children. The number of these middle- and upper-class Chinese who came to America was far less than the number of Chinese laborers. Moreover, well-to-do Chinese were considered to be less threatening to American culture.

106   *Chapter 5*

The Chinese Exclusion Act was America's first discriminatory immigration policy based on race and class. As a result, "the Chinese were the first illegal aliens in the United States, and indeed in the world."[5] Ironically, 39,579 Chinese, the largest number of any year, were admitted into the United States in 1882.[6] Perhaps anticipating the impending passage of the Exclusion Act that year, many Chinese rushed to come to America. Once the Exclusion Act went into effect, Chinese emigration came to an abrupt halt. For instance, in 1885, three years after the passage of this act, only twelve Chinese males and ten females were admitted. In 1888, eight Chinese males and two Chinese females came to America. Between 1883 and 1943, the latter being when the act was repealed, the average annual admission of Chinese into America was about 1,900. It never exceeded 5,000 except for in

Figure 5.1.   Race Inequality in America. *duncan1890 © iStock*

Figure 5.2. Anti-Chinese Mob in San Francisco. *duncan1890 © iStock*

1883, when 8,031 Chinese came to America.[7] During the exclusion period, the majority of immigrants were supposed to come from the exempt categories, such as merchants and scholars and their spouses and children.

The Exclusion Act, however, provided an opportunity for some enterprising Chinese to circumnavigate the rules. Chinese on both sides of the Pacific Ocean invented all manners of imaginative schemes and gimmicks to bring nonqualified Chinese into the United States. The Chinese Exclusion Act was not successful in achieving its intended outcome because a steady trickle of Chinese laborers managed to enter the Golden State. One of the illegal methods used by prohibited common Chinese was to forge fake identities. Many Chinese fabricated family relations on immigration documents, with hopeful immigrants becoming the children, siblings, or spouses of Chinese residents or citizens in America. Thousands of Chinese came to the United States with such fraudulent identities. According to one estimate, about 90 percent had entered the United States with fake identities during the Chinese exclusion period between 1883 and 1943.[8] The rampant use of false identities was possible because of social networks within a specific geographic region. In the second half of the nineteenth century and the first half of the twentieth, most Chinese who came to the United States were from the Pearl River Delta region of South China. The major cities of this region included Hong Kong, Macao, and Canton (Guangzhou). Chinese in this region had far more opportunities to emigrate because they had easy access to information, networks, and foreign recruitment. Both of the leased territories, Hong Kong and Macao, attracted numerous foreign companies and agents, and the two cities served as key harbors for international trade and transportation.

In particular, the county of Taishan sent more than half of all Chinese immigrants to the United States.[9] The Chinese from this region were more likely to know each other through kinship and other social networks. They spoke the same dialect (Cantonese) and were familiar with the local geography and customs. Since fraudulent immigration depended upon the pretense of those involved, success required a high degree of factual knowledge and physical familiarity of people and surroundings. Assuming a false identity, however, was a high-risk venture. It required a large sum of money to buy a false identity and prepare for inspection at US customs. Failure to fool immigration officers in America and be barred entry often led to disaster. There are numerous anecdotes of Chinese committing suicide upon being prohibited entry into the United States. Despite the high cost and chance of failure, many were willing to take the risk. The Golden State was too enticing to give up. During this exclusion period, many Chinese in the prohibited category were willing to risk almost everything to go to America.

In particular, California was perceived as a prosperous place with a high standard of living. If families were lucky enough to have relatives in California, the temptation was greater. For example, the average monthly income of a family with someone working in America was 54.38 dollars, three times greater than the average income of 16.95 dollars[10] for families without any American connection. After having lived a few hard years in the United States, some "Gold Mountain" wives chose to return to China to live a life of luxury with housemaids and servants. They could afford a pampered life at home with the money they received from husbands still working in America. These "Gold Mountain wives" (*Gam Saan poh*), although separated from their husbands for years, enjoyed a great degree of prestige in their villages.

In this game of manufactured identities, US immigration officers were often no match for the determined and well-prepared Chinese. Most inspectors in the US Immigration Service did not know the Chinese language, customs, the intricacies of human relations, or the complexity of family structure. They relied upon Chinese interpreters who were likely to be more sympathetic with their countrymen than with the US government. Those who could afford immigration lawyers, either white Americans or Chinese-Americans, had a much better chance of obtaining entry visas through the appeals process. Indeed, the US Immigration Service admitted they were unable to foil nearly nine out of ten cases of immigration fraud.[11] The cultural barriers between prospective Chinese immigrants and US Immigration officers was such that they had a difficult time fathoming the complex family structures and cultural practices of the Chinese.

Figure 5.3. San Francisco Chinatown. *ilbusca © iStock*

THE CREATION OF PAPER PERSONS

Since the passage of the Chinese Exclusion Act in 1882, only three categories of Chinese in the United States could sponsor family members or business partners for permanent residence. First, Chinese residents who belonged to the category of permitted Chinese immigrants[12]—such as scholars, students, businessmen, or diplomats–could bring spouses and children if they had been married before coming to America. During their stay in America, some would return to China to marry and have children. They would then invite spouses and children at a later time. The other two categories included American-born Chinese who married in China and had children during their extensive and subsequent visits to their homeland. Third, established Chinese merchants in America could sponsor a business partner. In turn, the sponsored business partner could sponsor his spouse and children.

Chinese laborers, however, could not sponsor any family member no matter how long they had resided in America, simply because they were not eligible for naturalization according to the Naturalization Act of 1790. The United States prohibited the naturalization of immigrants from non-Western

Figure 5.4. A Chinese Store in Chinatown. *ilbusca © iStock*

countries until 1953. Thus, Asian immigrants became so-called aliens ineligible for citizenship and remained perpetual foreigners. After 1882, if longtime Chinese laborers wanted to visit home, they had to obtain a "reentry permit"[13] from the US government before they left for China. Otherwise, their reentry could not be assured due to their working-class status. If an average Chinese outside the exempt categories wanted to come to America, they had to resort to an illegal scheme. Without exception, Chinese immigrants needed to produce proof that they belonged to one of the exempted categories, either by blood or marriage. The law of supply and demand went into effect, creating a black-market economy that revolved around creating forged identities.

Sometimes, acts of nature affect human life in unexpected ways. That was the case with the Great San Francisco Earthquake of 1907. In the twenty-fifth year of the Chinese Exclusion Act, San Francisco and its surrounding area was hit by a massive earthquake with a magnitude of 7.2 on the Richter scale. City streets twisted and buildings crumbled. The ensuing conflagration consumed as much as three quarters of San Francisco. Government records on most San Francisco Bay Area residents turned to ash. Official marriage, birth, immigration, and citizenship records disappeared overnight. Without back-up records, there was no way of verifying, authenticating, or cross-checking the validity of any information.

Some shrewd Chinese took this development as a golden opportunity to change their fates.[14] Many immigrants claimed citizenship by birth in the United States. Since there was no way to disprove it, many Chinese-American citizens were "born" in America. Another way that the San Francisco earthquake and ensuing fire benefited some Chinese families was the increase of American-born children. For instance, instead of two sons and two daughters, a family could now claim four sons and three daughters. In this way, the road was open for additional relatives or someone else who wanted to come to America. The added identities of these "new family members" were then sold on the immigration black market.

Most cases of "paper people" involved boys or young men for a number of reasons. First, the life story of a fifteen-year-old boy would be much shorter and simpler than that of a thirty-five-year-old man. The boy would have far less information to memorize and understand, thus less likely to make a mistake during the intense interrogation by American immigration officials. Second, it would be much easier to match young boys with paper fathers in America. A thirty-year-old alleged son in China would have a far more difficult time being matched with an appropriate Chinese-American father. The next reason was psychological guessing. The brokers assumed that American immigration officials would be less harsh in dealing with young boys than with adults. A child's mistaken response could be attributed to immaturity or innocence. An "I don't know" answer by a young boy had a greater likelihood of being excused. Finally, in a patriarchal, patrilineal, traditional China, males dominated almost every aspect of life. They were the breadwinners of the family. In addition, their earning potential in America would be greater as they would have far more active years. Their earnings would continue without disruption, whereas a woman's earnings could be disrupted by getting married and having a family. Obtaining a "paper identity" was a serious long-term investment, and families that bought them had a high expectation of economic return. This expectation did not preclude girls and young women from playing the role of paper daughters, but they played relatively minor roles in this scheme of faked identities.

THE CREATION OF A BOGUS FAMILY

The following story is fictitious, illustrating the process of creating a "paper" identity. This fictitious story is based on many case reports. Paul Wong was a Chinese merchant who came to America when he was twenty-seven years old. He began as a railroad construction worker in the Sierra Nevada. He worked hard and saved every penny, never affording himself any luxury. He never ate at restaurants or bought fancy clothes from the department store. He wanted to visit nearby American towns, but restrained himself from spending money for travel. He resisted the temptation to gamble, smoke opium, and visit prostitutes. His frugality resulted in considerable savings over the years. When he had a large enough nest egg, he moved to San Francisco, where he started a dry goods import business in Chinatown. With wise management and hard work, the business grew steadily. Nine years after arriving in the United States, he had enough money to allow himself the luxury of visiting home. During his month-long visit, he savored every moment with his family, friends, and fellow villagers. He threw a big party, first for his family and then for the entire village. More than anything else, he rediscovered the joy and happiness of family.

After Wong returned to America, he decided to bring over his wife and two children. When he had left China nine years earlier, the oldest son was six and the other four. Now, they were teenagers. Married at eighteen, Wong had been apart from his wife and sons for too long. Knowing Wong's intent to take his family to America, a Chinese broker approached him with the idea of creating extra paper children: one for an alleged oldest daughter and another for an alleged youngest son. Wong was tempted by the amount of money offered, and the broker assured him of payment either by cash or working at his store. Wong was aware of the illicit practice of bringing paper children from China, and it was not so difficult for him to create extra slots in the family registry. He consented to add a daughter and a son. In the fake family registry, the oldest daughter was seventeen and the youngest son ten. Supposedly, the oldest daughter was born in the second year of Wong's marriage and the youngest son one year before he had left China for America. If the broker did not find a child that matched the proposed son, he could use the slot for a young woman.

Although young men or boys were given preferential treatment in the practice of creating paper persons, young Chinese women were also brought to America for the purpose of marriage or of becoming concubines or prostitutes. If the broker successfully filled both slots, it would be a windfall for him. However, the risks of bringing two paper children at the same time would be greater. Brokers usually staggered the process to reduce the risk of being discovered. With Wong's consent, the broker in America contacted his counterpart in the region of Wong's village. First the broker in China looked for a boy who resembled Wong's two sons. As much as possible, the broker in China tried to find someone from Wong's clan, preferably one of Wong's distant relatives who was around the right age. If he could not find a ten-year-old boy from Wong's clan, he looked for one from Wong's village, ideal as the boy would be familiar with Wong's family and the physical environment surrounding the village. If he could not find a boy with similar physical characteristics in the same village, he would extend his search to nearby villages. Although there were many eager candidates, the broker needed to find an ideal one. Many would be passed over because they did not meet the requirements of height, weight, and complexion. When the broker finally found a boy that met his expectations, he contacted the local village clerk in charge of family registries. With a bribe, the boy's information was changed and his name was added to the Wong's family registry. The entire system was a well-oiled machine. The clerk did not see anything wrong as the paper people would send money home. It was a patriotic act. The broker then assigned the boy to a coach to teach him the finer details of Wong's family history and relations. In addition, the coach introduced the boy to Wong's wife and two sons so they could familiarize themselves with each other. The boy lived with Wong's family for two days every other week.

The boy was also given a book containing extensive information on the Wong family going back two generations. He was expected to study and know the genealogy of his paper family and other important information, including names, ages, birthdays, physical characteristics, personalities, occupations, hobbies, and other relevant information about his bogus family. In addition to his immediate family, the boy was also required to remember the names of his paper cousins and uncles and aunts on both his new father's and mother's side, including any major family events such as weddings, births, and deaths. Another element that the boy was expected to know was the physical environment of Wong's home and village. The coach asked the boy to have a clear picture in his head of Wong's house, the surrounding houses in all directions, the streets, the streams, the bridges, the rice paddies, the vegetable gardens, and the entire surrounding area within a ten-mile radius. Also, the boy needed to be familiar with the rhythms of village life and the names of prominent or peculiar villagers. Other than detailed family and village information, the coaching book[15] also listed all kinds of instructions, including those that covered proper physical appearance and manners the boy should display. It detailed how to interact with immigration officers and how to answer their probing questions. Sample questions and answers were provided for practice. This part of the coaching book was constructed based on information provided by interpreters who worked in American immigration offices. Since interpreters knew who would be more likely to pass or fail from their years of observation, their insightful suggestions were very helpful. Some immigration lawyers in the San Francisco Bay Area supplied valuable tips and legal information.

The coaching book was extensive and detailed. It was meant to be a multi-generation, operational book for many years to come. Someday in the future, Wong's children might bring their own paper family members to America. Since most coaching books were family and time specific, they needed to be updated and, as such, usually grew thicker as new names, both authentic and fabricated, were added. Usually, each clan kept a few copies of the handwritten book. If the family book was lost, the whole scheme of the paper family could be exposed. And if the lost book found its way to the US Immigration Service, many in Gold Mountain would be in jeopardy. For this reason, the coach instructed the paper person to throw the coaching book into the sea before arrival in America if there was a possibility it might be confiscated.

In time, professional coaching specialists emerged as paper identity operations became more complex. At the same time, US immigration inspectors in San Francisco grew more sophisticated in examining Chinese immigration applicants. Coaching specialists not only developed fabricated content but also coordinated activities related to the many people involved in the scheme. The coaches anticipated the type of questions immigration inspectors would ask and the amount of time each paper person needed to become familiar with the content of his or her coaching book. Accordingly, coaches then scheduled official interviews at the US consul in Hong Kong.[16]

Inventing and bringing a paper family member to the United States was very expensive, and costs increased with age. In the 1930s, for example, brokers charged around one hundred dollars per year of an applicant's age.[17] So a thirty-three-year-old man paid 3,300 dollars (around $51,000 in 2020) whereas a fifteen-year-old boy paid 1,500 dollars (around $23,000 in 2020) to go to Gold Mountain. Unless one's family had a lot of property to sell in order to pay for the forged identity, many paid with labor once situated in America. Typically, an advance deposit was required before departure and the remainder was paid upon arrival in Gold Mountain. If someone could not pay the entire amount upon successfully entering America, he or she had to pay the remaining balance plus interest over a period of time. Thus, many Chinese labored in restaurants, laundromats, or dry goods stores to pay off their debts.

At that time, average Chinese laborers in America earned anywhere between twenty and fifty dollars per week,[18] depending on the nature of work and their experience. If someone in his early twenties worked in a Chinese restaurant for thirty dollars (around $460 in 2020) per week, it would take an entire year to pay off the debt. If someone in his thirties earned fifty dollars (around $770 in 2020) per week, it would take almost two years to pay off the debt. In that case, not much money was left for one's living and personal expenses or their remittance payments home. Estimates suggest that nine out of ten ordinary Chinese came to the United States with false identities during the exclusion period.[19] In spite of the cost, effort, and risk involved, many Chinese were eager to take the chance to make their fortune in Gold Mountain, and many were successful.

AGONY ON ANGEL ISLAND

During the exclusion period, most Chinese bound for the United States entered Gold Mountain through San Francisco harbor. Nearly half of Chinese passengers were released on the day of their arrival; the other half were kept in a detention facility on Angel Island. Chinese passengers in the exempted categories, such as diplomats, scholars, businessmen, students, and their family members, were not suspected.

The initial US immigration station was located not far from San Francisco's Chinatown, and immigration officials considered it a less than ideal location. Besides the possibility of escape, easy access by Chinese residents to arriving Chinese nationals often interrupted the inspection procedures. To avoid undue meddling and influence, the US government decided to isolate suspected Chinese immigrants for further probing, and chose a new site, Angel Island, in the northern part of San Francisco Bay. The new site, which could only be reached by designated ferryboats, began operations in January 1910. From the top of Angel Island, beautiful San Francisco and its surrounding communities are in a full view. Although the island is roughly ten miles from San Francisco, Angel Island became known as the Ellis Island of the West. The similarity between these two island immigration stations, however, ended there. Ellis Island in New York was mainly for European immigrants, and most passed quickly through. Typically, European immigrants waited three or four hours at most while those who were quarantined stayed much longer. The entry process at Ellis Island was almost a routine formality for European immigrants.

Its counterpart on the West Coast was quite different, to say the least. Angel Island station was built for immigrants mainly from Asia. Since the US government was aware of the widespread fraudulent practices among Chinese immigrant applicants, the island facility was a detention center for intense examination and interrogation. Many Chinese stayed there for weeks and months while some waited for years. A considerable number of Chinese were sent back without ever making it past Angel Island, never realizing their dreams of walking on imagined streets paved with gold. A Chinese interpreter at the US Immigration Station on Angel Island made the following observation. "I used to think it was easier for a camel to enter the eye of a needle than for a Chinaman to pass through the Golden Gate."[20]

Upon arrival, Chinese were separated from Japanese, Filipinos, and other immigrants from Asia. These immigrants stayed on the upper floors of the main building while the Chinese stayed on the lower levels. Because many Chinese entrants were subject to intense scrutiny, the cost of examining each Chinese immigrant was fifty or sixty times more expensive compared to that of other Asian nationals.[21] The average customs inspection and immigration procedure for a Japanese family, for instance, took no more than three hours.

Figure 5.5. Angel Island in San Francisco Bay. *goldenangel © iStock*

If a Chinese family of four with two parents and two children arrived together, they were immediately separated by gender. The father and his son were sent to the men's dormitory while the mother and daughter went to the women's. Boys under the age of twelve were allowed to stay with their mothers, and teenage boys were allowed to visit with their mothers once a week. On a typical day, there were anywhere between two and three hundred men and boys and about fifty Chinese women between the two dormitories. More than anything else, the language barrier was the most challenging aspect in processing Chinese immigrants at Angel Island. Since Chinese spoke distinctive dialects, finding interpreters fluent in the correct ones could be difficult. Although the majority of Chinese immigrants came from the Canton region, sometimes there were immigrants from other regions speaking different dialects.

During the interview, each applicant was examined by a special hearing board composed of two immigration inspectors and a Chinese interpreter. In addition, a stenographer recorded the interview. Sometimes, the Immigration Service used more than one interpreter to prevent any collusion between the Chinese. The interrogations often took place a few days or a few weeks apart. Seldom were interviews conducted consecutively, a deliberate tactic to detect discrepancies in stories due to lapses in memory. In complicated cases, different immigration officers asked different questions, approaching the case from different angles. It was normal for potential immigrants to be asked up to nine hundred questions over a considerable period of time.[22] If officers detected any inconsistency, discrepancy, or contradiction that raised a red flag, further intense interrogation followed, which might result in deportation.

In the detention center, the exchange of messages between Chinese was strictly prohibited. Nevertheless, some parents used child visiting privileges to convey messages between themselves. Husbands sent messages through their sons to their wives, and wives used the same channel to reply.[23] Family members or relatives in San Francisco also sent notes hidden in fruit for those detained on Angel Island. The kitchen staff serving Chinese detainees sometimes played a part in the cat and mouse game between Chinese detainees and immigration officials. They acted as secret messengers between separated family members. For instance, if a kitchen staff member dropped one spoonful of soy sauce on a vegetable dish, it signaled that there was a note, while two drops meant two notes attached at the bottom of the dish.[24] The Chinese, more often than not, outsmarted customs staff.

The questions asked by immigration officers were specific and often unexpected. For instance, in order to confirm that an alleged Chinese merchant father in America and his paper son came from the same village, the officer would ask who lived in the third house of the second row in the village. In another question, the paper son might be asked to name the female shaman of his village. Some questions might be related to the siblings of one's mother, the marriages of uncles and aunts and their children. They also might be asked for the names of a maternal uncle's family two or three weeks later. Any mistakes made during the interrogation period raised suspicion. The considerable intervals between interrogation sessions was a deliberate tactic to further strain the limits of memory. Unless one remembered clearly names and facts based on a real relationship experience, it was not easy to remain consistent relying on rote memorization. The ability to answer unexpected questions depended on the thoroughness of preparation and practice done beforehand in China.

Sometimes immigration officers would ask about animals around the house. Typical questions were what color was the dog at the second paternal uncle's home and whether the dog was male or female. In one interrogation of a mother with a son, the mother told the inspector that her family had a dog, but her son had said otherwise. When the boy was confronted with this contradiction, he was able to provide an explanation by stating that the dog was killed and eaten by the family just before leaving for America.[25] If younger children could not answer, their inability to provide one was often attributed to their young age.

In the initial stage of examination, inspectors would probe each family member separately. When contradictions or discrepancies occurred, the husband and wife, along with their children, were questioned together. During family interrogations, immigration officers closely observed each member's reaction to their questions. Unlike as with family members, sponsoring a business partner from China was subject to far stricter scrutiny. The Immigration Service required thorough documentation of a sponsor's business activities in America as well as tax reports. When an invited partner from China was examined at the immigration station, the inspectors would thoroughly vet the sponsoring merchant too. Often the officers interviewed witnesses to prove that the merchant sponsor was an authentic business owner in America. Both Chinese and Caucasian witnesses were interviewed to verify the legitimacy of the sponsor's business.

In order to increase the chances of passing the initial immigration inspection, Chinese applicants used all manners of gimmicks. Making a favorable first impression on US inspectors was considered important, and some Chinese paid special attention to their appearance. Those who could afford bought tickets for first-class cabins, their reasons being far more than just for physical comfort during the long voyage. Presenting first-class tickets with their passports conveyed the message that they came from a well-to-do, upper-class part of Chinese society, which might reduce suspicion on the part of US immigration officers. They also wore expensive Western clothes and accessories to further this image of being from the upper echelons of Chinese society.

Besides physical appearance, potential Chinese emigrants were coached to speak properly to customs officers. As much as possible, they wanted to appear to be members of the well-educated, upper class. To demonstrate high socioeconomic status, some women walked gingerly with their feet bound, an age-old custom practiced by upper-class families. On the other hand, those who could afford only steerage class and ordinary, traditional clothes were more likely to be held longer and scrutinized more thoroughly. If someone's appearance and manner did not fit with the image of the exempted categories (scholars, students, businessmen, tourists, diplomats and their family members), immigration officers often suspected that a common laborer was trying to enter the United States with forged papers. Customs officers, for instance, might notice the incongruity between fashionable clothes and swarthy faces or calloused palms.

US immigration inspectors were always on the lookout for any sign that gave away a laborer. For example, if an alleged businessman from China had strong muscular development, they wondered how he was in such outstanding physical shape. This would prompt a close examination of the skin, hands, arms, and feet. Tanned complexions or calloused hands were a clear indication that the immigrant was neither a scholar nor student nor businessman. Another reason for paying close attention to the physical features of Chinese immigrants was to discern if there was a family resemblance between the applicant from China and his American sponsor. An alleged son from China was carefully compared with his alleged parents in the United States. If there was no discernable resemblance, the Immigration Service might summon the American siblings of the alleged son from China. If the siblings did not resemble one another, the burden of proof of their biological relationship was placed upon the family. This might be resulted in intensive probing and cross-examination that often led to the discovery of fraud. In the days of pre-DNA testing, proof of biological ties depended upon mere observation and impression. This probing process was long and arduous, often taking weeks and months. At its completion on each individual or family, the decision to admit or deport was made by a special hearing board. If the board voted to deport, the applicant could appeal. Rejected applicants hired immigration lawyers who handled the appeals process at Immigration Service Headquarters in Washington, DC. The entire process usually took about a month.

DENIAL OF ENTRY INTO GOLD MOUNTAIN

The final rejection of admission into the United States caused many Chinese to despair. Some chose to end their lives in the detention center instead of facing disappointed family members and friends back home in China. After investing so much money, time, and effort, they could not bear the shame of returning home a failure. Some would make an extreme choice to escape the debt incurred for the purchase of their "paper identity," which would be a heavy burden to one's family for many years to come.

The denial rate of admission for Chinese immigration applicants was much higher than those of other national groups. Following the Chinese Exclusion Act of 1882, immigration officers raised the intensity of inspection and interrogation many notches higher on Chinese applicants. In 1910, for example, a total of 1,770 Chinese applied for entrance into the United States; 909 (51%) were denied. In the following year, the rate of denial was even higher (59%) as only 41 percent (538) of 1,307 applicants were admitted. These two years were on the extreme end of the spectrum, however. Over a twenty-five-year period between 1908 and 1932, for instance, the annual denial rate of Chinese applicants was a little over one in four (28%).[26] During the same period, the denial rate among non-Chinese applicants sat at around 3 percent, with the highest denial rate for a non-Chinese group being no more than 5 percent.[27] There existed nearly a ten to one ratio of denial rates between Chinese and non-Chinese applications. Because the Exclusion Act targeted the ordinary Chinese, they attempted to enter Gold Mountain by any means available. The continuous, illegal flow of immigrants raised concerns in the US Immigration Service and caused them to increase its vigilance against potential fraud.

After many weeks or months of anxious waiting, oscillating between despair and hope, a visitation by an immigration officer often meant that the end was near. When a woman was allowed to see her male companion, often an alleged father or husband, she knew that she would be deported. Everyone knew what an official visitation meant, and the reunion of two separated persons was often bittersweet. If a detainee had come alone, relatives were allowed to come and visit. A deportation order, without any further hope of appeal, meant there was no chance of entering Gold Mountain. Although the thought of returning to China made detainees desperate, this pain was more acute for women. Their prospects of marriage had dissipated as soon as they had entered into the process of becoming a paper wife or daughter in China. They had become tainted in the eyes of many of their countrymen. Nonetheless, many Chinese were able to outsmart the US government. The paper scheme was a very complicated forgery meant to circumnavigate the Chinese Exclusion Act. Each scheme was the culmination of a delicate coordination, and the success rate in deceiving US immigration officers was high because the government inspectors often could not fathom the depths of Chinese culture and its family intricacies.[28]

One thing that many Chinese detainees could not understand was why the American government did not scrutinize applicants in Hong Kong or elsewhere in China. In this way, America could have saved not only money and time but also the agony of those who were rejected in America. Indeed, it was heartbreaking to face a deportation order after borrowing so much money and waiting for so long in the prison-like detention facility on Angel Island. The US government was concerned, however, that if it examined Chinese applicants in China, they would be unable to control undue influence from local officials, as bribery was a common practice. At one point in time, Chinese immigrants took their physical examinations in Yokohama, Japan, as the US government did not trust medical reports submitted by Chinese doctors and hospitals.

In order to avoid the intense scrutiny of Angel Island, some wealthy Chinese sailed to either London or Paris first. From there they sailed to New York, where immigration inspection was brief and routine as the majority of the entrants were European. For instance, a Chinese running a profitable restaurant in Indiana wanted to bring a young wife and a man to work in his restaurant. For his return trip, the restaurant owner traveled first to Paris with the two, whom he claimed as a daughter and son, then on to New York. The three of them memorized the facts of their coaching book to make sure that they would not contradict one another.[29]

When the Angel Island detention facility was closed in 1940, after thirty years of operation, it left the following records. Between 1910 and 1940, about 175,000 Chinese had passed through its halls. For admission into America, many Chinese pretended to be members of the exempted categories, but the reality was far from it. During the thirty-year operation, Angel Island handled an annual average of six thousand immigrants, mainly from Asia. This number included anywhere between 1,000 and 4,500 Chinese per year.[30] About two out of three Chinese applicants passed the immigration inspection and were released within two weeks. About 5 percent were eventually deported, with or without an appeals process.[31] Fifty-six Chinese died during detention and four babies were born. Nearly two hundred Chinese were held for more than a year, and three detainees were held for more than two years. Kong Din Quong holds the record for being held the longest: 756 days (two years and twenty-six days).[32] The anxiety and agony of these long-held detainees are scraped in Chinese poems on the walls of the detention center.

PAPER WIVES AND PAPER DAUGHTERS

From the beginning, the idea of going to Gold Mountain was mainly for young men in their prime. Leaving home and going to a faraway country was too foreign for most Chinese women, most of whom preferred to stay home and wait for the return of their fathers, brothers, or husbands. Schemes involving forged identities most involved young men. This tendency, however, did not preclude Chinese women from wanting to enter Gold Mountain. Many single Chinese men in America desired wives. As many Chinese established roots in America and decided not to return to China, they wanted to start families. Married men wanted to bring their wives and children, and others wanted to bring future wives arranged by their families at home. Yet after 1882, Chinese laborers could not bring family members or future wives. Instead of returning to China to join their spouses and children they had left behind years ago, or to establish new families, many Chinese men used paper identities to bring their family members. In addition, some wanted to bring young concubines or prostitutes.

Although there had always been Chinese women in the United States, their numbers were small. The wives and daughters of well-to-do Chinese, such as diplomats, scholars, and merchants, had followed their husbands and fathers. However, they usually lived in large cities where their husbands or fathers had worked. At that time, it was almost impossible for lower-class Chinese women to come to America on their own merits because demands for Chinese usually included hard physical work. Afong Moy was the first Chinese woman who came to America in 1834, many years before the Gold Rush in California. She arrived in New York, and her American sponsor displayed her oriental beauty and bound feet in an exhibition for Americans.

For the privilege of seeing an Asian woman for the first time, people paid fifty cents (around $15 in 2020). She dressed in a Chinese costume and sat on a chair for eight hours a day, from ten to two in the afternoon and from five to nine in the evening. Surrounded by oriental decorations in a display room, she demonstrated the use of chopsticks and spoke in Chinese for white spectators. In the capital, she visited the US Congress and the White House. Moy had an audience with President Andrew Jackson and some prominent congressmen. Her sponsor took her to many cities, from New York to New Orleans.[33]

After Moy, only a few Chinese women managed to come to America. Two years stand out for the lowest numbers of Chinese women entering America: 1882 and 1898. In 1882, just before the enforcement of the Exclusion Act, only three tenths of a percent (0.3%) of Chinese immigrants were women, or three females per one thousand Chinese. A total of 39,579 Chinese were admitted that year, but only 116 were female with a sex ratio of 340 males to one female.[34] Sixteen years later in 1898, Chinese women made up one half of 1 percent (0.5%). A total of 10,594 Chinese were admitted that year, but only ten were women. The male-female ratio was 1,058 men to one woman.[35] These very limited numbers of Chinese women might have been invited or sponsored by parents or spouses. It was highly unlikely that ordinary Chinese laborers could have invited spouses or other family members through legal channels. Women composed between 3 and 5 percent of total Chinese immigration.

According to the US Immigration Service, between 1870 and 1879, 97 percent of Chinese admitted to the United States were male and 3 percent were female. In some years during this ten-year period, female immigrants were less than 3 percent.[36] Female immigration numbers increased to an average of 16 percent in the following decade (1880–1889). In the first two decades of the twentieth century (1900–1920), however, the number fell to 5 percent.[37] No matter the exact percentages, the number of males far exceeded females many times over. This was the cause of much social discontentment among Chinese in America. Most Chinese laborers, either married or single, remained alone without a chance of reuniting with their families or of starting new ones.

Some Chinese women who came to America without family connections, either by blood or marriage, faced tough times in a strange land. Typically, they were lured with promises of marrying wealthy men in Gold Mountain. According to a Chinese woman's testimony, she thought she was coming to America to marry a rich man, but she ended up a prostitute in a brothel. Upon arriving in San Francisco, "she was sold for $400 to a slave dealer, who then sold her to another man for $1,700."[38] This was a common refrain of many single Chinese women lured to Gold Mountain. The Chinese who could afford to bring female family members with their own money or borrowed money could have normal family lives. Even before the Chinese Exclusion Act, many Chinese laborers could not afford visiting home and getting married there due to a lack of money. The cost of the voyage home and a wedding was prohibitive, and the Exclusion Act only served to exacerbate this situation.

This predicament spawned an industry designed to meet the sexual needs of single Chinese men. Brokers and brothels used all kinds of fraudulent schemes to bring Chinese women to America. Nobody knows how many Chinese women ended up serving as slave prostitutes, but the number was high enough that Chinese prostitution became a public outcry, adding fuel to an already to rising anti-Chinese sentiment.

The image of the Chinese prostitute was the female version of negative stereotypes of Chinese laborers. Newspapers and magazines, especially in California, argued that the degraded heathens from uncivilized China were corrupting the moral condition of the young republic of America. They claimed that Chinese prostitutes corrupted white men who had no immunity to the diseases that the prostitutes carried. In the nineteenth century, prostitution was a common practice in the West, yet Chinese prostitution was singled out as immoral and degrading. The public outcry led to a congressional response known as the Page Act of 1875. By and large, the Page Act was created to ban the admission of "undesirables" from Asia, which included

Figure 5.6.   Chinese Opium Den in America. *duncan1890 © iStock*

involuntary labor recruits, people with criminal records, and prostitutes. Although the law was applicable to all Asians, the Chinese were its main target.

In 2011, the US Senate expressed its regret for the passage of this discriminatory law against the Chinese. The Senate admitted that the Page Act of 1875 "was disproportionately enforced against Chinese women, effectively preventing the formation of Chinese families in the United States and limiting the number of native-born Chinese citizens."[39] It should be noted that the US Congress passed the Exclusion Act on Chinese laborers within seven years of the Page Act. To comply with this act, Chinese women had to go through several stages of inspection. Once they had compiled all necessary immigration documents, they underwent an initial interview with the harbormaster of the British colony in Hong Kong, then another inspection aboard the ship bound for the United States. However, the real inspection occurred at the US Immigration station in San Francisco. The main objective of this multiple screening process was to differentiate legitimate spouses or daughters from potential prostitutes. The real challenge was to distinguish between legitimate wives of Chinese residents and prostitutes from lower social class backgrounds. The inspectors carefully examined not only the moral character of the women but also their medical condition, especially pertaining to venereal diseases. It was shameful and humiliating for these women to undress for medical checks. During these inspections, women with rough manners would raise suspicion and were assumed to have come from lower social backgrounds. The US Immigration Service required Chinese women to attach photographs to their applications. In those days, taking a picture in a studio was expensive. This requirement was to ensure that no substitute would take the place of disqualified female applicants.

Between 1875 and 1882, several hundred Chinese women were sent back to China.[40] Expectedly, the proportion of the female Chinese population in the United States dropped by about 2 percent.[41] Unintentionally, the law "paradoxically encouraged the very vice it purported to be fighting: prostitution."[42] In other words, the enforcement of the Page Act reduced the number of Chinese women, resulting in an increase of demand for Chinese prostitutes in America. The male-female sex ratio continued to widen. Most families had to borrow money to send their daughters to Gold Mountain. The amount was as much as 4,000–5,000 dollars (around $52,000–65,000 in 2020) to finance their journey to America.[43] Unless the women were sold to wealthy men as concubines or worse, the incurred debt was a heavy financial burden for their families. In one case, after much waiting on Angel Island, a Chinese woman received a deportation order. She was in such despair that she tried to hang herself, yet she was saved by someone who saw the scene. Three months later, she was granted a temporary admission on a 1,000-dollar (around $13,000 in 2020) bond.[44] Those who left for America as wives and were deported back to China had little chance to start anew. For this reason, most deported women attempted to reenter America under false names.

SECOND CHANCES

The story of Lee Puey You[45] is one of the most complicated and tragic cases ever revealed by a Chinese woman. She landed in America twice using two different false identities. She had two husbands in the same fraudulent scheme, yet neither was authentic. Puey You's widowed mother persuaded her daughter to accept an arranged marriage to a wealthy Chinese merchant widower in America. The daughter resisted the proposal because the widower in America was almost twenty years her senior. Eventually Puey You yielded to her mother for the alleged wealth of this merchant. Her family, without a father, was struggling for existence. The merchant widower in San Francisco arranged for Puey You to travel to America. She pretended to be the daughter of a Chinese American citizen. In spite of her effort to remember the fabricated facts and family relations in the coaching book, she failed the interrogation at Angel Island and was deported back to China. Puey You wasted almost two years in the detention facility on Angel Island. She considered suicide but could not erase her mother's face from her mind.

Back in Hong Kong, she sold rice to support her family. Her mother insisted that Puey You try again because the family had already used the advance money from the merchant in America. When Puey You agreed, the merchant came up with a new scheme. This time, she would marry a Chinese American in Hong Kong and get a marriage certificate from the US Consul. This was to be a marital arrangement just for the transit period. The alleged husband was to act as a courier escort, but he demanded that Puey You sleep with him. His argument was that they had to act like a married couple during the journey to impress the inspectors in San Francisco. She consented, becoming more than a nominal wife to this courier during the transit period. Puey You passed the second immigration inspection as the wife of the Chinese American courier. When she was taken to her merchant husband, Puey You found out that he was already married and had children. From the beginning, the merchant had intended to make her his concubine, and his wife treated Puey You like a slave. Although Puey You did not want to be his concubine, she had no one to turn to in America. She took care of all house chores for the family. When she gave birth to a daughter, the merchant registered the child under the name of the escort courier to avoid any official suspicion. Years later, the merchant died without leaving anything for Puey You or her daughter. Somehow, the whole scheme was uncovered by the US government, and the Immigration Service ordered Puey You's deportation. She fought hard by insisting that she was an innocent victim from the beginning. In the end, the US government allowed her to stay in America. Although her life story was extraordinary on many accounts, the vulnerability of poor Chinese women was a common thread in their pursuit of American dreams in Gold Mountain.

THE CHINESE CONFESSION PROGRAM

The Chinese Exclusion Act was repealed in 1943 during the Second World War when China became an ally of the United States in the war against Japan. The repeal, however, did not affect the number of Chinese immigrants permitted into the United States. The National Origin Act of 1920 allowed up to 105 Chinese immigrants per year. This trickle continued until the US Congress passed the Immigration Amendment Act of 1965. This amendment reversed the previous immigration policy by increasing Asian immigration. Beginning in 1968, each Asian country could send up to 20,000 immigrants per year and the annual total for the eastern hemisphere was 190,000 immigrants, as opposed to 170,000 for the Western hemisphere.

In the first half of the twentieth century, China underwent a seismic political shift. After Japan's defeat in the Second Sino-Japanese War in 1945, for the next four years Chinese Communists and Nationalists vied for control of the country. Eventually the Communists, led by Mao Zedong, prevailed and drove the Nationalists to Taiwan. In 1949, China came under communist rule. Not long after the communist victory in China, the Korean War broke out in 1950 between North and South Korea. The North was supported by Communist China and the Soviet Union, and the South backed by the United States and its allies. China and the United States stood on opposite sides as key players in the Korean War. Moreover, communist expansion in Eastern Europe and East and Southeastern Asia caused a "red scare" in the United States, ushering in the McCarthy Era. Under the careful watch of Senator Joseph McCarthy, any American who was suspected of being a communist sympathizer or supporter was subject to harassment or worse. The US government became increasingly wary of possible infiltration and the spread of communism in the United States with the help of Chinese American residents, both legal and illegal. The US government feared that Chinese spies might have access to US passports through fraudulent documents. Realizing the countless numbers of paper citizens and residents among the Chinese, the US government opened the Chinese Confession Program from 1957 to 1965. It was a symptom of Cold War phobia.

About twelve thousand Chinese partook in the program and confessed fraudulent entries years ago. As a result, about twenty thousand others were implicated and forced to participate in the program.[46] Because of the legal implications of their confessions related to immigration fraud, many were hesitant. During these confessions, Chinese paper residents were required to report on everyone involved in the fraud. Revealing the network of paper relations, however, was a serious matter. Those who confessed revealed their real names, birthdates, birth places, and family composition. Once approved by the Immigration and Naturalization Service, they had to go through re-documentations of various certificates. This process included changes of name, birthdates, birthplaces, biological parents, and so forth. Identity changes involved a wide range of government-issued documents such as citizenship certificates, green cards, social security cards, driver's licenses, educational diplomas, tax records, property registrations, professional licenses, and the like. In spite of the complicated process, many Chinese welcomed the opportunity for a new start in America. For years, they were haunted by their fraudulent entry and afraid of discovery by law enforcement.

Understandably, the majority of confessors, about ten thousand, came from the San Francisco Bay Area. However, it was not a blind and blanket amnesty across the board. There was a statutory remedy for the illegal Chinese that provided a legal framework to remain in America. The suspension of deportation was applicable to paper spouses who married American citizens and those who entered America before June 28, 1940. Chinese who demonstrated good moral character were also considered for suspension of deportation. Another category of consideration was for those who might experience extreme hardship in the event of deportation by the Immigration and Naturalization Service.

The actual number of Chinese who came to America with false identities is anyone's guess. Those who died or returned were not counted at the time of the confession program. According to some estimates, each Chinese woman in San Francisco must have had an extraordinary number of children. The number for each Chinese woman exceeded the maximum human female average reproduction capacity (fecundity) of twelve by fifty times. "[I]f the story told in the courts were true, every Chinese woman who was in the United States twenty-five years ago must have had at least 500 children."[47] To that extent, many Chinese came to America by claiming a biological relationship with someone who lived there. This was the lure and fever of Gold Mountain to those living in China. At the same time, it testified as to the hardship many Chinese faced during the political and economic turmoil since the Opium War.

REFLECTIONS

In 2016, Microsoft's Chinese chatbot, XiaoBing, was asked about its dream. It responded by saying, "My dream is to go to America." This statement stirred discomfort as Chinese leadership was pitching for the realization of the Chinese Dream in Great China. The embarrassed Chinese company, Tencent, decommissioned the robot for its unpatriotic utterance. One can only speculate that the Chinese robot was expressing an unspoken aspiration for Gold Mountain through the deep learning process of the AI machine.[48] The chatbot utterance, however, was not a mere fluke. The US government has attracted rich foreigners through its "golden visa" program, also known as the EB-5 investor visa. Anyone who can invest half a million dollars in the United States can receive a permanent visa (or green card). In 2016, for instance, Chinese applicants grabbed 82 percent of investor visas. A decade ago, the share of Chinese investors was only 12 percent. As the investor visa program sets limits by nationality, the average waiting period for Chinese is now five years.[49] Some infertile Chinese couples use American surrogate mothers at a minimum cost of 30,000 US dollars. They prefer American surrogate mothers as their American-born children will be US citizens by birth. They believe, and rightly so, that American citizenship will benefit their children's educational and employment opportunities.

More than a century ago, the practice of immigration through fraudulent paper identities reflected the wide gap between China and the United States in standard of living and economic opportunity. When the US Supreme Court ruled in 1943 that the Chinese Exclusion Act was unconstitutional, it was no longer necessary to keep the Chinese out. Beginning in 1949, the Chinese communist government kept its citizens confined within the bamboo curtain. No foreign travel by ordinary Chinese citizens, let alone foreign immigration, was allowed until China adopted its open-door policy in the early 1980s.

The 1970 US census counted 435,062 people of Chinese ancestry. This figure included American-born Chinese and Chinese from other parts of Asia, such as Hong Kong, Taiwan, Singapore, Malaysia, and Indonesia. By 1980, the Chinese population in the United States had almost doubled to 806,027. Then between 1980 and 1990, it doubled again to 1,640,000. In the next two decennial US Censuses, in 2000 and 2010, people of Chinese ancestry numbered 2,432,585 and 3,106,005, respectively. The US census of 1900 recorded 89,863 people of Chinese ancestry. A simple calculation shows that the number of Chinese has multiplied twenty-seven times over a century.

As the political and economic status of China continues to ascend, the increase of Chinese in America may slow. It may not be so far-fetched to imagine that someday many Chinese in the United States may choose to return to China to seek a better quality of life. This has already happened in certain instances. Nowadays, many Chinese scientists, engineers, and scholars desire to go back home after finishing their advanced studies or training in America. This tendency is a far cry from the days when many Chinese students of advanced studies hoped to settle down and work in the United States or other Western nations. As the luster of Gold Mountain fades, the rising superpower of China may attract overseas Chinese and others to its Middle Kingdom. Like today's America, China may have to deal with the problem of illegal aliens from the West in the not so distant future. And it's not so great of a stretch of imagination to picture a future where immigrants clamor to partake in the prosperity of China and attempt to enter it with their own fraudulent identity schemes. As the venerable author and humorist Mark Twain once stated, "History doesn't repeat itself, but it often rhymes."

NOTES

1. Erika Lee, *At America's Gate: Chinese Immigration during the Exclusion Era, 1882–1943* (Chapel Hill: The University of North Carolina Press, 2003), 12.
2. Encyclopedia.com, "Denis Kearney," accessed December 17, 2019, https://www.encyclopedia.com/people/history/us-history-biographies/denis-kearney.
3. Madeline Y. Hsu, *Dreaming of Gold, Dreaming of Home: Transnationalism and Migration between the United States and South China, 1882–1943* (Stanford: Stanford University Press, 2000), 58.
4. Eric Fong and William T. Markham, "Anti-Chinese Political Movement in California in the 1870s: An Inter-county Analysis," *Sociological Perspectives* 45, no. 2 (2002): 183–210.
5. Elliott Young, *Alien Nation: Chinese Migration in the Americas from the Coolie Era Through World War II* (Chapel Hill: The University of North Carolina Press, 2014), 8.
6. Lee, *At America's Gate*, 117–19.
7. Ibid., The Chinese admission figures by years are missing two short periods: 1892–1895 and 1933–1943. It was not clear whether the omission was due to no admission or lack of record.
8. Hsu, *Dreaming of Gold*, 69.
9. Ibid., 3.
10. Ibid., 113.
11. Ibid., 71.
12. Lee, *At America's Gate*, 4.
13. Ibid., 41.
14. Ibid., 201–2
15. Ibid., 196–98.
16. Him Mark Lai, Genny Lim, and Judy Yung, ed., *Island: Poetry and History of Chinese Immigrants on Angel Island 1910–1940* (2nd ed.) (Seattle: University of Washington Press, 2014), 326.
17. Hsu, *Dreaming of Gold*, 87.
18. Ibid.
19. Lai, et al., *Island*, 316.
20. Angel Island Association, "About Angel Island," accessed March 19, 2015, http://www.english.illinois.edu/maps/poets/a_f/angel/about.htm.
21. Lee, *At America's Gate*, 87.
22. Ibid., 88.
23. Lai, et al., *Island*, 306.
24. Ibid., 305.
25. Ibid., 263.
26. Lee, *At America's Gate*, 143–44.
27. Ibid.
28. Ibid., 87.
29. Lai, et al., *Island*, 267–68.
30. Lee, *At America's Gate*, 117–19.
31. Lai, et al., *Island*, 315.
32. Ibid., 339.

33. Erika Lee, *The Making of Asia America: A History* (New York: Simon & Schuster, 2015), 31–33.

34. Lee, *At America's Gate,* 117–19.

35. Ibid.

36. Ibid.

37. Ibid.

38. Lee, *The Making of Asia America*, 69.

39. US Senate, "Expressing the regret of the Senate for the passage of discriminatory laws against the Chinese in America, including the Chinese Exclusion Act" Congressional Bills 112th Congress, May 26, 2011.

40. Eithne Luibheid, *Entry Denied: Controlling Sexuality at the Border* (Minneapolis: University of Minnesota Press, 2002), 43.

41. Geroge Anthony Peffer, "Forbidden Families: Emigration Experiences of Chinese Women under the Page Law, 1875–1882," *Journal of American Ethnic History* 6, no. 1 (Fall 1986): 28.

42. Kerry Abrams, "Polygamy, Prostitution, and the Federalization of Immigration Law," *Colombia Law Review* 105, no. 3 (April 2005): 702.

43. Lai, et al., *Island,* 289

44. Ibid, 252.

45. Ibid, 335–36.

46. Immigration History, "Chinese Confession Program (1956–1965)," accessed October 20, 2020, https://immigrationhistory.org/item/chinese-confession-program/.

47. Hsu, *Dreaming of Gold,* 75.

48. Shona Ghosh. "Tencent Removed Microsoft's Chinese AI Chatbot after It Posted Unpatriotic Messages," *Business Insider*. August 3, 2017, accessed August 5, 2018, https://www.businessinsider.com/tencent-pulled-microsots-chinese-ai-chatbot-2017-8.

49. DW, "Chinese Investors Chase 'Golden Visas' to the US," accessed August 5, 2018, https://www.dw.com/en/chinese-investors-chase-golden-visas-to-the-us/a-38816291.

Chapter Six

Koreans in Thorny Henequen Fields in Yucatan

At the beginning of the twentieth century, many Koreans in coastal harbor cities were buoyed by the news related to Hawaii. The tales of having a good life and earning good money on those balmy islands of paradise spread like a pandemic among Koreans. More than seven thousand Koreans, mainly single men, had already gone to the new American territory as sugarcane plantation laborers between 1903 and 1905. Although they made less than a dollar a day (around $18 in 2020) laboring from dawn to dusk, the news of men working abroad enthused many men idling at home. In a small country afflicted by frequent famines and epidemics and a population vying for scant resources, what Korean laborers in Hawaii were making sounded enticing.

The last Korean kingdom, the Yi Dynasty (1392–1910), was beginning to show signs of its demise after five hundred years of existence. Although the kingdom had adopted a new name in 1897, the Empire of Korea, it was crumbling under the weight of political and economic problems. The old system was too inadequate to cope with the stress coming from powerful, surrounding nations. Koreans viewed their nation as a shrimp constantly crushed between big whales in global power struggles. China viewed Korea as a buffer zone against aggressive Japan, while Russia hoped for easy access to open harbors for its navy and merchant ships during frigid winter months. Japan, on the other hand, needed a land bridge for its imperial ambitions in China and beyond. A newly modernized and powerful Japan wanted to extend its reach far and wide in the eastern half of the vast Asian continent.

Japan was obsessed with the idea of conquering Korea as the first step to expanding its influence in Northeast and Southeast Asia, thereby competing with Western imperial powers. To that end, Japan had steadily built up its military. Furthermore, a newly industrialized Japan had handily defeated

Qing China in the Sino-Japan War of 1895. This outcome substantially neutralized Chinese influence over Korea, which had served the Middle Kingdom as a suzerain in major political decisions for more than a thousand years. Ten years later, Japan defeated Russia in 1905 in the Russo-Japan War, thus removing one of the major Western influences over Korea. In fact, Japan's defeat of both China and Russia partially contributed to the fall of the Qing Dynasty in 1911 and the Russian Empire in 1917. After defeating these two continental powers to the north, Japan was given a free hand in manipulating the politics of a weakened Korea bereft of allies. Through all sorts of manipulations and tactics, Japan made Korea its protectorate in 1905, and from that moment, Korea became a perfunctory puppet of Japan, unable to control its defense and foreign affairs.

The dream of Hawaii was rather short-lived, however. King Kojong halted the emigration of all Koreans because of reports from Yucatan in the southeast corner of Mexico. While Korean laborers were recruited for sugarcane plantations in Hawaii, there was also a request for laborers from henequen plantation owners in Yucatan. They had heard of the hard-working Koreans in Hawaii and were interested in bringing Koreans to their plantations. They had a hard time recruiting and maintaining sufficient workers for their henequen harvesting, and they turned to East Asia as a new source of labor supply. At that time, Mexico was unknown to most Koreans, and no diplomatic relationship existed between the two countries. Nonetheless, what attracted and brought more than one thousand Koreans[1] to Mexico was henequen. The tough, cactus-like plant was green gold as the demand for henequen product, such as rope and sacks, was high. Asians called a similar plant dragon's tongue for its scary shape. Each leaf of the tough plant had thorns running along its edge and a sharp, terminal needle at the end, features which resembled the long tongue of the imagined dragon. To workers harvesting henequen, it evoked the thoughts of pain.

Rafael Peon, the leader of the henequen growers association in Yucatan, contacted British international labor supplier John G. Meyers. As a first step, Meyers set up a recruitment office in Korea with his Asian partner, a Japanese labor supplier named Kan Ichi Ouniwa.[2] The recruiters were able to raise sufficient interest among Koreans in working in Mexico. The source of interest was green gold (Oro Verde). During the feverish pitch of Hawaiian immigration, many potential laborers believed that the green gold of Mexico might bring the same fortune as the white gold (sugar) of Hawaii. They assumed that the living standards of any Western country would be much better than those of their own.

From the middle part of the nineteenth to the early part of the twentieth century, the demand for henequen products—especially ropes, sacks, and twines—was high. These were useful products in the age of mercantilism as large ships had carried manufactured goods and raw materials between European nations and their overseas colonies and other markets. The tough, tropical, agave fiber was ideal to make durable ropes and sacks, and the growers made fortunes from this green gold. In the beginning of the twentieth century, the Yucatan region produced about 90 percent of the rope in the world.[3] The henequen, used by Mayans for generations, brought sudden wealth and fame to this ancient Mayan territory, especially the capital of the Yucatan State, Merida.

In the 1880s, Yucatan was one of the richest states in Mexico, and Merida enjoyed modern amenities such as streetlights and a tram system many years ahead of the Federal Capital, Mexico City. During the peak of the henequen boom, many millionaires made Merida the place of their residence. Yet, henequen growers had a hard time attracting or retaining laborers for a host of reasons. First of all, Yucatan was hot and humid; often, daytime temperatures hovered over 40 degrees Celsius (104 Fahrenheit). Not many could withstand the heat and humidity for ten hours or more in the fields. Second, the tropical area had many poisonous insects and snakes, particularly rattlesnakes whose bites were often lethal. More than anything else, cutting and harvesting henequen was difficult. Because of the thorns running along the edge of its thick leaves, workers often injured themselves. After cutting leaves from the stem, workers had to remove the sharp and hardened thorns and needles with a knife. Workers labored ten to twelve hours a day dealing with this painful plant, yet their earnings were far from being commensurate with the physical hardships endured. Koreans on the other side of the Pacific Ocean had no clue about the physical and working conditions of the henequen farms in Yucatan. They were just dreaming of making a new life in an affluent Western country.

THE RECRUITMENT OF KOREAN LABORERS

Not knowing much about the outside world, let alone the Yucatan region on the Atlantic side of Mexico, the people of the Hermit Kingdom responded with enthusiasm to the recruitment campaign. Meyers and his Japanese partner used Korean newspapers to advertise employment opportunities in Mexico. The theme of their advertisements revolved around the idea of getting rich by working a few years in Mexico. The ads portrayed Mexico as a land of El Dorado (a legendary treasure city of South America), and this captured many people's attention. The recruiters also painted the opportunities in Mexico as comparable to those in Hawaii. In 1904, most Koreans believed that the living and working conditions in Hawaii and Mexico would be the same because both were in the Occident. Shrewd labor recruiters painted the opportunities to be found in Mexico with the same brush as those found on the balmy, tropical islands of Hawaii. In reality, Hawaii and Yucatan hardly resembled each other either in climate or geography. Furthermore, the sociocultural environments of the two regions were quite different.

Recruitment pamphlets contained the following promises. Each family could grow vegetables and raise chickens to supplement company provisions and sponsors would pay all expenses for the Pacific passage. Also, plantation owners would cover any medical expenses incurred. Housing and coal would be free, and children over seven years of age would receive a free education. Each workday would be nine hours long, and the daily wage would be one and a half to three Mexican silvers while daily rations would cost anywhere between 25 and 30 Mexican cents. Wages would be paid weekly only to the worker. Labor contracts would be for four years after which workers would be free to return home. Upon completion of the contract period, each laborer would receive one hundred Mexican silvers. The whole journey by ship and train would take about a month. Individual emigrants would be informed of their departure dates by local recruiters.[4]

The promise that the Korean workers could eat as much as they wanted was a particularly strong incentive. Famine was common in Korea, especially in the spring right before the summer crop. Many had heard of the plentitude of tropical fruits in Hawaii, and they thought Mexico would be the same. Some of the recruits were misled to believe that they would go to Hawaii. Others were convinced that it would be easy to move to Hawaii from Mexico if that was what they wished.

The majority of labor recruits were commoners, but some came from privileged backgrounds. Unusual labor recruits included a royal family member with his own household, a few former eunuchs, palace maids, about two hundred former soldiers, petty civil servants, and Confucian literati. In a twist of irony, some even pretended to be common laborers so as to be accepted for physical overseas labor.[5] Regardless of their social backgrounds, all thought they were heading for a land far better than Korea and for vastly improved economic and social opportunities.

By the early months of 1905, Meyer and his associates had recruited a total of 1,033 Koreans. The group consisted of 702 men, 135 women, and 196 children, some of whom were orphans less than ten years of age.[6] Local Korean recruiters were encouraged to recruit families as much as possible to reduce the risk of escape in Mexico, but they could not help attracting a large number of single men and some abandoned children. The departure date was set for April 3, 1905, aboard a British-registered ship, *IL FORD*. The foreign ministry of Japan, however, ordered a stop to all emigration from Korea. This unexpected action was in response to a number of concerns. First, there had been a report that labor immigration to Mexico was illegal. In 1902, the Japanese government had intervened in an attempt to bring about five hundred Japanese families to the Yucatan henequen farms. The offered daily wage had been less than one yen, a minimum set by the Japanese government.[7]

Second, anti-Asian sentiment in the United States was rising. The fear of yellow peril in California was partially attributed to the move of Korean workers from Hawaii to the mainland. The Japanese government suspected that the Koreans bound for Mexico might eventually move to the United States, thereby worsening anti-Asian sentiment there. In trying to restrict Korean immigration the Japanese government was trying to protect its citizens residing in the United States from discrimination.

After much discussion and negotiation, the already recruited group was allowed to leave for Mexico. This recruit group turned out to be the first and last Korean emigration to this country. The British steamer departed from Jaemulpo (or Incheon), a major harbor near the capital, Seoul. After crossing the Pacific Ocean, it arrived at Salina Cruz, the Pacific Coast entry port of Mexico. After passing through customs inspection, the Koreans took a train to Coatzacoalcos harbor on the Gulf of Mexico. From there, a steamer took them to Progreso, where they boarded a train for the Yucatan state capital of Merida.

Altogether, the journey took forty-five days. The travel distance between the Korean harbor in Jaemulpo and their final destination of Merida was around 8,000 miles (12,500 km), almost one-third of the earth's circumference. During the voyage, many suffered from seasickness. On the way, two children died of sickness, and one baby was born. The bodies of the two children were thrown into the sea according to the maritime customs of sea burial. The Koreans who had never sailed such a distance were quite disturbed by the notion that fish would consume the dead. Two Korean interpreters accompanied the labor recruit group. Most Koreans, if not all, wore their traditional Korean outfits: loose white cotton pants and coats. Many of them were wearing hand-woven rice-straw sandals with a few weeks of duration. At a glance, the peasant appearance of the Korean laborers seemed to testify as to the sorry state of the country they had left behind.

At their final destination in Merida, crude, temporary accommodations were waiting for the group. The sponsors had erected large tents in an open field, and the Koreans had to sleep on dirt, each family cooking their own food in an open area. After a few days of waiting in the field, the Koreans were displayed for inspection either by plantation owners or their managers. The buyers checked each recruit quite thoroughly from top to bottom with only one thing in mind: physical fitness for the grueling labor in henequen fields. The Koreans were shocked as the inspectors treated them as if they were livestock for sale, soon realizing that they had been sold to Mexico as slaves. The so-called labor contracts were in name only, yet it was too late to change their situation. They were so far removed from their country, which had become a powerless and helpless protectorate of Japan. The Koreans felt

Figure 6.1. Map of Mexico and Cuba. *Frankljunior © iStock*

deceived, betrayed, and abandoned in this desolate corner of southeastern Mexico. Many lamented their fate by beating their breasts and some pounded the ground with their fists while wailing loudly. This was a customary display of extreme despair and sadness in public. It was a sad day when the entire group was divided into small groups of different sizes and led by strangers to different henequen plantations.

For nearly two months, the group had stayed together, eating the same food and breathing the same air. The group dynamic had helped the more than one thousand recruits overcome their sense of separation, strangeness, uncertainty, and anxiety outside of their homeland. As the recruits were scattered in different directions, their fates and the fate of their country seemed to overlap. With a few exceptions, most Koreans were taken to one of twenty-two henequen fields scattered around Yucatan.[8]

CUTTING OFF TOPKNOTS

Before the work began in the henequen fields, plantation owners ordered the Korean men to cut off their topknots (Sangtu). They argued that topknots would hinder the work of cutting thorny henequen leaves. As the workers had to bend over to cut the bottom of the leaves from the stem, topknots could easily entangle with the plant's sharp thorns and its spiny needle. The order was a prudent preventive measure for worker safety and productivity, but the Korean men took it differently and regarded the order as an insult to their manly dignity. Cutting off one's topknot was considered an ultimate shame, almost like exposing oneself naked in public. Mexicans in Yucatan had no idea about the symbolic value that Korean men placed in the topknot. The tradition had lasted more than two thousand years in much of East Asia, signifying a man's age, marital status, and even social status. In Korean tradition, a married man without a topknot was almost unthinkable.

The shape and location of the topknot differed slightly among East Asians. Both Korean and Han Chinese adult males gathered and twisted every strain of hair and made a topknot at the center of the head. On the other hand, Mongols, Manchurians, and Japanese shaved a part of their heads, either the front or the sides. Their thin and long topknots were placed in the hind part of the head. Unlike the traditional Han Chinese and Korean topknots that sat straight, Samurai and Manchurian topknots were slanted.

According to the teachings of Confucius, men were not supposed to change or remove any part of the body they had inherited from their parents. It was a filial duty to keep their bodies healthy and intact. Over two-and-a-half millennia ago, Confucius set forth the alpha and omega of his core value: filial piety. This system began with taking care of one's body and ended with social honor for parents: "The body, hair, and skin, all have been received from the parents, and so one does not dare to damage them, that is the beginning of filial piety." Moving from the physical to the social aspect of one's obligation, Confucius commands the following: "Establishing oneself, practicing the way, spreading the fame of one' name to posterity, so that one's parents become renowned, that is the end of filial piety."[9]

For the same Confucian reason, women were not allowed to cut their hair until modern times. Adult women wore their hair in a bun placed at the top or the back of their heads. When women decided to cut their hair, it was regarded as a bold gesture to defy the age-old tradition. With Western dress and shoes, short haircuts became the symbol of rebellious, modern women. Not knowing the symbolic significance of a man's topknot, plantation owners were puzzled by the violent resistance to their order to cut them off. To Korean men, on the other hand, keeping the topknot signified their dignity as adult men in a foreign country. In the face of losing their topknots, Korean men felt degraded in a totally strange land.

When the Korean men refused to cut off their topknots, the local workers subdued them and forcibly cut them off. Feeling like helpless sheep in the hands of a shearer, the men felt extremely angry and forlorn at the same time. Betrayed and bewildered in their new situation, this act of humiliation must have felt as if the final strand connecting them to their ancestral land had been severed. Indeed, the Koreans who found themselves in Mexico placed great value on their topknots, for they had refused to cut them off even at the order of their king. Ten years prior, in 1895, King Kojong had issued a decree for all male subjects to cut off their topknots. He and the crown prince had cut off theirs to set an example for their subjects. Cabinet members and top government officials had followed suit, and this had sent huge shock waves throughout the tradition-bound hermit kingdom.[10] Many, however, refused to obey the king's order because they believed it signified a rejection of the traditional Confucian ethic upon which much of Korean culture was based. Furthermore, many Koreans saw the decree as a sycophantic act to the Japanese. During the Meiji Reform beginning in 1868, the Japanese had cut off their topknots almost en masse, abandoning tradition in a push toward modernization through Westernization. The Japanese embraced Westernization by cutting off their topknots and wearing western clothing. However, the men in Korea were stubborn and refused to change by wearing their topknots as a symbolic gesture of nationality and tradition. Their resistance was so great that King Kojong rescinded his decree two years later in 1897.

Although the decree was once again reinstated in 1900, many still refused to follow the order. Thus, the pain of having their topknots cut off by the hands of foreigners caused even greater pain. The men in Yucatan felt absolutely powerless and helpless. Although the removal of topknots perhaps spared Korean workers from many troubles and injuries in the hot and humid climate of Yucatan, this recognition was no balm to the bitterness they felt. Culturally insensitive plantation owners never gave Koreans a chance to find an alternative solution. Stripped of their symbol of manhood, many Koreans felt utterly broken. They regarded themselves like slaves who had no control over their choices.

LIFE ON A HENEQUEN PLANTATION

When Koreans were brought to Yucatan in 1905, there were about 125,000 laborers working on henequen plantations. The majority were Mayans, numbering around one hundred thousand, and the rest were made of the Yaquis people from Sonora State, the Chinese, and Puerto Ricans.[11] Korean laborers comprised not even 1 percent of the total work force. Of more than twenty plantations, five took in more than 140 Koreans each, and the rest took from seven to seventy-six Korean laborers.[12] These group formations, large and small, helped the Korean workers aid each other in a new environment.

Wealthy plantation owners were the dominant social class in the region. They enjoyed the support of longtime dictator President Porfirio Dias (1876–1880, 1884–1911),[13] and they maximized profits by squeezing farm laborers. The members of the ruling class were usually the descendants of Creoles, an exclusive class who maintained their Spanish ancestry by preserving their biological and cultural stock. These privileged individuals of "Casta Divina" (Divine Cast) had tremendous influence over much of the politics and economy of the Yucatan region.[14] In the 1850s, Creole owners were driven out by Mayan peasant rebels who challenged the system of indentured servitude. The owners and their families fled to Cuba across the Gulf of Mexico. Years later, they returned to Yucatan and reestablished their henequen businesses.

In contrast, the life of henequen farm workers was a constant struggle for survival. Daily work started at dawn and ended at dusk six days a week, with a ten- or twelve-hour work day being the norm. The heat posed a problem, with average temperatures in the hot months of May through August soaring above 35 degrees Celsius (95 in Fahrenheit). The intensive labor coupled with the intense heat took its toll on Korean laborers who were from a temperate zone with four distinct seasons. In order to protect themselves from the sizzling sun and sharp thorns, the workers covered their entire bodies. Yet, what they had for protection was barely adequate and suffocating. The heat, humidity, and strenuous work caused excessive perspiration. The work was also repetitive and monotonous. With a machete, laborers cut leaves and removed thorns and terminal needles. They then made a bundle of

Figure 6.2. Henequen in Yucatan. *mofles © iStock*

Figure 6.3. Traditional Mayan Hut. *Traditional Mayan Hut © iStock*

twenty-five cut leaves which they carried to the roadside. Each henequen leaf was about ten inches wide (30–40 cm) and 30–45 inches long (1–1.5 m), weighing around five pounds (a little over 2 kg). The daily quota for each worker was two thousand cut leaves. If they worked ten hours a day, they were expected to cut, clear, and bundle two hundred henequen leaves per hour. Laborers were also constantly exposed to the dangers of rattlesnakes, scorpions, and poisonous tropical insects in the fields. Whether one was sick or injured, each laborer had to fulfill his daily quota. Failure to do so resulted in punishment, either whipping or beating. Field overseers on horseback were constantly monitoring and ordering workers to keep pace. If workers fell behind, they were ordered to pick up the pace. A slow response was rewarded with a whipping. Some field overseers were former bandits, and they were cruel in dealing with workers.

According to the original contract the laborers had signed in Korea, each laborer would earn seventy-five Mexican cents (centavo) for cutting two thousand henequen leaves a day. Beyond the daily quota, the worker would be paid an additional forty cents for an extra one thousand leaves. In the beginning, many Korean laborers had a hard time cutting even five hundred leaves a day. As they grew accustomed to the work, the daily quota of two thousand leaves was within reach. Besides cutting henequen leaves, other field work included removing henequen stems. They earned thirty-five cents for digging out one hundred stems. Other jobs around the plantation involved clearing fields, splitting firewood, and the like. For the same adult wages, children of twelve years of age and older could do the same work.[15]

From wages, plantation owners deducted a fixed amount for the passage fare, money owed for food from company stores, and an automatic savings of two-tenths of their earnings toward the termination payment at the end of the contract period. This payment would only be received if the worker completed the four-year contract term. Attempting to escape or seek work at another farm would nullify the termination payment. Essentially, this clause was a gimmick to keep laborers at the original plantation throughout the contract period. To the laborers, the compulsory 20-percent deduction was an invisible chain tied to the first plantation. Because of this, many workers could not negotiate or bargain with their original owners when others offered better wages or working conditions.

On henequen plantations, indentured servitude among Mayans was maintained generation after generation by three schemes: the transfer of parental debt to children (*mayorazgo*), the operation of plantation stores (*tienda de raya*), and the supervision administration (*capataz*). Parental debt often resulted in the servitude of children, thus perpetuating inter-generational bondage. Debt forgiveness at someone's death did not exist. Moreover, high prices at plantation stores trapped many workers, often without choice, into perpetual debt. This was how many Mayans in Yucatan ended up working for Creole farm owners as bonded laborers.[16] Around the time of Korean arrival in 1905, there were about 80,000 indentured workers[17] in Yucatan out of a total population of about 310,000.[18] Over a quarter of the residents in Yucatan were indentured, quasi slaves. In the mid-nineteenth century, some owners in Yucatan sold their Mayan workers to Cuba, where they rioted more than thirty times.[19] Unless laborers worked extra hard and were extremely conscientious about spending, saving was almost impossible. Rather, many ended up accumulating debt to plantation owners. Sickness, drinking, gambling, prostitution, and the purchase of goods from company stores easily led them to being trapped in the quagmire of deepening debt. In such situations, laborers had only two choices: escape or serve in perpetuity to the same owner. Even death did not erase their debt as it was transferred to children.

Indentured laborers were not allowed to leave the plantation without a permit. Guards watched and monitored the movement of workers. Nonetheless, some Koreans, especially those without families, contemplated and even attempted escape. Yet the chance to succeed in an escape attempt was low. Neither knowing the language nor the surrounding geography, Koreans escapees were caught in short order. Punishment for escape was severe, ranging from fifty lashes to solitary confinement in a metal box without water or food. In extreme cases, plantation owners ordered cutting off of hands or feet. Such cruel punishment was to show the consequences of attempted escape.

There is anecdotal evidence of Korean laborers banding together in a show of unity. At one point, outraged Koreans surrounded the house of a plantation manager who was merciless in punishing captured Korean escapees. With machetes and rocks in their hands, the Koreans threatened to kill the manager. The plantation owner was only able to calm the angry mob of Koreans by firing the manager. Such leniency by complying with the demand of the workers was rare. A captured escapee was forced to pay fifty cents a day for each guard involved in search and capture. This penalty was truly severe because it often amounted to more than his daily earning. For instance, a captured escapee from a plantation was forced to pay one and a half pesos for each day that three guards were used for his recapture. If an escapee managed to hide for five days, he had to pay a total of seven and a half pesos for the five-day search by the three guards. It was more than half a month's earnings.

In spite of the dreadful physical and monetary punishments if captured, some managed to succeed. According to the Ministry of Foreign Affairs of Japan, about 140 Korean laborers were able to escape.[20] If the official count is accurate, that number would be close to 15 percent of the original group of 1,031, which included children. The report, however, does not indicate how many families or individuals escaped. It might be safe to assume that most escapees were single adults rather than those with dependents.

To the surprise of some plantation owners, eight Koreans were able to free themselves before the end of their four-year contractual term. The requirement for freedom was to pay eighty to one hundred pesos.[21] The eight freed Koreans were former soldiers of the Korean army who had become Christian. Perhaps discipline ingrained in the military helped them work hard and save every penny. At the same time, it was quite possible that a strict Christian moral code had kept them from many temptations, such as drinking, gambling, and prostitution, which were all readily available in the state capital, Merida.

By 1920, about twenty Koreans managed to return home after fifteen years of hardship in Mexico.[22] Roughly one out of fifty original immigrants made their dreams come true. They must have worked extra hard and saved for their return home. Henequen workers could increase earning by cutting extra leaves beyond the daily quota of two thousand. Although rare, some efficient workers were able to cut up to ten thousand leaves a day. To save money, these thrifty Koreans forwent the traditional Korean diet, which consisted of rice, kimchi, and hot paste, very expensive in this far corner of Mexico. Instead they subsisted on a meager diet of corn tortillas and salt. The fare from Manzanillo, Mexico, to Pusan, Korea, was more than one hundred pesos per person, so they would have needed to be quite thrifty.

Other than the twenty returned individuals, the only other successful group of Koreans to exodus out of Yucatan was in a group migration to Cuba. Some managed to move to the United States, and others tried to forge new lives elsewhere in Mexico beyond Yucatan. Some of these out-migrants often ended up returning to Yucatan as they could not establish themselves elsewhere. Without special job skills, their language and cultural barriers were too formidable to overcome. Ironically, the land of tears and sweat that they had tried to escape became their home. Although the thorny henequen fields had left many painful scars on them, it was the only place they were familiar with in this new world. And as a Korean proverb says, a lengthy attachment to a strange place makes that place one's home.

THE EXPOSURE OF KOREAN MISERY

No one in the Korean government paid attention to the conditions faced by Korean laborers in Yucatan. Besides, there were no means to reach out to them in the remote, southeastern corner of Mexico. No diplomatic relations existed between the two countries. Moreover, at that time, Korea was a protectorate of Japan, stripped of its diplomatic authority. Even if Korea had diplomatic relations with Mexico, no high-ranking Korean government officials would be interested in the well-being of commoners laboring in a foreign land beyond the vast ocean. The misery of Korean henequen laborers in Yucatan was unknown to the outside world until a few sympathetic witnesses felt compelled to reveal their misery. The Korean laborers in isolated and scattered plantations had no means of communicating their plight to anyone beyond Yucatan.

The first eyewitness was a Chinese resident in Merida whose name was Huhwei. He was so disturbed by the terrible conditions faced by Korean laborers that he wrote a letter to a Chinese newspaper in San Francisco. At the same time, he managed to contact a few Korean leaders in the same city. Huhwei wanted to ensure that the outside world was aware of the miserable conditions facing Korean workers in Yucatan:

> It is so pitiful to see the indigenous people [Mayans] laugh at the Koreans, who wear tattered rags and straw sandals. The Koreans appear to be less than cows, horses, and other house animals. When the parents walk to the henequen plantations either holding their children's hands or carrying them on their backs in the rain, you cannot see the scene without tears. Here the Mayans are considered either fifth- or sixth-tier slaves, but the Koreans are regarded as seventh-tier slaves. They live like cows and horses. They are beaten badly in a knelt position if they do not meet the assigned daily quota. The bodies of the punished are stained with blood, and their flesh is torn. Indeed, I feel so terrible and pained whenever I see the Koreans.[23]

Not long after this letter was published, a Korean ginseng merchant ventured into Yucatan to sell his products to his fellow countrymen. He had learned about Koreans laboring in henequen plantations from the Chinese newspaper as the letter had circulated in both the Chinese and Korean communities in the San Francisco Bay Area. When he arrived, what he saw shocked him. The plight of Koreans in Yucatan was far worse than what he had imagined. His letter to Korean leaders in California detailed the horrors that he witnessed:

> I inquired about the Koreans through some Chinese residents in Merida. They told me that the Koreans were sold to the henequen plantations, and the sold workers had no freedom to move beyond these plantations. Only two Korean interpreters are free to move around. On the way to a plantation, I happened to encounter three Koreans. One was wearing a Western suit and the other two were wearing loose Korean outfits with no shoes on. The two barefooted Koreans were being taken somewhere for having done something wrong, but I could not press on . . .
>
> Here, the Koreans are working in the thorny henequen fields under the sizzling sun, and many of them are whipped for moving slowly at work. At night, they sleep in the field dugouts. . . . They barely extend their lives on watery gruel, and their lot seems to be worse than the plantation-owners' dogs. . . . When the plantation owner appears in the field, the field overseers prod the workers like ranch cows with their whips. The Korean interpreter, Kwon Byung-sook, acts like the local overseers in dealing with the Korean workers in order to please the owner. He swears and whips his fellow countrymen worse than the indigenous overseers, and the Koreans are very angry at him. If Mr. Kwon [interpreter] spots someone who comes to the plantation to investigate the condition of the Koreans, he reports to the owner to prevent any digging up information on the workers. He reported my visit to the owner, and a policeman has followed my every move. The policeman keeps asking me when I will leave the area, and I cannot continue my investigation anymore. [24]

The letter was dated November 17, 1905, about six months after the Koreans had started working on the henequen plantations. A few years later, a major Korean newspaper reported on the condition of Korean workers in Mexico in a retrospective way. The source was a Korean who claimed to have studied in Mexico for two years. It was not clear if the report was based on his own observations in Yucatan or on secondhand reports.

> When the Koreans realized that they were sold to Mexico as slaves, they wailed pounding the ground with fists. They questioned if such a miserable fate was the fault of the Korean government, Korean society, or their own. Many wondered if it was a predestined fate beyond their control. Their continuous wailing reverberated the Yucatan peninsula on the other side of the earth. Out of despair, a dozen of them committed suicide, and many were beaten and locked up by the owners for crying. [25]

King Kojong, the Korean monarch, was quite disturbed when he heard of the terrible suffering of his subjects in Yucatan. In response, he ordered a stop to all immigration to any overseas territory, including Hawaii. He realized that Korea, as a Japanese protectorate, could do nothing for its people beyond the Pacific Ocean. By then, the last Korean Dynasty was only five years away from its 1910 demise.

Legally speaking, the Koreans in Mexico were not slaves. They had labor contracts written in Korean and Spanish which they had signed in Korea. Wage and contract periods were specified, and when the contract period was complete, they would be able to leave the henequen plantations. The reality, however, was very different. Conditions were often unbearable and the physical hardships, economic despair, mistreatment, and sense of isolation overwhelmed many of the workers. Helplessness and hopelessness pervaded their lives and, to many, the four-year contract period seemed an eternity. As a Korean saying goes, each passing day felt like the passage of three years.

FAMILY LIFE

Most Korean laborers lived in tiny Mayan huts provided by the plantations. These simple, primitive huts had grass roofs, mud walls, and dirt floors. As there was no designated kitchen, cooking was done outdoors. Each family occupied a single hut, and single workers shared a hut. This type of housing did not allow for any privacy. It was very hard for the Korean workers to learn Spanish under the circumstances, and this limited their social activities. Their Korean-born children, however, tended to be bilingual. Besides Spanish, they picked up conversational Mayan as they worked with Mayan laborers. In extremely rare cases, a few of them spoke only Mayan as they had lived with only Mayans most of the time. Small henequen farms could use only one or two Korean laborers who were surrounded by Mayans.

For their own convenience, plantation owners or field supervisors changed the names of Korean workers. It was very difficult for them to pronounce and remember the strange, foreign Korean names. Common Spanish names were added to their Korean ones, and workers became "Pedro" Bongchan Kim or "Maria" Sooni Lee. Over time, even Korean last names were changed into familiar-sounding Spanish surnames: Choi into Sanchez, Kim into Kin or King, Baek into Peck, Ho into Jose, and the like. In addition, the mother's maiden surname was included, according to Spanish custom. The longer Spanish version of Korean names, for instance, was "Maria" Sooni Lee Park or Pedro Bongchan Kim Suh. As the workers began to intermarry with Mexican women, Korean names began to sound more Spanish. Some examples are Jesus Kildong Hong Gonzales, Amanda Bokja Bakeido Lopez, and so forth. Mr. Hong married a local woman whose last name was Gonzales, so their children's surname became Hong Gonzales.

Due to the extremely skewed ratio of men to women (802 adult men out of total of 1,033), it was almost impossible for single members of the latter to find and marry Korean women. Thus, the majority of Korean men married Mayan women or local mestizos. A few even managed to marry white Creole women. In general, Korean men were quite popular with the local women due to their reputation as being hard workers and possessing a strong sense of family responsibility. Also, their relatively strict moral code, derived from either Confucianism or Protestantism, impressed the local women. As a result, intermarriage between Korean men and Mexican women became common.

Unlike their counterparts in Hawaii, the laborers could not afford the practice of bringing picture brides from Korea. Mexico was simply too far away and too unknown to most Koreans at home. Moreover, the henequen farm laborers were too poor, and the cost of long-distance travel and other marriage-related expenses prohibitive. Even if some could afford the expense of bringing a Korean woman from Korea, they lacked the courage to ask her to leave her homeland and live in the isolated, southeast corner of Mexico.

Any sizable Korean community with one hundred members or more would run a Korean school to teach children Korean. Some communities in Yucatan started Korean schools for as little as five children.[26] Besides the Korean language, these schools taught Chinese characters that were heavily used in writing, especially among educated Koreans. Learning Korean was easy as it is a phonetic language, but Chinese required a great deal of time and effort because it is an idiographic language, whereby a learner has to memorize the shape of each Chinese character and its meaning. Although many Korean parents were struggling laborers with meager earnings, they made great sacrifices for the education of their children. These community-based language schools did not last long, however. When the labor contract was over, free Korean workers tended to move away in search of better economic opportunities elsewhere. Another reason was that neither Mayan nor Mestizo mothers shared the same enthusiasm for education as their Korean husbands.

Over time, the identity of many Koreans was diluted not only biologically but also culturally. A grandchild's memory of his or her Korean grandparents' teachings or customs faded quickly from memory. On Sundays and holidays such as Easter or Christmas, Korean men who were not churchgoers would go to the city of Merida to spend their free time. While drinking at local cafés, it was not uncommon to hear them shouting, crying, or murmuring *Jaemulpo*, the harbor near Seoul from which they had departed their homeland. One sympathetic café owner changed the name of his café to *Jaemulpo* in honor of his Korean patrons, and the section of Merida the

Koreans frequented became known as *Jaemulpo* corner. The nostalgia felt by Koreans laborers, isolated and far removed from their homeland, was visceral. Each and every day they longed to return.

COMMUNITY LIFE

The four-year labor contract expired in May 1909 and Korean workers were free to leave their plantations. Unexpectedly, some owners claimed the children who were born on their plantations. The owners insisted that Korean laborers' Mayan wives and children were their property and asked the Korean workers to pay if they wanted their families to leave with them. Some of them offered an alternative option if the workers could not afford the price: work for five more years in order to gain custody of their Mayan wives and children.[27] This demand reflected the mindset of plantation owners toward their indentured laborers from Korea. In their eyes, the Korean contract laborers were no less than slaves.

Some Koreans extended their labor contracts with the same owners as they had no other option for their livelihood. Others represented their own interests as free laborers. A few set up small shops in the Chinatown section of Merida, but the majority continued to work on henequen plantations. The freed Koreans began to hold church gatherings at a private home. These religious gatherings occurred two or three times a week and attracted about eighty Koreans. Centered around the church group, they formed a branch of the Korean American Residents Association in Merida. The headquarters of the association in San Francisco dispatched two representatives to help the Korean community in Yucatan. The highly respected president of the association, Ahn Chang Ho, came and spent many months among the Koreans in Yucatan. He provided both organizational and moral instructions on how to make Koreans exemplary citizens in Mexico.

The association helped Korean residents identify themselves as a part of a much larger community at home and abroad. As an overseas Korean community, they had a clearly defined goal: the liberation of Korea from the colonial rule of Japan. This lofty goal gave many Koreans a sense of purpose beyond their daily mundane struggles for existence and helped them transcend individual hardship. Deeply influenced by Ahn Chang Ho, the Korean community in Merida established self-imposed rules to maintain high moral standards among its members. Any member who violated the community's moral standards would be punished in the form of a fine and the threat of expulsion. For instance, the association set a minimum age for marriage: eighteen years for men and sixteen for women.[28] Engaged couples had to obtain a wedding permit from the association. Any married man involved in extramarital affairs was subject to the sanctions of the community. Gambling, excessive drinking, and prostitution were violations of community ethics. To enforce these strictures, each local Korean community appointed judges and policemen. Strong community solidarity made such enforcement upon free members possible.

The community supervised individuals working in henequen fields through an appointed Korean labor contractor. Individual workers were hired or transferred through the designated Korean labor representative to prevent undue competition among Korean workers, thus maintaining reasonable wages and benefit standards. The Korean community had what they called the "henequen honesty rule,"[29] applied to all Korean laborers in the region. Some dishonest workers cheated in making henequen bundles with less than the required twenty-five leaves. Since their earnings were based on the number of bundles they carried to the loading area, some workers were less than honest. If a worker was dishonest with ten to twenty less cut leaves per one thousand (forty bundles), that person would be fined five pesos. If the shortage exceeded twenty leaves per one thousand, the fine was doubled to ten pesos.[30] Anyone who protested the imposed fine was expelled from the community. No henequen plantation in the area would hire an expelled Korean laborer. Most first- and second-generation Koreans complied with these self-imposed community rules. They thought of themselves as part of a larger community. Isolation from home and the host society resulted in ethnic cohesion.

FREEDOM FIGHTERS IN YUCATAN

When the Korean laborers left for Mexico in April 1905, they had already felt the tightening grip of Japan on their country. In the previous year, the Russo-Japan War had erupted over the control of Manchuria and the Korean peninsula. After defeating China in 1895, an assertive Japan asked Russia to recognize Japanese control of the Korean peninsula in exchange for Japan's recognition of Russian control of Manchuria. Russia, however, insisted that Japan control only the southern part of Korea below the thirty-ninth parallel (in 1945, Korea was divided along the thirty-eighth parallel). Japan rejected the Russian proposal and decided to control the entire Korean peninsula. On February 8, 1904, Japan declared war upon Russia. In numerous key battles in the Yellow Sea (or East China Sea) and East Sea (or Sea of Japan), Japan destroyed much of Russia's Far East battleships. Through the mediation of the American President, Teddy Roosevelt, the two countries signed a treaty at Portsmouth on September 5, 1905. Neutralizing one of the major Western influences in Korea, Japan made the Korean peninsula its protectorate. Japan gained America's support in this move in exchange for its approval of America's rule over the Philippine Islands. The recruitment of Koreans for Yucatan henequen plantations took place in the midst of the Russo-Japan War, and Korean workers knew what was happening.

Within half a year of beginning work in Yucatan, the laborers learned that their homeland was under the control of Japan and were asked to contact the Japanese Consul in Mexico City with any concerns. This news distressed many Koreans and compounded their feelings of misery. As foreigners in Mexico, they were now under the authority of another foreign country, Japan, who took steps to colonize their homeland. Working and living almost like quasi slaves in a foreign country was very painful. Now they had become a people without a sovereign nation.

When the Japanese Consul in Mexico City requested that Koreans register as Japanese citizens following Japan's annexation of Korea as a colony, most Koreans ignored the order. The only documents that proved their status were old passports issued years ago by the now defunct Korean government. By refusing to be Japanese subjects, they became a stateless people, making themselves more vulnerable without the protection of any government. During economic downturns in Mexico, anti-foreigner laws were passed that affected their employment.

At the same time, the political turmoil of the Mexican Revolution began in 1910, and it lasted for the next ten years. The rebels fought against the central government, which was aligned with the interests of wealthy plantation owners. Many haciendas in Yucatan were the targets of Mexican rebels, and this disrupted operations in many plantations affecting the Korean workers. Some Koreans responded to the call of the rebels and joined them in fighting against the forces of the status quo. Many Koreans became quite fatalistic about their unfortunate situation both in Korea and Mexico. They felt ill-fated as they were caught in the middle of political turmoil in both Korea and their host country, Mexico.

Guatemala, Mexico's southern neighbor, was also thrown into a revolutionary swirl, and a considerable number of Koreans were sucked into it. Some of the Koreans in Yucatan became involved in the Guatemalan revolution, either siding with the government or the rebels. In 1915, the Guatemalan Underground Revolutionary Army induced thirty-three Korean mercenaries to fight against the longtime dictator Manuel Estrada Cabrera (1857–1924). The Guatemalan rebels promised to pay huge sums of money and give a piece of land for the nation of "New Korea" if the revolution was successful.

Many Koreans, aiming for Korean independence, had a strong desire to establish a Korean exile government in Guatemala. Although there are contradicting reports of Korean involvement in the Guatemalan revolution, about thirty Korean mercenaries were recruited through the arrangement of a few local Korean leaders. Later, some Korean survivors testified that they had been mistreated by the Guatemala revolutionary army, and that the rebel army had used them as human shields on the front lines. Four Koreans were killed in combat.³¹ The idea of a New Korea in Guatemala was an unrealized hope among the patriotic laborers. This bold political conception came years before the establishment of the first Korean exile government in Shanghai in 1919, which occurred after a nationwide demonstration against Japanese colonial rule in Korea. Known as the March-First Movement, this patriotic uprising had been inspired by the American President Woodrow Wilson, who had endorsed the principle of self-determination for new nations following the First World War. Former Korean soldiers who had served under the Empire of Korea opened a military training center in Merida, which they called the Military Honor School. At one time, this place trained thirty-two students using imitation wooden rifles. Eventually, the Yucatan government forced its doors to close.

This type of military training among Korean expatriates was not unique to the Yucatan Korean community. In Hawaii and continental America, this phenomenon was repeated as Korean expatriates opened and ran military training schools for the same purpose. In the United States, the first Korean military training school was established in Nebraska in 1909. Called the Korean Youth Military Academy, it trained twenty-seven Korean cadets in Hastings, Nebraska. Following the example of the Nebraska military school, former Korean soldiers set up two similar schools in California and one in Kansas and Wyoming, respectively. At a later date, a pilot training school was established for Koreans in Willows, California. Running such an aviation school for Koreans was possible with the support of Kim Chong Nim, a wealthy rice farmer. He donated three light planes for flight training and supported the Korean pilot school with a monthly contribution of 3,000 dollars (around $40,000 in 2020). This considerable donation was fueled by his sincere patriotism.³²

The largest Korean military training operation, however, took place in Hawaii. Initially, three different Korean communities in Hawaii operated three military schools located on different islands. Later, school leaders decided to consolidate the three schools into one on Oahu. At its peak, this military academy had as many as 311 enrolled cadets. Most were former army soldiers of the Empire of Korea. Trainees worked on either sugarcane or pineapple plantations during the day and received military training at night.³³ Koreans in the Americas, from Hawaii to Yucatan, were able to transcend their personal hardships by holding dearly to the noble cause of Korean independence. Any activity to benefit their colonized homeland gave a profound meaning to their own struggles in these foreign lands. Korean communities in Hawaii, California, and Yucatan were part of a larger, close-knit network for the liberation of Korea.

FROM YUCATAN TO CUBA

A few Korean workers managed to move to Cuba in the years following the expiration of their labor contracts. They were the first Koreans to ever step on the island of Cuba. When they returned to Yucatan as labor recruiters for the sugarcane fields in Cuba, a large number of fellow Koreans responded. This group included Mexican-born or Mexican-grown second-generation Koreans who were fluent in Spanish and well versed in Latin culture. Besides employment opportunities in Cuba, the Koreans were pushed by deteriorating socioeconomic conditions in Mexico during its ten-year revolutionary conflicts. On top of that, the demand for henequen products had declined considerably after the First World War, as the price of henequen fiber had peaked during the war. For instance, in 1916 henequen workers earned up to ten pesos a day,[34] thirty times more than what they had earned five years earlier. When the First World War ended, however, prices fell and remained depressed. Other places in the Caribbean region, especially Cuba, posed some competition when it came to henequen production. In addition, modern synthetic fibers steadily replaced natural fibers. Many Korean henequen farm laborers in Yucatan had difficulty surviving and began to look elsewhere for a better future.

Around this time, Cuba was experiencing a massive labor shortage as sugar was in high demand. Although Cuba was another country, getting there was only a matter of crossing the narrow Yucatan Channel. A group of 288 Koreans were filled with hope in starting a new life in the island nation.[35] When their ship arrived in Cuba, customs officials refused to allow them to disembark as their nationality was unclear. The Koreans insisted that they should be treated as Korean citizens. Some carried expired, invalid passports issued by a Korean government that had been out of existence for years. At the same time, the Japanese Consul in Havana refused to recognize them as subjects of Japan. Years before, many Koreans rejected the Consul's advice to register as Japanese subjects. After keeping the Korean passengers seventeen days aboard the ship, the Cuban government decided to recognize them as Koreans. The prolonged frustration and bitterness at the port seemed to portend what was waiting for them in Cuba. Not long after they landed, sugar prices plummeted unexpectedly, and their economic future in Cuba looked dark.

From the beginning, the lives of Korean laborers were intertwined with the international demand for agricultural commodities. The demand for henequen had brought them to Yucatan in 1905 and the demand for sugar had pulled them to Cuba. But even sugar prices were not immune to fluctuation in the international commodities markets. When Korean laborers in Yucatan were recruited for work in Cuba, the price of sugar was 22.5 cents per pound. When the price fell to 3.75 cents per pound in 1921, it had lost more than 80 percent of its value in just one year. A decade later, during the Great Depression, sugar sold for less than a penny, at 0.57 cents per pound.[36] Like henequen, the price of sugar was volatile as its worth was determined by supply and demand around the world.

It was indeed a double blow to the former henequen laborers from Yucatan. The sugarcane field operators reduced their labor force in order to survive falling prices. This cutback affected not only wages but also the amount of work available. The newly arrived Koreans were unable to find work in the sugarcane fields. The heavily sugar-dependent Cuban economy tends to be very slow from June through November, known as *tiempo muerte* (time of death). The Koreans managed to find some work in their Cuban henequen fields in Matanzas. Although henequen, unlike sugarcane, was harvested year around, global demand was also ebbing. The Koreans could not find full-time work even in henequen fields. Thoroughly shattered by their short-lived Cuban dream, they contemplated moving to Brazil—the largest South American country—which had accepted a large number of Japanese immigrants for its agricultural development. The remigration plan to Brazil did not materialize, and some had no choice but to return to Yucatan.

Those who remained in Cuba maintained their ethnic solidarity by forming an association called *Coreano Associacion de Matanzas*. The members carried out their duties by supporting the cause of Korean independence. They sent money to the headquarters of the association in San Francisco and mobilized its members for the goal of Korean independence. They organized parades of a political nature on special occasions. When Japan attacked Pearl Harbor in 1941, Koreans in Cuba wore pins of the Korean flag lest they should be mistaken for Japanese. In the early months of the Pacific War, five Koreans were arrested by the Cuban police. They were released with the help of the Korean association which proved that those arrested were Korean, not Japanese. As the Cuban government applied legal restrictions on foreigners, thus detrimentally affecting their economic life, many Koreans became naturalized Cubans.

EXODUS ATTEMPTS

Since most Koreans in Mexico hoped to settle down in America, the Korean Residents Association in San Francisco wanted to move them to Hawaii when their labor contracts expired. The association planned to ask the US government to grant these laborers and their families admission to Hawaii. To cover the expense of the proposed move, Korean residents in Hawaii and the mainland had raised almost 1,100 dollars (around $15,000 in 2020).[37] After so much suffering and hardship, the Koreans in Yucatan were filled with hope and excitement. Hawaii was much closer to Korea and had a sizable Korean community as well as other Asian communities. Their Hawaiian dreams, however, were shattered by an imprudent few. A group of four Koreans decided to go to Hawaii as an advance team via San Francisco. These Korean men told US customs officers in San Francisco that they were in the process of immigrating to Hawaii. When the Immigration Service could not find any official documentation for them, they were detained for forty-three days. After paying a hefty fine, they were sent back to Yucatan. As they were so anxious to leave, they acted emotionally while the Korean Residents Association and the American government were still in negotiation on their expatriation.

However, the association did not give up hope for bringing their fellow countrymen to America. It contacted white farmers in Northern California who had shown interest in bringing Korean workers as laborers. Fruit growers needed farm hands to pick fruit during the harvest season. This mutual interest, however, did not result in concrete action. Although Mexican migrant farm workers could cross the border without passports, Koreans in Yucatan had to show valid passports and other necessary documents, and the passports many of the Korean immigrants carried were invalid.

Running out of remigration options in the Americas, the sympathetic association and the Yucatan Koreans even considered the eastern Siberian region of Russia as an area for potential group resettlement, particularly the major harbor city of Vladivostok. The main attraction of Far East Russia was the proximity of the region to Korea, then a Japanese colony, as the two countries shared a short border. However, news of the mistreatment of Korean residents by the Soviet Union government during the Stalin era dissuaded them. The new communist country was also experiencing political turmoil following the 1917 Russian Revolution, which overlapped with the latter part of the ten-year Mexican Revolution.

Since most Koreans in Yucatan wished to go to Hawaii or the mainland of the United States, some of them moved to the Pacific Coast of Mexico. It was a long diagonal move from the Gulf of Mexico to the northern end of Mexico's Pacific Coast. As much as possible, they wanted to be closer to home on the other side of the Pacific Ocean. Over the years, one by one they arrived at the border city of Tijuana, directly across from San Diego. Tijuana was perceived as a gateway to California and the United States, and they hoped to be closer to a much larger Korean community in Southern California. As a result, today Tijuana has the highest concentration of descendants of the early Korean immigrants to Yucatan, and some of them found ways to make the move to the United States.

Chapter 6

REFLECTIONS

The story of Korean henequen laborers in Yucatan shows that personal fates can be profoundly affected by major political events within and outside of one's country. Their tragic stories cannot be fully understood without a knowledge of the last Korean kingdom subsumed into an ambitious Imperial Japan. At the same time, the ten-year revolution in Mexico and Guatemala was inextricably intertwined with the lives of Korean laborers. Yet their sad past was nearly forgotten, only coming to light recently. Their lonely struggles in a remote southeastern corner of Mexico and a high rate of intermarriage had buried most of their stories for almost a century. When their stories resurfaced, Koreans at home and abroad identified them as "henequen" Koreans, which have become synonymous with Korean Mexicans. In many ways, the agave-like henequen symbolized the thorny, rough fate of most Korean laborers and their descendants in Mexico.

Today, some young Korean Mexicans, often with only one-quarter or one-eighth Korean ancestry, have woken up to their Korean roots and heritage. The 1988 Summer Olympic Games in Seoul was a turning point for them. Witnessing South Korea and its impressive achievements during the Olympics exposed a very different Korea from the one they had heard about from their grandparents or great-grandparents. Whether they were just one-quarter or down to one-sixteenth Korean, they began to be interested in the land of their ancestors. As a dynamic South Korea continues to make news with giant corporations such as Samsung, Hyundai, and LG, as well as a global footprint in popular culture through the phenomenon of K-pop, many Mexicans of Korean ancestry have come out of their ethnic closets. Mostly third- or fourth-generation Korean Mexicans have begun to search for faded ethnic roots and to claim a part of their ancestral identity. They are now proud of their Korean connections. At the same time, Mexico is an important country for South Korea's global trade in the Americas. As a member country of NAFTA (North American Free Trade Agreement; also called USMCA—US, Mexico, Canada), Mexico has attracted Korean investment and business. Many Korean corporations, large and small, set up their manufacturing or assembly operations near the US-Mexico border, commonly known as *maquiladoras* in order to take advantage of the free trade agreements among Canada, the United States, and Mexico. The increasing Korean economic activities in Mexico have become valuable economic opportunities to some Korean descendants and their exposure to and interactions with Koreans and have reinforced their Korean identity.

In addition, Korean Mexicans had encounters with Korean immigrants from South America, mainly from Argentina, Bolivia, Brazil, and Paraguay, in the 1970s and 1980s. The Koreans from South America regarded Mexico as a base for crossing the US-Mexico border when opportunities arose. Contacts and interactions with Koreans from Korea and South America reinforced their partial Korean identities. This awakening has resulted in the official attention of the Korean government. The Korean Prime Minister, Kim Whang Shik, visited Mexico at the invitation of the Mexican government in 2013. Two novels about Korean Mexicans, *Henequen* (three volumes) and *Black Flower,* were published in Korean in the 1990s and a movie, *Henequen,* was released in 1996. The Korean government began to include Korean Mexican youth in cultural programs and training for overseas Korean youth leadership.

In 2015, the Korean government recognized eighteen Korean patriots in Mexico and three in Cuba, posthumously. They were the first-generation Korean immigrants to Yucatan who helped the Korean independence movement in the Americas. The Korean government awarded them with Presidential medals or National Foundation medals according to the significance of their contribution to the cause of Korean independence during the thirty-six-year Japanese colonial rule (1910–1945).

Unlike other overseas Korean patriots who were active in America, China, Russia, and other countries, the governmental recognition of Korean patriots in Mexico came much later. Nonetheless, the Korean government honored the history of the henequen Koreans. To most Koreans, Yucatan is remembered as a place of suffering for Koreans. The almost forgotten history of vanished groups of Koreans has emerged as a reminder of the painful history of modern Korea at the turn of the twentieth century. At the same time, their key identifier "henequen" symbolized the rough fate of Korea in modern times. Like the green gold, the Korean people have proved to be tough and tenacious.

NOTES

1. Kyoo Whan Hyun, *Hankook Yu Iminsa* [A History of Korean Wanderers and Emigrants] vol. 2 (Seoul: Hungsa Dan Publishing Department, 1976), 978.
2. Ibid., 976–77.
3. Mike Nelson, "Modern Henequen Production in Yucatan, Mexico," accessed July 14, 2015, https://www.mexicomike.com/stories/henequen.htm.
4. Hyun, *A History of Korean Wanderers and Emigrants*, 978.
5. Ibid., 979.
6. Ibid., 978.
7. Ja-Kyung Lee, *Mexico Imin Yaksa* [A Brief History of Korean Immigration to Mexico: A Macro Perspective] (Unpublished Paper in Korean, 2010), 2–3.
8. Hyun, *A History of Korean Wanderers and Emigrants,* 981.
9. Charisma, "Sinchae Balbu Suji Bumo" [The Body, Hair, and Skin, All Have been Received from the Parents], accessed September 17, 2020. http://blog.naver.com/PostView.nbn.?blogId=honesh&logNo=150141486360.
10. Namu Wiki, "Danbalyung" [Creed on Topknot Cutting], accessed September 17, 2020, https://namu.wiki/w/단발령.
11. Lee, *A Brief History of Korean Immigration to Mexico*, 6.
12. Ibid., 7.

13. Ibid., 6.
14. Ibid.
15. Ja-Kyung Lee, *Hankukin Mexico Iminsa* [The History of Korean Immigration to Mexico] (Seoul: Jisik Sanup Co., 1998), 76.
16. Lee, *A Brief History of Korean Immigration to Mexico*, 8.
17. Lee, *The History of Korean Immigration to Mexico*, 60.
18. Ibid., 50.
19. Ibid., 49.
20. Lee, *A Brief History of Korean Immigration to Mexico*, 8.
21. Ibid.,10.
22. Ibid.
23. Hyun, *A History of Korean Wanderers and Emigrants*, 982.
24. Ibid., 983.
25. Ibid., 982.
26. Lee, *The History of Korean Immigration to Mexico*, 351.
27. Ibid., 313.
28. Ibid., 353.
29. Ibid., 354–56.
30. Ibid., 356.
31. Ibid., 324–34.
32. Won K. Yoon, *The Passage of a Picture Bride* (Loma Linda: Loma Linda University Press, 1989), 90–93.
33. Ibid.
34. Lee, *The History of Korean Immigration to Mexico*, 359.
35. Ibid., 490.
36. Ibid., 486.
37. Ibid., 344.

Chapter Seven

A Korean Picture Marriage

The Lure of Hawaii

More than a century ago, thousands of Koreans went to Hawaii to escape from poverty at home. In the first wave of Korean immigration to the balmy tropical islands, a little over seven thousand Koreans left for the new US territory. Of the total 7,226 Koreans who left for Hawaii between 1903 and 1905, 84 percent (6,048) were men: the rest were women (637) and children (541).[1] As these figures indicate, the sex ratio of the early Korean population in Hawaii was almost thirteen males to one female.[2] Like the Chinese and Japanese immigrants before them, the majority of these labor recruits were single and in their twenties and thirties. Initially, most of these Koreans had no intention of settling down in a foreign land.

Not long after their arrival in Hawaii, however, two major events took place. In 1905, Korea became a Japanese protectorate, then eventually its colony in 1910. And Korean immigration to Hawaii discontinued in 1905 due to the shocking report on the situation faced by Koreans in Yucatan, Mexico. At the same time, the protectorate Korean government was stripped of its diplomatic authority by Japan. These major political changes at home upset the Koreans in Hawaii. As their country was under Japanese colonial rule, many Koreans decided not to return home.

The second event was the Gentlemen's Agreement between Japan and the United States in 1907. According to this agreement, Japan would not issue new passports to its citizens who wished to move to the United States. However, Japan could send its citizens to Hawaii, and the Japanese government would discourage its citizens in Hawaii from moving to the mainland.[3] This informal agreement was the culmination of the rising anti-Japanese sentiment on the West Coast, especially in California. Both Japanese and Korean immigrants were subject to the opposition of white exclusionists. Following the Chinese Exclusion Act of 1882, many white residents in California resented the increasing presence of Japanese, either from Hawaii or Japan. This resentment resulted in the formation of the Japanese and Korean Exclusion League in 1905.[4] The Gentlemen's Agreement between the two governments was to appease the American majority's xenophobic attitudes toward East Asians. Nonetheless, the US government would permit the entry of wives, children, and parents of Japanese residents into the United States. That included future spouses, mainly young women, to be married to Asian residents in America. This policy spurred the coming of a large number of picture brides from Japan and Korea. As a result, about one thousand Korean picture brides found their way to Hawaii between 1910 and 1924. Far more Japanese workers in Hawaii managed to find their wives in the same manner. About fifteen thousand Japanese picture brides came to Hawaii between 1907 and 1923, with about ten thousand to the West Coast during the same period.[5]

Mainly due to the distance, time, and cost of travel between Hawaii and Korea, most Korean bachelors could not afford to go home and choose a bride. Also, the loss of wages during the travel time and wedding in Korea would be quite considerable. Thus, the use of photographs came in handy for matchmaking between women in Korea and bachelors in Hawaii. The advantage of photo exchange was far more than just savings for the bachelors. By the time a Korean worker was ready to consider starting his own family in Hawaii, he was likely already in his thirties or forties. Moreover, their bodies had shown signs of long, hard labor in the sugarcane fields. Years of exposure to the tropical sun had turned their skin dark brown and wrinkled, and their hands and feet were as calloused as stone. Some of them were already bent from years of weeding, cutting, and bundling sugarcane. No women with any expectation involving the male physique would be attracted to such coarse farm laborers in Hawaii. Some Korean men married locals, such as Polynesian or Portuguese women, but most turned to the help of Korean matchmakers. A few shrewd people set up matchmaking businesses to link Hawaii and Korea. In this chapter, the process of picture marriages between Korean bachelors in Hawaii and Korean women in Korea is detailed based on the story of a Korean woman from the small town of Haman in a southeastern province of Korea. The story of the late Lee Young Oak is retold as she revealed her Hawaii venture. The story was recorded in the 1980s.[6]

MARRIAGE BROKERS

Realizing the necessity of finding wives for Korean sugarcane plantation workers in Hawaii, a matchmaking business was set up in Honolulu. Simultaneously, marriage brokers recruited local matchmakers in large Korean cities. The most challenging task was to find young Korean women who would be open to the idea of marrying older Korean men in Hawaii. Marrying a total stranger in a faraway land was not a favorable prospect. Marrying someone without seeing them in person let alone checking their personality and family background was too risky. Thus, persuading reluctant, skeptical women and their parents was the most difficult task for matchmakers.

In 1917, one arrived in Haman, a small town in the southeast region of Korea. She spread a rosy picture about life in the tropical paradise of Hawaii, and managed to sway several girls. In a land of destitution and despair under Japanese colonial rule, the promise of plenty sounded enticing. Once the matchmaker succeeded in arousing interest and curiosity, she took the girls to a local photo studio for pictures. The girls would borrow the best dress they could find from their neighbors, and the skillful photographer would improve the faces of the women and present them in a favorable light. On the back of each picture, the agent put down the name, birthday, and hometown of the woman in the picture. After taking pictures, the matchmaker told the girls that it would take about two months to hear any news from Hawaii. She also promised to bring back two things from Hawaii: pictures of their future husbands and money. Some girls were excited about receiving money for marrying a stranger in Hawaii, but they all begged the matchmaker to keep their venture a secret. None of them wanted to risk losing the chance of marrying someone in their own town in case the picture marriage proposal did not go through.

In some towns, the girls' curiosity about America dated back to their Sunday school days. When they saw the fair-looking American missionaries and their families for the first time, they were quite impressed by the well-dressed and well-mannered Americans. The fair-skinned Westerners looked like angels, and their halting Korean sounded angelic. Every time the potential picture brides heard the magic word "America," they got excited. Sadly, this dreamland existed only in the imagination of these poor village girls. Then unexpectedly, they were offered a chance to realize their dreams; their imagination could become reality.

As promised, the matchmaker returned to the town with the pictures of Korean men in Hawaii. Some men took their pictures by fancy cars, others in front of impressive houses with beautiful gardens. The Korean men in Hawaii used these backgrounds to improve their viability. They would also use a wedding suit available at the studio to impress their potential brides. Photographers, with heavy-handed makeup techniques, transformed older, farm laborers into acceptable young men. Some used old pictures they had taken ten or fifteen years earlier to display a youthful face.

When the Korean men in Hawaii received the pictures of the Korean women with their names and birthdays on the back, they made their choice mainly based upon appearance and age. In response, they took their pictures and jotted down their names and birthdays on the back of their pictures. In addition, they added the name of the woman in the picture they had picked. This benign process was what ultimately paired thousands of young women to older men and a life of domestic bondage.

When the matchmaker returned, the girls who had sent their pictures two months before gathered in a secret place. The matchmaker handed a specific picture to a specific girl. On the back of each picture, a girls' name was written in Korean; the matches had already been made without a word from the girls. It was one-way selection by total strangers in Hawaii. Girls had absolutely no say on their lifelong commitment, a stark contrast to the age-old tradition of matchmaking done by the parents of both families. It was a nervous moment as the matchmaker read the reaction of the girls, for whom it was a moment of fate.

Each girl stared at the man in the picture, and then they looked at his age. nineteen-year-old Sunhee was matched with a thirty-seven-year-old man and the twenty-one-year-old Subi was matched with a thirty-eight-year-old man. fifteen-year-old Young Oak was matched with the oldest of the three men. On the back of the picture handed to her was written in pencil: "My name is Chung Bong Woon, and I am 42 years old. I picked Lee Young Oak." Young Oak protested to the matchmaker, "Jinjoo Grandma, how come I was matched with the 42-year-old man? Didn't you know that I am the youngest of the three? I am sure the marriage broker or the man in Hawaii mistook my picture for someone else's. Otherwise such a match could not happen." The other girls joined Young Oak in complaining that their men were too old.

With an understanding voice, the matchmaker tried to calm the girls, "I know the men are a bit old, but old husbands know how to treat their young wives right. They went to Hawaii many years ago when there were hardly any Korean women there so they lost the chance to marry in their 20s. But if you girls marry these men, it will bring you and your family a great fortune." Nevertheless, Young Oak was quite disturbed by the fact that the man she was matched with was older than her mother. She felt the irony of fate. Her mother had told Young Oak many times never to marry an older man, ironic as Young Oak's father was ten years the senior of her mother. Young Oak had observed that there seemed to be no joy and happiness in her parents' marriage, which seemed duty-bound and without affection.

This background made Young Oak concerned about what her mother's reaction would be to her fifteen-year-old daughter marrying a man twenty-seven years her senior, nearly three times her age. The apprehensive matchmaker told the girls that she had received one hundred dollars (about $2,500 in 2020) from each man. Each woman would get fifty dollars (around $1,250 in 2020) and the matchmaker would take the other fifty, thirty dollars for her commission and twenty for the photo studio. The experienced matchmaker told the girls to go home and take the night to think it over and come back the next morning with their final decisions. She told the girls in a serious tone, "You girls should not take this matter lightly. If you accept the money and fail to comply with the contract, I am the one who goes to jail for the breach of contract. So, take it seriously."

After the other girls left, the matchmaker told Young Oak about her match with Mr. Chung Bong Woon: "According to the letter of my broker in Honolulu, Mr. Chung is the best of the three men. The broker felt that Mr. Chung deserved the best picture bride. So he gave Mr. Chung the first choice, and he picked you from the three pictures. Not only is he a good man, but also he has quite a bit of money. Therefore, don't feel so bad about his age." Young Oak was pleased to know that she was the first choice of the best man of the three. The next morning the three girls met again with the matchmaker. The older girls looked somewhat resigned, and told the matchmaker that things had gone too far to change their minds. They became sympathetic with the men in Hawaii who might be very disappointed if they should turn them down. They thought that receiving a picture and money from an unknown man so far away couldn't be a mere accident: it must be the work of fate. They had heard so many times the age-old Korean saying, "Even an old straw sandal has a matching one and chopsticks are in a matching pair." The matchmaker was relieved as the girls accepted the arrangement. From her handbag, she took out one hundred dollars and gave fifty to each of the older girls. She told Young Oak that she had not received money yet from Mr. Chung but she would hear from him soon.

Before leaving the town, the matchmaker gave final instructions to the girls: "Don't forget to write to your men in Hawaii as often as you can until you leave Korea. Good luck with your marriages in Hawaii." By accepting the pictures and money from Hawaii, they consented to marry their picture grooms. They then proceeded to register their names in the family registries of their future husbands. This action was for the legal proof of their marriage in Korea. With this legal document, they began to apply for passports from the Japanese government and immigration visas from the American Consul in Seoul.

VOYAGE TO HAWAII

Young Oak did not feel any particular emotion toward her future husband. He looked slim but stern, and his crew cut and mustache made him look strong-willed. The only question she had was why he had taken the picture seated. She hoped that nothing was physically wrong below his waist. The two girls who received money from the matchmaker were supposed to write a letter to their men in Hawaii, but they didn't know how to write a letter, let alone a love letter. Blaming Young Oak for luring them into the picture marriage business, they demanded that she write their letters for them. Since Young Oak had yet to receive either a letter or money from Mr. Chung, she had no obligation to write to him, yet she jotted a few words on a piece of rice paper. It was almost like a business letter, reading "I am still waiting for your letter and money."

As each day passed, Young Oak began to feel some affection toward the man in the picture. She kept his picture at the bottom of her cloth basket, and every morning she took it out to look at. After such close studying, Young Oak touched her lips to those of the picture groom (she learned that this affectionate act was called a "kiss" after she came to Hawaii). As time passed, the age of Mr. Chung and his sitting position didn't bother her anymore. Even if he turned out to be old and lame, she would still marry him. The fact that he was living in Hawaii and had a lot of money made other conditions almost insignificant as far as she was concerned. Finally, she received a letter and a fifty-dollar check. According to the letter, Mr. Chung had given the broker in Honolulu one hundred dollars and a letter for his picture bride in Korea. When he received Young Oak's note, he had found out that the broker had used the money and withheld the letter. He sincerely asked her to understand the delay and promised to write often and send more money later. Upon receiving a letter from a man for the first time in her life, she seemed to feel the heat of love. It was November 1917.

Finally, the day came. Young Oak was supposed to go with the other girls she had induced into picture marriages, but one had failed a customary eye-disease examination, and the other had not yet received passage money from Hawaii. Since Young Oak could not wait indefinitely for her friends, she had to leave alone. Many villagers came to say "goodbye." Without exception, the women wiped tears away as they left the gate of Young Oak's house. No matter how beautiful and abundant Hawaii might be, the poor little girl was leaving her parents and hometown. They compared Young Oak to the legendary girl, Shim Chung, who was sold for three hundred bags of rice on behalf of her blind father. Later, Shim Chung had been used as a sacrifice to calm the stormy sea. Such a comparison made Young Oak and her family sad. As the women left Young Oak's house, they murmured: "The little Shim Chung is going to Hawaii for her poor family." Young Oak's mother could hardly control her emotions as she packed her daughter's things for the long journey. Young Oak's mother had warned her daughter not to marry a man much older than herself. Also, she had cautioned Young Oak many times not to marry a widower. Neither of the warnings had been heeded. The young picture bride, however, was not as sad as her mother.

Inside Young Oak felt relief because she had never wanted to marry a peasant boy from the other side of the hill, nor tread the same path as other women she had seen in the countryside. She thought that she was destined for a better fate than most village peasant wives. Yet she was careful not to show any trace of her inner contentment while others were expressing sadness for her. A horse-driven carriage was ready to take her. After embracing her crying mother with a few words of comfort, she boarded the carriage. Young Oak felt numb as she left her hometown, and she was anxious to get to Hawaii and meet her future husband. The carriage arrived at a southern harbor, Masan, and from there she took a passenger ship to Pusan. Without much thought about leaving the country, she boarded a Japanese steamer bound for Yokohama. It was March 1918, and Young Oak became one of the almost one thousand picture brides who left Korea between 1910 and 1924.

WAITING IN YOKOHAMA

On the ship, Young Oak's mind was occupied by imagining her future husband in Hawaii. Memories of her childhood and family life in Haman hardly crossed her mind. Finally, the ship reached Yokohama, near Tokyo. At the harbor, her brother and a Korean innkeeper were waiting for her. Most of the Korean passengers bound for Hawaii and the American mainland stayed at this Korean inn while waiting for their final passage. The Korean innkeeper handed Young Oak a letter and a check he had received from Mr. Chung. She was a bit surprised by the effective network of Korean immigrants that connected Korea, Japan, and Hawaii. The amount of the check was 200 dollars (around $5,000 in 2020). In the letter, Mr. Chung instructed his picture bride to take a first-class cabin to make her voyage more comfortable. He warned her about terrible seasickness during the voyage. Furthermore, he told her that first-class passengers would be exempt from physical examination. Once again Mr. Chung's thoughtfulness touched Young Oak, and she felt already closer to Hawaii than the hometown she had left a few days before.

Young Oak had a different idea, however, about how to use the money sent by Mr. Chung. She decided to take a third-class cabin, which only cost sixty-five yen. She didn't want to pay the hefty 300-yen price for the comfortable first-class cabin. Instead, she gave 300 yen to her brother in Tokyo for his studies, leaving her with only 100 yen. Young Oak had not forgotten why she had ventured into the picture marriage in the first place. In her numerous letters to Mr. Chung, she made it very clear that she wanted to help her brother in his study in Japan. While staying at the Korean inn in Yokohama, she met other picture brides, some of whom were waiting indefinitely for passage fares from their husbands-to-be in Hawaii. Young Oak realized for the first time how lucky she was to be matched with someone like Mr. Chung, who was willing and able to spend so much. She also discovered that some of the so-called picture brides were widows and divorcees, a few of whom even had children from previous marriages. Occasionally the Korean innkeeper would lend money for the passage fare if some of his guests had to wait too long in Yokohama. At that point, he was more concerned about their well-being than a possible loss of lent money; he simply counted on the conscience of the guests he would help. Young Oak was deeply moved by the good deeds of this innkeeper, who helped fellow countrymen in a foreign land.

Like any third-class passenger, Young Oak had to take a physical examination in Yokohama for entrance into the territory of the United States. It mainly consisted of an eye infection check and a stool test. Others told Young Oak that the Yokohama test was more stringent than the one she had in Seoul, and this made her nervous. She passed the eye infection examination the first time but failed the stool test. The Japanese doctor told her that she was carrying common parasites, and he put her on a heavy dosage of medication in order to eradicate them. From other Koreans staying at the inn she heard that sometimes it took two or three months to clear parasites, a fact that worried Young Oak. The prospect of waiting so long made her depressed and she now deeply regretted not taking Mr. Chung's advice to pay for the first-class fare.

After carefully thinking over the parasite problem, Young Oak decided to use a trick. She approached another picture bride who had passed the physical examination but was still waiting for passage fare from her future husband in Hawaii. Young Oak noticed that the lady was quite upset about her pitiful situation, blaming herself for having been drawn into the picture marriage. The desperate woman told others that she was already experiencing what was in store for her in Hawaii. Young Oak presented her with cosmetics in exchange for her clean stool. They both knew it was a serious violation of the law. If such a trick were uncovered, both would be deported back to Korea, but mutual sympathy outweighed the fear of potential risk. It was a friendly deal between two picture brides in a time of agony. Young Oak submitted the other woman's stool in the container clearly marked with her name and was declared medically cleared a few days later. She was delighted that things were going in her favor. The other Korean women at the inn envied Young Oak, whose future husband seemed considerate and wealthy.

As Young Oak was preparing for the final leg of the voyage, she had mixed feelings of joy and sadness. Yokohama was a foreign city, yet she could speak Japanese and was quite familiar with Japanese customs. In addition, her brother's frequent visits from Tokyo and her accommodations with a group of Korean guests made her feel at home. Furthermore, her homeland was not that far away from Japan. The night before her scheduled departure, the innkeeper and the other picture brides gave Young Oak a farewell party, and she bought rice cakes (*Mozzi*), sweet candies, and cider. She was in a good mood, but the other girls who were still waiting for passage money or medical clearance were sullen and even sad. As the farewell party progressed, the girls began to sing popular Korean folk songs. As they sang familiar songs about love, homeland, and separation, they all cried. Their hopes and curiosity about the romantic life in Hawaii had faded quickly. Instead they were overwhelmed by self-pity and homesickness. Some cried uncontrollably, calling "Mother," "Father." They pleaded: "Please take me home. Take me home." As they regained their calm, they wondered why they had ever wanted to marry someone they had never met and who lived so far away from Korea. Many of them wanted to escape from poverty, heavy domestic chores, and the dullness of village life. At the same time, they wanted to see a new world and enjoy freedom in America. A few ambitious women hoped to pursue higher education and careers in the land of promise.

ENCOUNTERS IN HONOLULU

Amid hugging, handholding, and farewell wishes, Young Oak boarded an ocean-going steamer. Her brother was deeply emotional as his little sister embarked on the long journey alone to a stranger in a foreign land. Moreover, he had a painful heartache when he realized that his little sister had chosen a picture marriage mainly to help him and their family. On the ship, there were only three Korean passengers; the rest were Japanese. The ship left Yokohama on April 23, 1918. As the land of Japan slipped away below the horizon, Young Oak suddenly felt the pain of separation from loved ones. Although Japan was a foreign country, she had a brother there, but now she was bound for a land of total strangers. This realization made her feel much closer to Mr. Chung Bong Woon. Now he was the only person to whom she could turn and trust.

As the voyage continued, many passengers were lying flat, terribly weakened from seasickness, but Young Oak did not experience any of that. She enjoyed every moment of the voyage. It was fun to watch jumping fish during the day and shimmering stars hanging over the Pacific Ocean at night. She ate and slept well. Full of excitement, she walked around the deck, singing her favorite songs. As the days passed, she felt closer to Hawaii. After nine days, the ship finally docked in Honolulu on May 1, 1918. Her first impression of Honolulu was somewhat disappointing. The city was not comparable to either Seoul or Yokohama in size and appearance. The drab buildings looked small and scattered.

First-time immigrants were led to a separate building by officers. The immigration station appeared stark, and the windows were covered with heavy steel bars. Young Oak wondered why the building looked almost like a prison. She was a bit surprised by the meals served there, all of which were typically Japanese: a bowl of rice, miso soup, pickled yellow roots (*takuan*), and either roasted or fried fish. As she looked out the window, she saw mostly dark-skinned people (Hawaiians) in the street. Those waiting in the station seemed to be mostly Japanese. She didn't quite feel that she had come to the fairyland she had dreamed of for so long.

Soon she met the two Korean picture brides who had left Yokohama a few days before her. Young Oak wondered why they were still being detained at the immigration station. One of the depressed girls explained: "We are still waiting for our men. Somehow they cannot leave the sugarcane plantation. We don't know how we got mixed up in this picture marriage business!" Young Oak discovered an even worse case, a picture bride who had left Yokohama exactly two ships before her. According to this disgusted woman, she had developed an eye infection during the voyage, and the Immigration Service had refused to admit her into the country, ordering her to return to Japan for treatment. She would be admitted only after her infection was completely cured. This woman kept cursing the service for refusing to take care of her eye problem in Honolulu. Young Oak wondered if Honolulu was so rudimentary in medical care that no one was able to treat an eye infection properly.

Unexpectedly, Young Oak received a package from Mr. Chung, sent by a Korean innkeeper in Honolulu. In it she found five large oranges and a note from the innkeeper that read: "A hearty welcome to Hawaii. Mr. Chung Bong Woon will come to meet you by the first ferry leaving Maui Island where he works. Chung Yoon Phil." Young Oak enjoyed the juicy, sweet oranges and was buoyant at the thought of soon meeting her future husband. She also loved the fresh pineapples she bought with her last seven yen from a Japanese vendor in the compound. Contrary to her first visual impression of Honolulu, her first taste of Hawaii was sweet. On the third day of waiting at the station, a Korean interpreter called out Young Oak's name. He handed her a package and told her that Mr. Chung had come for an interview with the immigration officer. The interpreter told her that she would see Mr. Chung when her own interview was over. Then he cheerfully teased her: "Mr. Chung is a lucky man to marry such a cute and well-mannered woman." When Young Oak realized that her future husband was in the same building and breathing the same air, she felt like jumping up and down like a little child. Her joy and excitement were indescribable. Finally, it was time for her interview. The Korean interpreter briefly told Young Oak what to expect. He cautioned her that he was not supposed to explain the interview procedure. She tried to recall the English words that she had memorized, and tried to sort out the right words for the different phases of the interview.

Then the interpreter led Young Oak to an immigration officer. She was nervous, but the presence of the Korean interpreter helped. She was really glad to be assisted by a compatriot at a tense moment such as this. When they entered the office, the interpreter received something from an officer and gave it to Young Oak without saying a word. It was a sheet of paper and a pencil. On the paper, a sentence was written in both Korean and English. The written instruction was simple: "Take this paper and pencil to the right side of the immigration officer and give them to the officer with both hands." It was a literacy test for foreign immigrants. The interpreter kept silent while watching Young Oak somewhat nervously. As instructed on the paper, she took the paper and pencil to the officer, who sat behind a large desk. As she passed cautiously before the officer to reach his right side, Young Oak politely said, "Excuse me," in English. This surprised the officer, who turned to the interpreter and said: "Mr. Cho, this lady can speak English. She doesn't have to go through all the routines. She passed." As the interpreter conveyed the message, Young Oak was delighted about the easy pass, and she felt good about the English lessons she had initiated at home. Later she heard that some illiterate picture brides had been sent home. The Immigration Service believed that a person illiterate would be a burden to the United States.

After a while, both Mr. Chung Bong Woon and Lee Young Oak were called in before the officer who had tested the latter. The two stood side by side for the first time, but Young Oak was too shy to look at Mr. Chung. Through the interpreter, the immigration officer asked Mr. Chung: "Mr. Chung Bong Woon, is this the woman you have invited to marry?" "Yes, sir," Mr. Chung replied firmly. Young Oak was then asked a similar question through the interpreter: "Miss Lee Young Oak, is this the man you saw in the picture, and did you come to marry him?" She answered without hesitation: "Yes, I came to marry Mr. Chung Bong Woon." The officer smiled at them. After hastily filling out a form, he turned to the couple and said: "Congratulations. Now you are ready to go. I wish you a happy married life here in Hawaii." The two walked out of the office and Mr. Chung led the way; according to Korean custom, Young Oak followed about three feet behind. As the two entered the station lobby, they turned around and looked at each other for the first time. He stood about the same height as his bride. As seen in the picture, he had a mustache that did not quite match his right-angle crew cut. The hem of the old black coat he was wearing almost touched his knees. Young Oak thought that it might be the style in Hawaii. Somehow, the outfit made him look clumsy.

For a few moments, she stared and smiled at him, until he spoke: "I feel very sorry to make you wait so long for me." Bowing politely, Young Oak finally ventured to speak: "With the money you sent me, I had a pleasant voyage. I am deeply grateful for the things you have done for me and my family." Mr. Chung smiled: "I hope you had an enjoyable voyage. Did you get seasick?" "Not at all. I ate and slept well," his bride cheerfully answered. Mr. Chung gave his right hand to Young Oak to lead her out of the station lobby. Young Oak slightly jerked when she held his hand. She seemed to be holding a palm that was as hard as rock. As he opened the lobby door, half a dozen Koreans waiting outside the immigration building warmly welcomed the couple. The ladies in the welcoming party kindly patted Young Oak on the back. One of the women said, "Mr. Chung, you are a lucky man to bring such a nice bride from Korea. She must have been born into a good family." Mr. Chung just smiled, not saying much. They drove an old Ford to a Korean inn located less than a mile from the Immigration Service building. The couple checked into a special corner room the innkeeper had reserved especially for Mr. Chung. Young Oak began to feel at home in Hawaii.

Her first meal at the inn reinforced her comfortability. On the table, she saw nothing but familiar Korean dishes, including kimchi, hot bean paste (*gochoojang*), and lettuce for rice wrapping (*ssam*). The innkeeper's wife was so pleased that Mr. Chung had brought such a cheerful bride. She had seen many Korean picture brides who did nothing but cry day and night from the moment they checked into the inn. Their men almost went crazy not knowing how to handle their strange brides. Even after the crying phase, some picture brides remained so upset they wouldn't speak a word to anyone for days. They would emerge from their room to eat and then withdraw. Only the men's threats to deport the women back to Korea finally forced them to accept their fate.

The innkeeper's wife had also heard many heartbreaking stories about picture marriages. As the women spotted their future husbands from the decks of the ships they arrived in, their dreams of a new life in Hawaii were absolutely shattered. Although they were mentally prepared for disappointment, the men they had come to marry looked so old and boorish. The bachelors, usually in their thirties and forties, were badly tanned, wrinkled, and even bent from years of hard labor under the sizzling Hawaiian sun. Plantation life without the care of a family had made them look much older than their age. So shocked were some picture brides that they refused to leave the ship and desperately begged the crew to take them back to Korea, but such pleas were ignored. The crew knew that the brides did not have money to pay for their return passage. Even if the brides promised to pay the fare upon return, most crews doubted their parents' abilities to pay, let alone their willingness to take their daughters back. Thus, the picture brides were forced off the ship by the crew while their men watched helplessly from the pier. They would then be led into the Immigration Service building as if they were being taken to a slaughterhouse. Some turned hysterical and let out the agonizing cry: "Mother, Mother, take me home. Take me home."

THE WEDDING CEREMONY AND HONEYMOON

After lunch, the innkeeper suggested that Mr. Chung be married that evening for a number of reasons: "Today is Wednesday. If you marry this evening at church right after the midweek worship service, that takes care of inviting people. I can arrange for your wedding with the pastor. Second, if you have to wait until Saturday or Sunday, you will have to use two separate rooms until the wedding day. This will double the lodging cost." Mr. Chung and Young Oak appreciated these practical considerations. Neither Mr. Chung nor his picture bride raised any objection to the strict Confucian moral code practiced at the inn. The enforced norm of Korean tradition was that no boy and girl would occupy the same room without the presence of adults once they reached the age of seven. So, they agreed to marry that evening. In fact, many Japanese and Korean picture couples had their wedding ceremonies in the immigration station building right after their interviews.

The wedding was less than eight hours away, so Mr. Chung asked Young Oak to go shopping for their wedding. Accompanied by two Korean men who were residents of Honolulu, the two went to the downtown shopping district. Mr. Chung bought Young Oak a pair of shoes, a gold wedding ring, and a fancy comb studded with colorful corals. Young Oak made sure that the pair of shoes she was trying on would not make her taller than her husband during the wedding ceremony. The two accompanying bachelors teased Mr. Chung for his willingness to buy anything his bride asked for. They were surprised by the amount of money Mr. Chung was spending without any hesitation: "Mr. Chung, you have worked so hard for so many years on the plantation. What is the money for? Buy anything for your new bride on this once-in a-lifetime occasion. Isn't money for spending?"

They hurried back to the inn so they would not be late for the wedding. In their best dress, the couple sat in the front row of the Honolulu Korean Methodist Church. There were no pews in the church, and people were sitting on the floor. About fifty people attended the midweek service. When it began, the pastor of the church, Reverend Bang Ha Joong, announced that there would be a brief wedding ceremony right after the service. He made a special appeal to his congregation to stay for the wedding of Mr. Chung Bong Woon and Miss Lee Young Oak, from Korea. As soon as the service was over, the pastor asked the two to come forward and stand before him. There was no wedding march, neither bridesmaid nor best man. Yet the pastor seemed to follow the procedures of a typical Christian wedding, including the wedding vows. After the closing prayer, the pastor introduced the newly married couple, Mr. and Mrs. Chung Bong Woon, to his congregation. As if it were a custom of the church, the pastor asked the couple to march around the congregation for an introduction. The two walked slowly around the people seated on the floor in a circle. Young Oak was holding her husband's left arm. The church members clapped for the couple, who looked more like a father and daughter than husband and wife, but no one seemed to care about the obvious age difference of twenty-seven years between groom and bride. The bride appeared to be slightly taller than the groom.

Young Oak heard some people whisper to each other with a surprised look: "Look at the bride. She is smiling and holding her head up. She must be happy." Young Oak said to herself: "Why shouldn't anyone be happy on her wedding day?" Only later did she come to realize the meaning of their negative comments. During the circular march, the groom whispered to his bride: "Aren't you shy?" Young Oak only smiled without saying a word. As the two completed the circle, the pastor invited the well-wishers to go to the inn for the wedding reception.

When they got back to the inn, Mr. Chung left his bride alone in the reserved corner room. He asked her to wait until the party was over. Then he went downstairs where the wedding reception was about to begin. Soon Young Oak heard the loud noise of laughter and singing. She wondered if it was an American custom to not let the bride attend the reception. Even in Korea, the reception would be held in the presence of both bride and groom. The brave bride was about to venture into the reception hall, but she restrained herself so as not to offend her husband. About half an hour later, Mr. Chung brought a bowl of ice cream and cookies to his bride and left the room again without saying much. Young Oak really liked the sweet ice cream and cookies. Suddenly, she felt fatigue overwhelming her. It had indeed been a hectic day. So many important things in her life had taken place in such a short time. Going through the tense entry interview at the immigration station, meeting Mr. Chung, shopping, and finally the wedding—everything had taken place within twelve hours.

One more passage rite in her life awaited her, to face the first night with the groom, but she was too tired to worry about it. When the groom returned to the corner room, he grumbled that the guests had just left and seemed a little bit apologetic to his bride: "I am sorry for having left you alone so long. I could not leave the party while the guests were celebrating for my own wedding. We are very tired. After changing clothes, let's sleep." He went behind the special pictorial folding screen by the bed and changed his clothes. For the first time, Young Oak faced a man without street clothing on. At the same time, she realized that she was the only other human being in the room. This made her feel tense, even scared. Again, looking at his bewildered bride, Mr. Chung asked her to change her clothes behind the screen. It was a signal to prepare for their first night together. "The touch of my hand may feel hard to you. My palms and fingers are calloused from repeated blisters," the groom cautioned with a forced smile.

Then he jumped on the bed and lay with his right arm under his head as if he wanted to see every movement of his young bride. Young Oak changed into the dress her mother had specially made for this first night. She was puzzled because her mother had told her that on the first night the groom would be the one to undress the bride. Coming out from behind the folding screen, Young Oak didn't know what to do next. As she hesitantly approached the bed, Mr. Chung pulled her hand toward him. At that moment, she began to tremble, not knowing how to react under the circumstances. Out of desperation, she pleaded with him: "Can we marry without touching each other?" Then she dropped to the floor beside the bed. Every time the groom tried to touch her in the dark, she shrank into a crouched position like a shrimp. She cried while trembling like a lost young bird, and the frustrated groom kept puffing one cigar after another. She had not quite understood what the pastor had meant when he said that two bodies would become one. No one had given her any adequate instruction as to how she should approach the first night. Again, pulling her hand toward him, the groom said: "Well, this is part of married life." The first night was full of fears and tears for the young bride. She hardly slept.

The next morning Young Oak could not dare to look at her husband. For the first time, she felt an indescribable shame. When she kept her head down, Mr. Chung raised her chin and asked: "Why don't you look at me? Don't be ashamed. We are married now. I am your husband and you are my wife." Then he chuckled. As they entered the dining room for breakfast, the innkeeper's wife met them with a big smile. Other guests staying at the inn congratulated the couple. Again, the innkeeper's wife began praising Young Oak: "Mr. Chung is indeed a lucky man. His wife is a rare kind of picture bride. I never take it for granted seeing a newly-wed couple coming to breakfast so happy. I have been in this business long enough to see all sorts of sad things happen to picture marriages. Sometimes I cannot sleep the whole night when I have to mediate between fighting couples. Usually the disappointed brides desperately fight back against their husbands who try to approach their newly married wives. Then the women scream as their husbands hit them out of anger and frustration. Sometimes we have to break into the rooms when we think that the couples have become too violent. I think picture marriages have made many young women and old men crazy."

After breakfast, the innkeeper volunteered to drive the couple around in his Ford. Young Oak was pleased to see so many different tropical trees and flowers in Honolulu. For the first time, she tasted wild bananas and other tropical fruits that she picked from the trees. She began to love Hawaii for its weather and beautiful scenery. During the honeymoon, Young Oak came to know more about her husband's life story and personality.

Mr. Chung Bong Woon was born in Boryung county in the Choong Chung province of Korea on January 1, 1876. He was the only son in his family. The preceding two generations of Chungs had also had only one son. This fact made him a very special figure because the continuity of the family depended on him. He had an older sister who had married a Royal Korean Army general. Perhaps through this connection he joined the Royal Korean Army, but his military career hadn't lasted long. In 1904, he left Korea for Hawaii only three months after his first marriage. His plan was to return to

Korea after making enough money, but not knowing how long it would take to do so, he asked his wife to wait until she heard from him. Mr. Chung was sad when he found out that his wife had married another man within a year of his departure. His first wife thought that he had gone too far to return, and Mr. Chung couldn't do anything about his wife's decision. He worked very hard and saved every penny with the intent of returning home. He restrained himself from spending money on items such as fancy clothes and shoes. He told Young Oak that he was still wearing the same clothes he had brought from Korea fifteen years before. He did not have a wrist watch, a very popular status symbol among men at the time. So, Young Oak understood his ability to spend money for her and her family.

LIFE ON THE PLANTATION

The sweet honeymoon in Honolulu was soon over. The time came to return to the reality of plantation life, and the couple took a small ferryboat bound for Maui Island. The Koreans on the Maui sugarcane plantation were surprised to see Mr. Chung accompanied by a young, cheerful woman. One man bluntly told Mr. Chung: "Since you took so long, we thought that you had deported your picture bride for refusing to marry you. Otherwise you would not have stayed so many days in Honolulu. At least you could have informed us that you would stay longer in Honolulu for the honeymoon." No one dared to imagine that the thrifty man would take a ten-day honeymoon in the big city. Skipping so many workdays and spending so much money in Honolulu was completely uncharacteristic of the Mr. Chung they knew.

The company house that awaited the newly married couple was a small but neat dwelling spaced a hundred feet away from their closest neighbors. The house had a living room, a bedroom, a small storage space, and a detached toilet and kitchen. The roofed outdoor kitchen had a dining table beside an open fireplace for cooking, which was done with firewood. In the bedroom, Young Oak saw a doublebed with a mosquito net drawn over it and a shiny Singer sewing machine. Young Oak loved the brand-new mosquito net, a luxury item in Korea. Here and there, she also noticed gas lamps and candles for lighting (electricity would not be brought to the plantation for another year). Mr. Chung took his wife around the house, giving brief instructions. He also showed her where food was stored and how to use the outdoor kitchen. Everything was neatly arranged. He said he would start working the next day and that breakfast should be ready by no later than 4:30 in the morning.

In the evening, the couple went to the Korean Methodist Church. All six Korean workers and their families living on the plantation compound gathered in the church. Some bachelors also came to the reception. There were about ten Korean families on other Maui plantations, but they could not come because of the distance. The workers and their families dressed properly for the occasion–celebrating the marriage of their community head (*dong jang*). The deputy head formally welcomed the couple, and Mr. Chung politely thanked him and his fellow workers for the hearty welcome.

Young Oak could not fall asleep. She was nervous about cooking her first breakfast for her husband because she had not learned much about cooking at home. It was about 2:00 a.m. as she got up quietly to cook. When she slipped out to the outdoor kitchen, it was still dark. In the clear sky, stars were shimmering. Not knowing the proper ratio of rice and water, she poured too much rice into the cooking pot. As the rice cooked, she could smell it burning, so she kept pouring in water to cool the pot. At the sound of the alarm clock, Mr. Chung got up exactly at 4:00 a.m. and looked for his wife. When he could not find her anywhere in the house, he instantly thought that she had run away. Only after he found her cooking in the outdoor kitchen was he relieved. Mr. Chung told his wife to use the alarm clock next time. Without a word of complaint about the badly burned rice, he finished the meal and left for the plantation at 4:30 a.m., saying that he would come home around 5:00 p.m. in the afternoon. In the morning hours, Young Oak cleaned the house, but there was not much to do. She waited for her husband the whole afternoon. As soon as she saw him coming home she ran to him, like a little girl awaiting her father's return from a long trip. Taking his lunch pail, she walked happily next to him. He looked extremely tired, and his trousers were covered with wet red mud up to the waistline. After supper, Mr. Chung went straight to bed and fell asleep in a few seconds. Young Oak didn't know that this would be the daily routine on the plantation for many years to come. Following his suggestion, she asked other Korean wives on the plantation how to cook rice and other Korean dishes properly.

One day, Mr. Chung asked his wife for clean work clothes. Young Oak told him that she had piled the soiled work clothes in the backyard. She never thought of reusing these heavily soiled clothes. As the dirty clothes dried with mud, they weighed about three pounds and were as stiff as raw leather. Her irate husband shouted at her: "Are you stupid? How can anyone afford throwing away work clothes after just one-day wearing? I wonder about the state of your mind. I must have brought an immature child, not a mature woman." He kept shaking his head in disbelief. Not long after the incident of rice burning and soiled clothes, she heard from other Korean women that Mr. Chung might consider sending the teen bride back home. He had complained to his fellow workers that his young wife didn't know how to cook or wash clothes. Moreover, he felt pity for his sixteen-year-old wife struggling all alone far away from home. He said that some nights his wife would call out in her sleep: "Mother, Mother, give me water." He felt terribly guilty living with such a young wife. Of course, he had not forgotten the first night when his bride had trembled like a baby.

The sympathetic Korean women who lived on the plantation told Young Oak to be careful not to repeat the same mistakes. They also advised her to act like an adult, even in bed, but Young Oak wondered how she could control what she said in her sleep. This report scared her because if she was sent back home, not only would this bring shame to her and her entire family, it would also greatly reduce her chances of remarrying a decent man in her village. More important than such personal reasons would be the discontinuance of the financial support from Mr. Chung. She felt that her brothers would need Mr. Chung's help to finish their education in Japan.

One evening, after supper, she said to her husband: "Father, I am quick to learn new things. Please teach me and show me how to do things right. I know my lack of experience in life has caused much inconvenience and trouble to you." Moved by the sincere attitude of his young wife, Mr. Chung confessed: "I don't know much about housekeeping either. As you know, I have lived alone for almost 20 years in Hawaii. I will teach you the things I am familiar with. You must remember that I am an impatient man. Therefore, I want you to be quick and alert." He also suggested that Young Oak ask other women if she had questions about domestic chores around the house.

LOPSIDED MARITAL RELATIONS

From the moment Young Oak met Mr. Chung, she never called him *yeubo* (dear or honey), a common, affectionate expression between spouses in Korea. She always called him *abuji* (father), even before they had children together. (Calling one's husband "my children's father" is quite common among Korean wives when children are born. Men use a similar expression in calling their wives "my children's mother.") Young Oak felt more comfortable calling him "father" than "dear" or "honey." As a matter of fact, she never considered him a dear, sweet husband because of the age difference of twenty-seven years. Moreover, around the plantation Young Oak noticed that some Japanese wives called their husbands *odosan* (father). She thought that a wife was supposed to call her husband "father" in America. The strict, old-fashioned Mr. Chung considered a woman calling one's husband "yeubo" quite improper. He said only a harlot would use such a vulgar term. Not knowing the proper American custom for addressing her husband, she didn't feel awkward at all calling him "father." And Young Oak meant it when she called him "father."

The relationship between the two was always that of a father and daughter rather than that of husband and wife. She considered Mr. Chung a benevolent father figure who had saved her family in a time of financial hardship. On top of this, they were more than a generation apart in age. Mr. Chung's formative years belonged to the nineteenth century and hers to the twentieth. Young Oak calling him father was reciprocated by Mr. Chung calling his wife "child." Any expressions of affection were a rare occurrence for the couple. To the forty-three-year-old man, his sixteen-year-old wife from Korea was hardly an equal. This was reinforced by his young wife's absolute obedience and respect.

Almost every night, Young Oak felt like crying. The loneliness and homesickness were unbearable, yet she could not cry because such an act might be regarded as a lack of love for her husband. She cried alone during the daytime while he was at work. She told herself that she would never let her own children marry someone far away and at too young an age. From time to time, Mr. Chung cautioned his young wife about the temptations of the bachelor workers on the plantation. He firmly ordered her to keep the doors locked during the daytime and advised his wife not to walk alone around the plantation while he was at work: "Many Korean families have been ruined by bachelor workers. These men are fond of seducing married women. They are usually lazy, constantly skipping work, using all kinds of sickness, including homesickness and woman-sickness, as an excuse. They barely can feed themselves. Without money, they cannot afford to bring a picture bride from Korea. Their faces look fair and their hands are soft. While married men are at work, they prey on the naive wives whose husbands are rough and dark from backbreaking work in the sugarcane fields. Foolish wives cannot resist the smooth talk and good looks of some former civil servants and scholars." Young Oak replied: "Don't worry, father. I will heed your warning."

PLANTATION LIFE

One day, Young Oak noticed a big round scar on her husband's abdomen. She asked what had happened. "For years, my job was to irrigate the sugarcane field," he explained. "It was indeed hard work. Often I had to work for hours in cold water reaching up to my waist. That irrigation job caused severe stomach pains. I often had terrible, terrible pains. After all sorts of Western treatment and medicine, which did not cure the pain, I went to a Korean doctor of oriental medicine. He applied a tiny ball of herb fire a few times to my stomach. I was really scared to death but that took care of the stomach pain. According to the doctor, the vacuum created in the earthen cup by the burning fire sucks the cold out of the stomach. I didn't quite understand it, but believed the effects of the treatment."

On a typical day, Young Oak's husband worked from 6:00 a.m. in the morning until 4:30 p.m. in the afternoon. Usually, he worked seven days a week with some exceptions. His daily wage in the earlier years was sixty-nine cents. When he reported to the plantation workstation, he would be assigned to a gang of twenty to twenty-five men, a mixture of Koreans, Japanese, Chinese, and Filipinos.

Each day's work was determined by the needs of the growing sugarcane plants: planting, weeding, fertilizing, irrigation, and harvesting by cutting. The hardest work was weeding and cutting the cane. Ten hours of continuous hoeing under the burning sun made many weep in despair. The workers were under the constant supervision of the luna (field supervisor), who always watched their movements. If he spotted any irregularity, such as standing straight to ease the pain, he would shout at or whip the offender. During work, chatting with others was prohibited, and the workers had only a thirty-minute break for lunch and rest. So, when they went home, they barely managed to finish supper and went to bed without delay. This caused many wives of plantation workers to be severely discontented with their married life.

In particular, cutting the sugarcane was demanding work. Before cutting, the workers burned the dry leaves in order to save just the stems. This produced an excessive amount of ash, and the field workers looked like ghosts during the harvest. Only their eyes and teeth showed their original color as the rest of their faces were covered with gray ash. With a heavy machete as long as twenty inches, the workers cut off the dusty canes that were twice as tall as they were. Continuous cutting caused blistering and, eventually, thick, calloused palms. Mr. Chung had already worked for fifteen years in the sugarcane fields when he brought Young Oak. Years of hard work had conditioned him into a tenacious, diligent man.

Sugarcane plantation owners used incentives at different levels to increase worker productivity. To anyone who worked at least twenty days a month, the company would pay a monthly bonus of five dollars, which rose to nine dollars if a worker worked thirty days. Thus, a typical worker putting in at least twenty days could earn about twenty dollars a month (fourteen dollars of regular wages plus the five-dollar bonus). Hard workers such as Mr. Chung earned about thirty dollars a month (twenty-one dollars of regular wages plus a nine-dollar bonus). In addition, the company would pay an end-of-year bonus. Usually, the yearly bonus ranged from two hundred dollars to five hundred dollars, depending on the annual profit, although one year Mr. Chung received 1,500 dollars (around $20,000 in 2020). A bachelor worker would pay ten dollars a month for boarding (three meals a day) and two dollars a month for clothes washing. As a bachelor, Mr. Chung could save more than five hundred dollars (around $6,500 in 2020) a year. From the beginning, Korean workers formed a village council (*Dong Hoi*) on each plantation. The council was a self-governing organization to maintain order among workers. If someone engaged in deviant behavior, such as excessive drinking, gambling, and fighting, the council members would punish the violator. Most Korean workers, if not all, were sensitive to not tarnish the reputation of their country and community.

About nine hundred Koreans, including a small number of picture brides, chose to return home.[7] This was a little over 10 percent of those who had left Korea years before. The remaining Korean community in Hawaii played a major role for the overseas Korean independence movement. Unlike their husbands, the picture brides had had first-hand experience with Japanese colonial rule in Korea and had developed a strong desire for Korean independence. At the same time, the patriotic activities provided meaning and significance for their lonely and often empty lives in Hawaii.

The practice of picture marriage ended in 1924 when the US Congress passed the Oriental Exclusion Act. From this year on, each Asian country could send no more than 105 immigrants per year. By the time this law was enacted, almost one thousand Korean families had been formed by picture marriages. As a result, the initially skewed sex ratio of the early Korean community in America became normalized and more balanced. Some couples were happy, but many filled their days with tears, regrets, and sighs, lamenting the age and culture gap and suffering from homesickness. Due to the considerable age gap between husbands and wives, many picture brides became widows when they were still young, even in their thirties and forties. These widows continued to struggle for many years to raise and support children. For most, life was never easy.

REFLECTIONS

During the thirty-five-year Japanese colonial rule of Korea, Hawaii was one of the major overseas Korean independence movement bases. In a sizable, young Korean community in a relatively small territory, Dr. Syngman Rhee was a key resident who earned a doctoral degree in international politics from Princeton following an MA degree in political science from Harvard. Dr. Rhee was a leading figure in the overseas Korean independence movement, and he became the first president of the Republic of Korea in 1948. Lee Young Oak was a lifelong devotee to Dr. Rhee's political cause from his days in Honolulu. As a result of her close personal relationship to him, she had opportunities to interact with Korean independence movement figures and high-government officials when Korea regained its sovereignty. Old photos show her taking pictures with President Rhee, as well as other Korean luminaries: the vice president, the speaker, four-star generals, and diplomats. She received a presidential commendation for her contribution to the cause of Korean independence and efforts toward a new nation-building at home.

On her seventy-fifth birthday party in Honolulu, in 1976, more than six thousand well-wishers, including the mayor of Honolulu, attended. A brand-new red Lincoln Continental, a gift of her children, was displayed at the party. Five sons with their wives, twenty-nine grandchildren, and six great grandchildren were at the celebration. Two prominent family members were missing from her birthday party: her husband, who passed away in 1952, and her fourth son. The couple had six boys. The eldest owned a family-operated furniture store and was a longtime fundraiser and campaign manager for Honolulu Mayor Frank F. Fasi. Robert Chung, her fourth son, had been a medical doctor. He was a key figure in establishing Castle Memorial Hospital in Kailua on the windward side of Honolulu. Dr. Chung had also served as Honolulu Police Commission Chairman until an airplane crash ended his life at the young age of forty-seven. It was 1973. Then in 1982, her first son died during an operation to remove a brain tumor. The mother had carried two of her sons, the first and fourth, buried in her heart until she passed away. Otherwise, she had led an extraordinary life by anyone's standard, let alone when comparing her with her fellow picture brides from Korea.

The first Korean picture bride to Hawaii, Sarah Cho, arrived in Honolulu on November 28, 1910, and a little over one thousand Korean women had followed, until 1923.[7] Without the Oriental Exclusion Act of 1924, the practice would have continued until the last Korean bachelor in the United States had found himself a picture bride in Korea. The coming of the picture brides lowered the gender ratio of the Korean residents in Hawaii to three men per

Figure 7.1. Mrs. Young Oak Chung around President Syngman Rhee, the first president of Republic of Korea. *A Photograph from* The Passage of a Picture Bride *(1989) by Won K. Yoon*

Figure 7.2. Mrs. Young Oak Chung with General Sunyup Baek of Korean Army. *A Photograph from* The Passage of a Picture Bride *(1989) by Won K. Yoon*

one female. By 1930, the ratio had become almost equal with 1.5 men to each woman.[8] In the meantime, many American-born, second-generation Koreans had reached adulthood, and this helped reduce the adult sex ratio quite considerably. The one-time male dominant Korean community resembled a normal community in terms of gender and age distribution. The introduction of picture marriage also significantly changed the quality of Korean community life. Married men with wives and children became stable and reliable in their work and social life. Moreover, Korean families could preserve their ethnic identity through reproduction and cultural transmission.

In spite of the contributions picture brides had made to the revitalization of the Korean communities in Hawaii, their personal lives often bordered on tragedy. Physical separation from their loved ones and villages were the source of constant sadness and loneliness. Many could not afford to visit their families in Korea as they did not have the money to pay for the long voyage. Marrying a total stranger who was much older and often illiterate was difficult to take. Finally, the monotonous, meager lives of tedium they experienced on the isolated sugarcane plantations drove many women into despair in these early years. Many picture wives struggled with a sense of regret, guilt, and shame. They carried bitter stories deeply buried in their hearts because the picture marriage was their choice.

Lee Young Oak could retell proudly her life story because she was one of a few who had a happy life in Hawaii. Many years after her much older husband passed away, she lived with a sense of gratitude and pride. A small church in her hometown, Hamahn in South Korea, displays her legacy on a bronze plaque attached to a cornerstone of the church building: "Deaconess Chung Young Oak Memorial Church, Dedicated on May 23, 1987."[9] It is one of many places in Korea that received her help.

NOTES

1. Dongailbo, "Agricultural Immigration to Hawaii in the Last Years of Korean Empire," in dongA.com February 24, 1998, accessed July 28, 2015, http://news.donga.com/View?id=7324743&date=19980224.

2. Won K. Yoon, *The Passage of a Picture Bride* (Loma Linda: Loma Linda University Press, 1989), 18.

3. Eric Foner and John A. Garraty, "The Gentlemen's Agreement," in *HISTORY*, accessed August 25, 2020, https://www.history.com/immigration/gentlemens-agreement.

4. Ibid.

5. New York Historical Society, "Picture Brides and Japanese Immigration," accessed August 25, 2020, https://www.history.com/topics/immigration/gentlemens-agreement.

6. Yoon, *The Passage of a Picture Bride*, 19–70. This chapter is a condensed version of a portion in the book.

7. Dongailbo, "Agricultural Immigration to Hawaii in the Last Years of Korean Empire."

8. Yoon, *The Passage of a Picture Bride*, 18.

9. Ibid., 185.

Chapter Eight

Peruvian Japanese in US Relocation Camp

Japan had become confident about its economic and military power after defeating two much larger neighboring nations within a decade: China in 1895 and Russia in 1905, respectively. Some leaders of Imperial Japan, the nation of the "Rising Sun," dreamed of establishing a vast empire much like another powerful island nation: Great Britain. This imagined Japanese entity was to be called the Greater East Asian Co-Prosperity Sphere. On paper, this sphere included India to the west, Australia to the south, and the Caribbean islands to the east. It did not, however, include any major nation in the Americas except for a narrow strip along the West Coast of Canada. The idea was more a cultural or civilizational sphere than a clearly defined political territory. Some ambitious Japanese leaders, however, wanted to have direct control over much of Northeast and Southeast Asia because the two contiguous regions lay within easy reach of the mighty Japanese navy and army.

An alleged justification of the proposed sphere was for Asia, much of which was under European colonial rule during the first half of the twentieth century, to gain autonomy. For instance, the nations of Indochina, save Thailand, were under the colonial rule of Great Britain (Burma and Malaysia), France (Cambodia, Laos, and Vietnam), and the Netherlands (Indonesia). Furthermore, the small island territories dotting the South and West Pacific Ocean were under Western control. Many parts of China's major cities were Western extra-territorialities, including Shanghai, which was divided into a number of foreign extra-territorialities. Even Japan had a piece of the city.

After hastily modernizing during the Meiji period and remodeling itself after the West in less than eighty years, Japan wanted to project itself as a counterforce on behalf of Asia. As the most industrialized nation in the region, Japan wanted to present itself as the liberator of Asia from Western colonial dominance. Although Japan's claims sounded altruistic, its behavior in the region contradicted these stated motives. The Pearl Harbor attack on December 7, 1941, was Japan's initial step in the creation of the Greater East Asian Co-Prosperity Sphere. Hawaii, the home base of America's Pacific fleet, happened to be located in the center of the imagined sphere. Almost simultaneously, the Japanese army attacked or invaded Thailand, Malaya, Burma, the Philippines, and the Dutch East Indies (Indonesia). At one time, it crossed the Burma-India border. During much of the Pacific War, Japan had to deal with four major war theaters against ABCD nations (America, Britain, China, and Dutch): Central Pacific, Southwest Pacific, China, and Southeast Asia. The invaded Asian countries were under Japanese control until the end of the Pacific War on August 15, 1945.

It was no accident that Japan wanted to call the Pacific War the Great East Asian War. The government of Japan wanted to justify and even glorify the Pacific War in the name of Greater East Asia Co-Prosperity, which implied a cultural clash between the East and the West. By labeling the war in such terms, the Japanese government wanted to make its citizens proud and obtain moral support from other Asian nations. Ironically, China had been in a war with Japan since 1937 and Korea under its colonial rule since 1910. When Japan established a puppet government, Manchukuo, in Manchuria and Inner Mongolia in 1932, it controlled much of northeast China. At the time of Pearl Harbor in 1941, Japan had already ruled Korea for thirty years and had been at war with the Republic of China for nearly five years. Most Chinese and Koreans, therefore, hoped that Japan would be defeated by America and its allies.

The shockwave of Pearl Harbor reverberated rapidly across the Pacific. From Canada down to Chile, the tremors from the attack continued to shake nations in the Americas. Reactions were swift and hostile to such outright Japanese aggression. Although the attack on Pearl Harbor was a surprise assault that occurred on a Sunday morning, December 7, 1941, it was not totally unanticipated. Since the formation of the Axis alliance and Hitler's invasion of Eastern European nations in 1939, countries in the Americas were watching the movement of the Axis nations. In the years preceding the Pearl Harbor attack, foreign ministers from the American States (OAS, Organization of American States) had met several times to discuss potential threats from the Axis. The Pacific War, however, was to have unintended consequences not only for millions of Japanese civilians at home, but also overseas Japanese nationals and their descendants throughout the Americas. Japanese residents in both North and South America were suspected instantly of having allegiance to their country of origin, particularly in nations along the Pacific Rim. As a result, Japanese nationals in the Western regions of Canada, the United States, Panama, Peru, and other Central American countries were subject to wartime controls by their resident governments.

More than 120,000 people of Japanese ancestry were interned in the United States during the war. The official reason or excuse offered was to prevent any potential collaboration of Japanese residents with an invading Japanese army on the Pacific Coast. The interned group included more than two thousand people of Japanese ancestry forcibly removed from Latin America. During the Pacific War, they were transported to the United States against their will. These Latin American Japanese were mainly from Peru and Panama, and the US government kept them in its relocation camps until the end of the war in August 1945.

This chapter is primarily about Japanese Peruvians who were deported and interned as enemy aliens in the United States, an act that was possible only with the cooperation of the Peruvian government. Tragically, Japanese Peruvians became double enemy aliens during and after the war, becoming "pawns in a triangle of hate."[1] These Japanese deportees to the United States were caught in the hostile crosscurrents of war between Japan, Latin American governments, and the United States. Since their wartime predicament interlaced with their counterparts in the United States, the stories of detained Japanese Peruvians need to be understood in the larger context of the relocation of Japanese Americans. In fact, the forced deportation and internment of Japanese Peruvians was only part of a much grander scheme hatched by the United States.

THE RELOCATION OF JAPANESE AMERICANS

Immediately following the Pearl Harbor attack, President Franklin Roosevelt called December 7th a "Day of Infamy," and the US Congress declared war upon Japan. Until that time, the United States had remained a reluctant bystander to the Second World War. Although Hawaii was an American territory almost 5,000 miles (7,800 km) and six time zones away from Washington, DC, the incident was the first major foreign military attack on the United States since the war of 1812. The strategic value of Hawaii as an American outpost in the middle of the Pacific Ocean was very significant as the United States wanted to be a major Pacific power. Forced to engage in the Second World War following the attack, President Roosevelt issued Executive Order 9066, which ordered the relocation of people of Japanese ancestry. Anyone with ancestry in their genealogical records down to one-eighth Japanese who resided west of the Mississippi River was to be placed in military camps. The criterion of one-eighth Japanese ancestry meant that some people who were barely Japanese culturally or racially were relocated. An individual with one-eighth Japanese ancestry and seven-eighths Caucasian ancestry, for instance, might hardly show any physical trace of his or her Japanese ancestry. Such a person's great-grandparent might have been the only full-blooded Japanese in the preceding three generations, either on the paternal or maternal side, but it did not matter.

Since most Japanese American residents were concentrated in the states along the Pacific Coast, from Washington down to California, the US government justified the evacuation order on the pretext of a possible Japanese invasion of the continental United States. At that time, many Japanese were already American-born US citizens (*Nisei* and *Sansei*), yet the US government suspected their loyalty. It argued that Japanese Americans might provide assistance to an invading Japanese army. When the Japanese military began to occupy numerous Pacific islands, including Guam in Micronesia, and to engage in covert submarine activities along the California coast, the suspicions of the US government were reinforced.

Japanese American residents were given a few days to pack up personal necessities and ordered to report to sixteen assembly centers. The majority of these centers were located inland, in central California, a clear indication that a high percentage of Japanese residents in California were rural farmers. Other states such as Washington, Oregon, and Arizona had only one assembly center each. Many Japanese Americans left their belongings and properties to the mercy of their neighbors. Those who could sell their properties had no choice but to accept whatever price buyers offered.

About 113,000 Japanese Americans were rounded up in the Western states, accounting for approximately 80 percent of Japanese residents, either foreign or American born, in the United States. Most Japanese residents of Hawaii and those living east of the Mississippi River were exempt for different reasons, but within those rounded up there included 1,118 from Hawaii and 219 non-Japanese companions, mostly the Caucasian spouses of Japanese evacuees.[2] The assembled Japanese were then transported to ten relocation camps located west of the Mississippi River.

California, Arizona, and Arkansas had two relocation camps each, and four Western states-Colorado, Idaho, Utah, and Wyoming-had one. The camps furthest from the Pacific Coast were located in Arkansas, in Jerome and Rohwer not far from the Mississippi River. Most relocation camps were established in desolate and isolated areas, and the hurriedly built barracks resembled those of the military. Each relocation camp was separated from the outside world by a perimeter, barbed wire fence. Soldiers watched the activities of the internees from guard towers. Canada also removed 27,000 people of Japanese ancestry without any charge during the war.

Family members stayed together, but all ate communally in a mess hall. School-aged children attended classes, and these schools provided extracurricular activities such as sports, music, and acting. Adults were assigned various tasks, including camp operation and maintenance. Individual freedoms were restricted, but the relocation camps were not like prisons. Internees were allowed to leave if they could produce official letters of school

Figure 8.1. Temporary housing for Japanese internees. *ChrisBowell* © *iStock*

admission or letters of employment from companies located east of the Mississippi River.

In relocating Japanese residents in the West, the US government allowed for one exception: most Japanese residents on the Hawaiian Islands. In December 1941, more than a third (38%) of Hawaii's residents were people of Japanese ancestry. In fact, there were more Japanese in Hawaii than on the entire mainland. The evacuation of about 150,000 people of Japanese ancestry from Hawaii, whose total population was about 400,000, would have paralyzed both private and governmental sectors. Thus, Hawaiian business owners and government leaders strongly opposed the idea of interning everyone of Japanese ancestry. Following the Pearl Harbor attack, the Hawaiian Islands were already under martial law with curfews and blackouts. Impressed with the dedication and diligence of Japanese American civilian volunteers during the emergency and recovery activities following Pearl Harbor, the US government approved the idea of forming a Japanese American combat unit for the European theater in February of 1943. President Roosevelt officially called the unit the 442 Infantry Regimental Combat Team. Initially, the four thousand-soldier unit was composed of Japanese Americans from Hawaii as many mainland Japanese Americans were unhappy about their forced internment. Nonetheless, soon some of the internees

Figure 8.2. A guard tower at the Manzanar Relocation Center. *fotogal* © *iStock*

volunteered to be a part of the military unit. Those who were bilingual served in the Pacific theater of war as intelligence officers and interpreters, and proved that they were loyal Americans.

The reputation of Japanese Americans during the war helped Hawaii become the fiftieth state of the union in 1950, within five years of the end of the war. Before, the US Congress had turned down Hawaii's applications for statehood more than once as some members of the US Congress were somewhat uneasy about the fact that Hawaii's dominant ethnic group was Japanese. Many Japanese Americans, however, fought hard for the country that had betrayed them. Their combat unit, the 442 Regiment, was the most decorated in the US Army during the Second World War. Altogether, fifteen thousand Japanese American troops were sent to Europe, mainly to Italy, southern France, and Germany. Originally, the US military classified Japanese Americans as 4C, enemy aliens, not subject to the draft.

The constitutionality of the relocation of Japanese Americans was legally challenged during the war, and the US Supreme Court ruled it unconstitutional on December 18, 1944, eight months before the end of the war. Yet most internees chose to stay on at the relocation camps until the end of the war. They were afraid of American public hostility and not sure of their economic security in the outside world. The last relocation camp was closed in 1946. Against this backdrop, the story of the internment of Japanese Peruvians during the war can better be understood.

PRELUDE TO THE PERUVIAN DEPORTATIONS

On a much smaller scale, yet far more tragic, are the wartime relocations that happened to a considerable number of Japanese residents in Peru. Yet the story of this relocation has been a mere footnote to the much larger, well-published story of Japanese American internment. The wholesale injustice done to the people of Japanese ancestry in America was one thing, but what the governments of the United States and Peru did to Japanese Peruvians is beyond any legal or moral justification. Peru was not a participant in the Pacific War in any way, shape or form. Moreover, the way Japanese Peruvians were treated at the end of their captivity was far more tragic than its beginning.

The forced deportation of Japanese Peruvians was not a sudden knee-jerk reaction to the Japanese attack on Pearl Harbor. A sentiment of xenophobia had been brewing in Peru for some time before the war. As the relationship among Germany, Italy, and Japan evolved into a military alliance with the Pact of Steel in 1939 and the Tripartite Pact in 1940, the United States had become concerned about a possible military threat from the Axis nations. At the Eighth International Conference of American States held in Lima, the capital city of Peru, in 1939,[3] the delegates pledged that member nations would be united in their efforts to defend the hemisphere from all hostile activities on either side of the Atlantic or Pacific oceans.

Not so certain about the commitment of Latin American nations to the pledge, President Franklin Roosevelt ordered American embassies and consuls in the region to gather information on German and Japanese communities and their leaders.[4] The American government found these two particular communities worrisome because both maintained strong ties to their home nations and had ethnic solidarity. The US intelligence agents attached to these Latin American foreign offices developed profiles on certain influential Japanese and German community leaders and residents. When Japan attacked Pearl Harbor, most countries in the Americas severed diplomatic relations with Japan, some promptly while others took a bit of time. A few countries, however, remained neutral in their relations with Japan; nations on the Atlantic Ocean, such as Argentina and Brazil, had a somewhat different outlook from those on the Pacific. In most of the latter nations, Japanese embassies and consuls were closed and diplomatic personnel were ordered to withdraw. Because Hawaii was not so remote from these Pacific-Rim nations, they feared possible attacks from Japan.

With America's sweeping relocation of people of Japanese ancestry, many Latin American countries promptly followed suit. For some, the economic successes of Japanese immigrants had been a cause of jealousy and even fear over the years, and the Pacific War triggered widespread anti-Japanese sentiment. In addition, by virtue of America being a leading member of the OAS, Latin American countries were generally supportive of the actions of the US toward its Japanese residents. Also, Latin American countries with sizable Japanese populations had become uneasy about possible clandestine acts by their own Japanese residents. At the same time, the US government was concerned about the actions of Japanese residents in Latin America that could affect its own national security. US authorities could not ignore the possibility of Japanese espionage and sabotage in Latin America helping the Japanese war effort against the United States. Immediately following the Japanese attack on Pearl Harbor, the US government's surveillance of Japanese residents in Latin America increased. Intelligence officers paid special attention to Japanese residents settled along the Pacific coasts of Mexico, Panama, Peru, and Chile.

Among other sites, the US government was determined to protect the Panama Canal by all means necessary as it was vital for connecting the Atlantic and Pacific coasts of the United States. It was possible, but quite inefficient, to detour around the tip of South America for maritime transportation between the two coasts. Undisrupted passage of merchant and naval ships through the canal was critical for US national security, the economy, and the war effort. Under pressure from the US government, some Latin American countries began to detain high-profile Japanese residents listed in American intelligence files. A few of these suspect Japanese residents managed to escape or hide, but most were apprehended. Realizing the gravity of the war and their situation, many Japanese detainees accepted their condition with a fatalistic attitude. When Japanese Latin Americans were apprehended for deportation to the United States, local police did not give them much time to deal with important business matters and other life concerns. They were taken to the capital cities and kept in jail. Without specific charges or evidence of wrongdoing against them, they were treated somewhat differently from common criminals. Nevertheless, the conditions in the detention centers were a stark reminder of the wartime hostility toward enemy aliens.

WHY PERU?

Why was Peru so eager to deport its Japanese residents to the United States during the war? Slightly more than eight out of ten deported Japanese Latin Americans came from Peru.[5] Up to the years leading to the Pacific War, Peru had the second largest Japanese community in Latin America after Brazil.

This fact had something to do with the geography of Peru. Most Japanese arrived in South America through the entry port of Callao, adjacent to the capital city of Lima. Japanese access to South America either for immigration or trade was straight and shorter when they used the Callao/Lima harbor. To many Japanese bound for South America, Peru was the first country of arrival in the continent. From there, they headed for other countries by various land routes. Besides Peru's need for Japanese labor, the convenience of the port of entry attracted many Japanese. Even before the war, many Peruvians were uneasy about the rapid growth of the Japanese population in their midst. For instance, a little over five thousand Japanese lived in Peru in 1910. By 1940, the Japanese population had increased fivefold to 26,388. Among them, 17,598 were Japanese citizens who had immigrated while the rest, 8,790 (33%), were Peruvian-born Japanese, or Nisei.[6] The rapid increase of Japanese people and their economic success resulted in an increase of uneasiness among the Peruvian people.

Over the years, Japanese residents in Peru were highly successful in their economic endeavors. The sizeable community and its concentration in the capital city helped to generate considerable economic power. In time, this bred resentment toward the Japanese among the Peruvians. The influential newspaper, *El National,* agitated its readers by arguing that "the Chinese and Japanese are silently conquering Peru."[7] The same newspaper maintained that the government should cease immigration from these two Asian countries. At the same time, the Peruvian public suspected that many Japanese were ultimately loyal to their emperor. They believed that the Japanese in Peru might play a role in expanding the Japanese empire beyond its island nation. Such a suspicion was fueled by two actions by the Japan in East Asia. In 1932, Japan established a puppet government, Manchukuo, in the northeast region of China, including a part of Mongolia. A few years later, in 1937, Japan invaded China.

By the time of the Pearl Harbor attack in 1941, Korea had been under Japanese colonial rule for more than three decades. Such imperialistic behavior of Japan on the other side of the Pacific Ocean raised Peruvian suspicions that the Japanese residents were also coveting Peru as a potential colony of Imperial Japan. A riot against Japanese residents subsequently broke out in May of 1940. Ten Japanese lost their lives during the riot and about six hundred Japanese properties—including homes, schools, and shops—were burned down.[8] The violent incident was preceded by three legislative actions against the Japanese, which contributed to the anti-Japanese sentiment.

In 1936, the Peruvian government halted the naturalization of Japanese immigrants. In the following year, second-generation Japanese were prohibited from claiming citizenship based on their nation of birth. Then in 1940, any Peruvian-born Japanese who returned to Japan either for study or any other purpose were stripped of their Peruvian citizenship.[9] It was almost a

Peruvian version of the Japanese exclusion law. Thus, anti-Japanese sentiment was already high before the outbreak of the Pacific War in 1941. When Japan attacked Pearl Harbor, Peruvian suspicion and hatred of Japanese residents grew to a fevered pitch. The war seemed to confirm Peruvian suspicion all along, and they reacted swiftly. The Peruvian government restricted the Japanese community by complying with the request of the US government for the deportation of Japanese Peruvians to America.

Peru's neighboring country to the east, Brazil, had a quarter million Japanese residents, including many Brazilian-born citizens. It was home to the largest overseas Japanese community in the Western hemisphere, and Brazil's response to its Japanese residents differed from that of Peru for a number of reasons. First of all, it was almost impossible to detain that many people. Second, most Japanese were farmers and productive members of society. Lastly, being a country not facing the Pacific Ocean, Brazil did not anticipate any direct military threat from Japan. At least, that was the attitude of the Brazilian government in the early stages of the Pacific War. Nonetheless, over time, even Brazil could not help but feel uneasy and suspicious toward its Japanese residents. Some law enforcement personnel were rough in dealing with Japanese residents during the war. The relatively tolerant Brazilian government moved four thousand Japanese from the Sao Paulo-Santos Harbor area to a small harbor city of Paranagua, about 180 miles (295 km) to the south. The Japanese in the northern state, Para, were relocated to Tome-Acu in the same state. Although the domestic relocation[10] was not comparable to forced deportation-internment in another country, it was a painful experience nevertheless.

TRANSIT FROM SOUTH AMERICA TO THE UNITED STATES

A little over a dozen Latin American countries responded to the request of the United States by participating in the wartime deportation program. These countries sent about three thousand nationals from the Axis powers to the United States during the war.[11] Although Peru deported the largest number of Japanese residents, other countries that sent deportees included Bolivia, Colombia, Costa Rica, Ecuador, El Salvador, Guatemala, Haiti, Honduras, Nicaragua, and Panama. Even three Atlantic-facing Latin American countries—the Dominican Republic, Haiti, and Venezuela—cooperated with the United States.[12] It is also interesting to note that the two largest Pacific Coast nations, Mexico and Chile, did not comply with deportation requests of the United States. Instead, Mexico moved its Japanese residents in Baja California to areas further inland. The two largest Atlantic-coast nations, Argentina and Brazil, did not participate in the deportation of their Axis nationals either. They tried to remain neutral during much of the war, so the ABC

(Argentina, Brazil, and Chile) nations of South America did not cooperate with the United States. Japanese Latin Americans made up about two-thirds of the total Axis nationals deported to America. German and Italian detainees made up the rest. A total of 2,118 Japanese Latin Americans were deported to the United States, and Peru sent the majority of them with 1,771 (84%).[13] Among the Japanese detainees, half (1,024) were suspected community leaders while the other half (1,094) were family members who joined up later through transportation arrangements made by the US government.[14]

On the surface, the Latin American countries seemed to justify deportation of their Japanese residents because of their concerns regarding wartime security. It was, however, only a remote possibility that Japan would engage in military action with any Latin American country. The hidden agenda for deporting Japanese residents was other than the security concern: "Peru, obviously considering the wartime period an excellent opportunity to rid itself of many Japanese, was somewhat in advance of American thinking, . . ."[15] At the same time, the US government had prevailed in its hidden agenda in pushing for the relocation of suspect Japanese from South America.

The United States intended to use its Japanese detainees from Latin America to exchange for American citizens held by the invading Japanese army in certain Pacific nations such as Indonesia and the Philippines.[16] In a way, the South American Japanese were to be used as pawns to be exchanged for captured American civilians in Asia. The US government could not dare to use its Japanese American detainees for such a shameful purpose. Sensing the intent of the Americans, the Japanese government strongly protested the deportation of its Latin American nationals to the United States.

The first ship, the *S. S. Etolin,* left Peru with 141 Japanese detainees[17] in April 1942, less than five months following the Pearl Harbor attack. Most of the detainees in the first group were men, either unmarried or with spouses in Japan. On the way, the ship picked up Japanese detainees, Germans, and Italians from other Latin American countries. The voyage from Calla/Lima to Panama took a little over two weeks. Panama was a transit point, and the US government was in charge of operating the canal. While waiting for transport from Panama to the United States, the detainees were assigned to labor. Like their counterparts in Peru, the Japanese in Panama had been under the watchful eyes of both the governments of Panama and the United States before America's declaration of war against Japan. When the Axis nations had formed a formal alliance in 1939, the US government had taken extraordinary measures for the safety and security of the Panama Canal from a potential attack either from the Atlantic side by Germany or from the Pacific side by Japan. Therefore, citizens of Axis nations were under special surveillance. No sooner had Japan attacked Pearl Harbor than the Panamanian government arrested about 250 Japanese outside the Canal Zone. This was according to a prearranged consensus between Panama and the United States, with the US government paying for the cost of deportation. Thus, the small country of Panama was eager to cooperate with the US government, deporting 250 Japanese residents, a distant second to Peru.[18] In fact, the two Latin American countries had established plans for detaining every single Japanese in the event of war. In addition, Panama was willing to set up detention centers for Japanese deportees during their transit from South American countries to the United States.

The transporting of Japanese detainees from Panama to New Orleans required a great deal of military-style logistics. The distance between the two locations is about 1,600 miles (about 2,600 km), but a straight voyage route was avoided so as to evade any enemy attacks. At that time, German U-boats were a serious threat in the Caribbean Sea and Gulf of Mexico. The transport ships were escorted by a variety of US Navy ships including destroyers, cruisers, submarines, and even military airplanes. It took about two weeks from Panama to New Orleans, and the US government took every precaution to avoid the embarrassment of losing civilian life during transport.

From New Orleans, the detainees took a passenger train to reach internment camps in Texas. Single detainees were separated and interned either in Kennedy or Seagoville. Not long after they arrived, the US government began to arrange for the reunion of detainee families. Unlike the men, wives and other family members were given time to deal with important matters such as the selling of property or businesses. Family members followed the same route and procedures as their husbands or fathers before them. The reunited families were given separate living quarters where they could resume their family life together. The last transport ship, the *Frederick C. Johnson*, left Calla/Lima in October 1944, ten months before the end of the Pacific War. Most passengers in the last group were the wives and children of Japanese detainees already being held in the United States. Some family members who missed the last transport ship out of Calla/Lima had to wait for more than ten years to be reunited. A husband or father had to wait either in the United States or in Japan for his wife and children in Peru because some deported men could not reenter Peru until the Japanese Exclusion Law had been rescinded.

LIFE AT THE RELOCATION CAMPS

Japanese detainees from Latin American countries were grouped together in relocation camps, separated from the Japanese American detainees. Similarly, Latin American Germans and Italians were grouped together at detention facilities. Among the deported groups from outside the United States, the largest were the Japanese from Latin American countries and the territory of

Hawaii. The relocation camp in Crystal City, Texas, was a restrictive compound with its outer walls topped with barbed wire. It was not, however, a prison. Each family was given an enclosed unit with basic amenities, and they were free to spend their leisure time by pursuing various activities offered at the camp. Controlled contact with the surrounding communities was allowed as some internees worked on farms or in factories. Yet information about the outside world was restricted as the internees had no access to radio, newspapers, or magazines, so they had no idea as to what was happening in the United States and beyond, particularly with regard to the war.

Formal education was provided for school-age children in three languages: English, German, and Japanese. The camp schools offered extracurricular activities such as sports, band, and arts. Many former teachers served as classroom instructors, and some were hired from the surrounding communities. For adults, a variety of hobbies was provided including classes on the tea ceremony, flower arrangement, martial arts, and the like. The camp had a swimming pool and vegetable gardens. All internees ate meals at the camp mess hall, and the camp authorities tried to serve ethnic foods as much as they could arrange, including bringing in Japanese food from Hawaii. Often, Germans and Japanese exchanged food according to their palates. As many as forty Japanese Buddhist priests were interned in relocation camps, and they performed religious rituals for Japanese internees on various occasions. Some of the Japanese expressed their resentment in small ways. They would deliberately drop serving dishes or bowls in the mess hall. To them, it was a small way of damaging the property of the US government.

The camp for foreign detainees in Crystal City, Texas, also held a number of American-born Japanese for a special reason. They were the ones who had renounced their US citizenship in protest for the mistreatment they were receiving from their own government, and thus were treated as foreigners. These repudiated citizens were regarded as enemy aliens and were separated from the general Japanese American internees. They were treated as enemy aliens in their own native land.

On the other side of the Pacific Ocean, about fourteen thousand American civilians were held by the Japanese military in occupied Asian nations, which included the Philippines, Indonesia, Singapore, and Vietnam.[19] In contrast, the US government detained a little over 115,000 civilians of Japanese ancestry, including about 2,000 Japanese taken from Latin America. Thus, the US government held a little over eight times more civilians than did the Japanese. Both Japan and the United States attempted to exchange civilians through mediation, with Spain representing Japan and Switzerland representing the United States. The repatriation negotiations for the detained civilians were based on a principle of reciprocity: a tit for tat based on numbers. This effort came to be known as the Gripsholm World War II Exchanges named after the Swedish cruise ship, the M. S. Gripsholm, that served as a transport vessel for the United States.[20] About three thousand men, women, and children of Japanese ancestry were repatriated to Japan through the exchange program. Japan reciprocated by sending the same number of American civilians. Each government established a list of detainee names according to its criteria and priority. Both governments gave high priority to diplomats, journalists, scholars, businessmen, and their accompanying family members. The Japanese government prioritized another category: longtime Japanese community leaders in the United States.[21]

The first exchange of civilians took place in October 1942. Each side repatriated about 1,500 people. In September 1943, the second exchange took place with about the same number from each side. Both countries managed to bring back about three thousand civilians. This amount turned out to be the entirety of exchanged civilians during the war. Since America was winning by that point and sensed an inevitable victory, the US government became less eager to exchange civilian detainees on equal terms. Among those held in America, volunteers for repatriation were given high priority. Of the approximately 3,000 Japanese repatriates, 737 were from Latin American countries. This was more than one-third of the Japanese Latin Americans detained in America. Instead of being humiliated by another foreign country, they chose to be repatriated to their country of origin.[22] After the war, about one thousand additional Japanese detainees from Latin America were sent to Japan as their former resident Latin American countries refused to accept them.[23] They could no longer endure the ambiguous state of being a stateless people held in the United States.

POST-WAR PREDICAMENTS

When World War II ended in August of 1945, the US government appealed to Central and South American countries to repatriate the Japanese Latin American internees being held in America. Most refused. According to a pre-war agreement signed in Mexico City, these Latin American nations had decided not to allow the deported Japanese to return home. Thus, the Japanese Latin American detainees faced a double rejection both in America and back in their pre-war resident countries. Suddenly, they had become a people without a country.

On legal grounds, the US government tried to expel the Japanese being held in internment camps. The absurd legal argument was that the Japanese Latin Americans had not entered the United States with proper admission documents, and therefore could not stay. They were thus considered undocumented aliens by the US government. President Truman issued Proclamation 2662 within three weeks of the war's end. On September 8, 1945, he passed final judgment on the legal status of Japanese detainees:

All alien enemies now within the continental limits of the United States (1) who were sent here from other American republics for restraint and repatriation pursuant to international commitments of the United States Government and for the security of the United States and its associated powers and (2) who are within the territory of the United States without admission under the immigration laws are, if their continued residence in the Western hemisphere is deemed by the Secretary of States prejudicial to the future security of or welfare of the Americas as prescribed in Resolution VII of the Inter-American Conference on Problem of War and Peace, subject upon the order of the Secretary of State to removal to destinations outside the limits of the Western Hemisphere in territory of the enemy government to which or to the principles of which they have adhered.[24]

It was an ultimate injustice. With the collaboration of Latin American countries, the US government had forcefully removed Japanese from their homes in Latin America, transported them thousands of miles, and then kept them in internment camps in America. Yet the same American government planned to deport them because they did not obtain proper immigration visas upon entering the United States. Thus, the US government, which had forced Japanese Latin Americans to become an undocumented people, treated them as illegal aliens and threatened them with deportation. Furthermore, the Japanese were seen as a security concern to the United States. Under the circumstances, the US government had only two options in repatriating the Japanese Latin American detainees: send them to Japan or to their former Latin American countries. Many of them, if not all, desired to return to their former homes in Latin America.

Out of anger and disgust, some chose to return to Japan, but the prospect of starting all over again in that war-devastated country was a bleak option. The physical destruction of some Japanese cities, including Hiroshima and Nagasaki, was beyond description. The shortage of food, shelter, and other basic necessities was a widespread problem in post-war Japan. The US government had spent huge sums of money and effort to remove more than two thousand Japanese from Latin America. Now it faced the problem of removing them from the United States. The success of the Japanese repatriation program by the US government appeared to depend upon two conditions: the compliance of the Japanese detainees with the US government order and the willingness of Latin American countries to accept them back. The Japanese detainees would have seemed to have three options for their post-war resettlement: their former Latin American country of residence, Japan, or the United States. Their choice for the Americas, either North, Central, or South America, however, was not legally feasible as no country in the Americas was willing to accept them. And the prospect for resettlement in post-war Japan was grim.

To many, nevertheless, the only viable solution to the quandary seemed to be to return to Japan. It was a reluctant, last choice. According to a survey of the Japanese detainees, only 10 percent wanted to return to Japan.[25] That surprised both the US and Japanese governments. In spite of being detained unlawfully in relocation camps, Japanese Americans were uncertain about returning to Japan. This was evident among many repatriated American-born Japanese during the war. They ended up working for the American occupation army in Japan and eventually chose to return to the United States.[26] Japanese Latin Americans were rounded up and transported to the United States as wartime suspects, yet the same government used the coerced entry for the cause of a forced repatriation. A Japanese detainee from Peru recollected his encounter with an INS officer: "You are illegal entrants to the United States. Therefore, the INS shall deport you to the country of your birth." To that, the detainee countered: "We were forced to enter this country against our will by armed American M.P.s. At that point, most of the INS officers fell silent, with forced smiles on their faces."[27]

Between November 1945 and June 1946, more than nine hundred Japanese Peruvians were repatriated to Japan.[28] The Peruvian government continued to refuse to accept those who wanted to return to Peru. It allowed only seventy-nine Peruvian-born Japanese to reenter the country on the grounds of their Peruvian citizenship by virtue of birth.[29] Such a response was a reflection of the deep-seated, pre-war anti-Japanese sentiment in Peru. In the meantime, some Japanese families could not bear their prolonged separation. A detained husband in the United States and his wife waiting in Peru volunteered to return to Japan. They were finally reunited, but their new life in post-war Japan was desperate. Without a support network, the couple ended their lives by committing suicide.

The real challenge, however, arose in dealing with those who refused to leave America. A total of 364 Japanese Latin American detainees, including children, wanted to remain in the United States.[30] Caught in a triangular emotional trap of Peru, America, and Japan, they saw a chance for a better life in the United States. Neither Peru nor Japan was even an option: the former had rejected them and the other was in ruins.

Wayne Collins, an American lawyer, was willing to represent the Japanese Peruvians as he had prior experience in handling cases where Japanese Americans had renounced their American citizenships because of their illegal internment during the war. This experience had prepared him to advocate for this group of 364 Japanese from Peru. As a result of Collins's arguments on behalf of his Japanese clients, the US government approved a "relaxed internment" with the status of "restricted parolee." The internees were also allowed to move freely in and out of the camp. Moreover, they could leave the camp permanently if they found an "employment guarantor" for a "provisional release."[31] The entire group found an employer who would be their guarantor in a small, rural town of about two thousand residents in southern New Jersey. Seabrook Farms was a company employing about three thousand people working both on its farms and in a food-processing factory. In 1954, the US government finally removed the status "illegal entrant" for these Japanese Latin Americans. It had taken almost ten years to change the status of those who had insisted on staying in the United States.[32]

In time, they qualified to become naturalized American citizens, the earliest being Mr. Higashide and his wife. They received American citizenship certificates in August of 1958. They had waited thirteen years since the closure of the internment camps. As they were so eager to become American citizens, they had started studying English and civic knowledge for the citizenship test. No sooner had they met the five-year residency requirement than they applied for US citizenship: "We had finally been freed from a lingering fear of possible forced deportation; we had been allowed the right of acquiring permanent residency in the U.S. . . . Acquiring U.S. citizenship no longer merely a dream."[33] The pre-war Japanese transplants to America were the beneficiaries of a change in the law that prohibited the naturalization of foreign-born Asian immigrants regardless of the length of their residence in America. In 1954, the US Supreme Court ruled that the Naturalization Act of 1794 was unconstitutional as Caucasian immigrants had always been eligible for naturalization. This race-based prejudicial law had lasted 164 years.

OTHER AXIS NATIONALS OVERSHADOWED

The detention of Germans and Italians is another obscure footnote in the history of America's violation of civil rights during World War II. About a thousand German and Italian citizens in Latin America had been relocated like the Japanese Latin Americans. When the United States declared war against Japan and its Axis allies in December of 1941, both German and Italian nationals were considered "enemy aliens" according to the Alien Enemy Act of 1798 and the Alien and Sedition Act of 1918. In addition, President Roosevelt signed three proclamations on the day of the Pearl Harbor attack on December 7, 1941. His reaction was prompt and swift:

> President Roosevelt signed into law Proclamation 2527, which branded approximately 600,000 non-naturalized Italians as potential 'alien enemies.' . . . The proclamation announced the United States' concern of an invasion by Italy: therefore the U.S. government would keep under observation any non-naturalized person of Italian descent over the age of 14 years. The same dictate was introduced to the American people by Proclamation 2525 and Proclamation 2526, naming the Japanese and Germans, respectively.[34]

Any foreign-born resident fourteen years or older from Germany, Italy, and Japan was subject to the American government's wartime control. In 1941, there were at least 1.1 million registered enemy aliens in the United States, and they were mainly Italians, Germans, Japanese, and others.[35] However, less than three hundred Italian nationals were kept in detention centers in the early years of the war, and they were released when Italy surrendered on September 8, 1943.

In the case of German nationals, about twelve thousand were held in detention centers during the war. The figure included those Germans who were temporary residents in the United States when war was declared. They were students, diplomats, business people, sailors of confiscated merchant ships, and so forth. Only a small portion of German and Italian nationals were detained while the Japanese were rounded up and relocated en masse, down to one-eighth Japanese ancestry. Like Japanese Latin Americans, some Germans and Italians from Latin American countries were deported to the United States at the request of the US government.

The Nazi party had tried to recruit sympathizers among overseas Germans in the Americas. The party's overseas arm, the NSDAP/AO, had active recruiters embedded in ethnic German communities in the hemisphere. They had some success in forming Nazi organizations by enrolling German nationals. Such secret activities caught the attention of many host governments and the US embassies and consuls in Latin America. As soon as the United States was attacked, the American government requested that Latin American governments deport suspected Germans to the United States. The US government received about four thousand five hundred German nationals from various Latin American countries.[36] Among the German deportees, 10 to 15 percent were registered Nazi party members. The following Latin American countries, however, did not comply with the US request to expel suspected Germans: Argentina, Brazil, Chile, and Mexico. These larger, more independent Latin American countries took internal, precautionary measures. In contrast, smaller Latin American countries were more willing to submit to the demands of the United States. German and Italian deportees were mainly held in the same detention centers in Texas but were kept separated from the Japanese detainees.

AN OFFICIAL APOLOGY

Deeply traumatized and shocked by the surprise attack on Pearl Harbor, both the American people and their leaders were caught in a wartime hysteria. The result was the relocation of around 120,000 people of Japanese ancestry from the United States and Latin America. Following Executive Order 9066 by President Franklin Roosevelt, the ensuing round-ups and internment of

Americans of Japanese ancestry left a huge blemish on American history. It took nearly forty-five years for the US government to offer an official apology to Japanese Americans who had been interned during the Second World War. The US Congress passed the Civil Liberties Act in 1988 to compensate the surviving members of the internment. It made a monetary reparation payment of 20,000 dollars to each surviving member of the internment, and President Ronald Reagan signed an official letter of apology.

Two American ACLU (American Civil Liberty Union) lawyers, Wayne M. Collins and A. L. Wirin, launched another fight for the Japanese Latin American internees. When the Pacific War ended, they worked hard to obtain freedom for those who refused to be deported back to Japan. They demanded the same official apology and monetary compensation from the US government, which wittingly chose to limit such compensation to only Japanese American citizens and residents. The former internees from Latin America complained about the omission of a compensation program for them. In response, the US government argued that the Japanese Latin Americans had not been admitted legally into the United States. The same absurd argument was repeated. The former internees thus initiated a class action suit against the US government. In the case of *Mochizuki et al. vs. United States*, the court ordered a somewhat different compensation to the plaintiffs: an official letter of apology and one-time cash payment of 5,000 dollars to each surviving member. The monetary reparation was one-fourth (25%) of the compensation paid to Japanese American internees.

Japanese Latin American internees were dissatisfied with the different ruling, and they kept fighting for equal treatment from the US government. They felt that they had suffered far more because they had been uprooted from their homes forcibly and transported to a foreign country. They felt that they deserved at least equal compensation if not more as they had been subjected to far more emotional suffering and economic loss. Furthermore, their host resident countries hadn't even been involved in the Pacific War.

During the war, they had been treated as "double" foreigners, as enemy aliens first by their own Latin American resident countries, and then by the United States. It was a double tragedy. They had been victimized simply because they happened to be of Japanese ancestry. The Japanese Latin Americans had been like innocent bystanders who had been mistakenly viewed as criminals and thrown in jail.

REFLECTIONS

It was almost unprecedented that a host government would deport its immigrant residents and its native-born citizens to another country. The almost two thousand deported Japanese Peruvians became double foreigners in the

United States. The real tragedy and shock was that democratic countries in the Western hemisphere had coordinated such an action. It was a clear violation of the deportees' basic human and civil rights. Even at the height of the wartime hysteria following the Pearl Harbor attack, this brutal act on innocent civilians was unjustifiable and indefensible on any legal grounds.

The massive internment of Japanese in the United States and throughout the Americas should be viewed in the larger picture of US racial policy. In the United States, only two non-white groups have ever been relocated against their will: the American Indians in the nineteenth century and people of Japanese ancestry in the twentieth century. The former group was forced to abandon their ancestral lands to make room for European settlers. The end of "the trail of tears" was, for many indigenous Americans, Oklahoma and the bleak Southwest region of the United States. Almost two-thirds of Japanese American detainees were American-born US citizens, yet they were treated like aliens of an enemy nation.

Nationals from the other Axis powers, while monitored, did not suffer the mistreatment of Japanese Americans. In California, there were a large number of German and Italian Americans at the outbreak of the war. Although a German attack on the West Coast was a remote possibility, the lives of Germans east of the Mississippi River were hardly disrupted. America's Atlantic coast was as vulnerable as its West Coast to an enemy invasion. The only explanation of the differing treatment between German and Japanese Americans is race. The numerical and racial minority of Japanese Americans had no political clout to defend themselves in the midst of the wartime hysteria. The mistreatment of Japanese Americans was bad enough, but to bring and detain German, Italian, and Japanese from Latin America was unjustifiable under any circumstance. As a dominant force in the Americas, the United States exercised a gross misuse of its power to coerce smaller Latin American countries into extracting their own citizens of foreign ancestry. This act reveals how America defied its core values of freedom, equality, and justice for all.

Karl Marx stated: history repeats itself, "once as a tragedy, and again as a farce."[37] After the war, the US government's arguments and efforts to deport the helpless Japanese detainees back to Peru was a farce. Many helpless Japanese succumbed to external pressures and ended up in war-devastated Japan. To this date, some of the former detainees and their descendants are demanding fair compensation at par with their counterparts in the United States. One of the tragic global stories in 2016 was the flight of the Rohingya people from Myanmar (previously known as Burma). The Muslim minority in the Buddhist country was forced to leave their villages mainly in Rakhine State because of the horrible acts being committed by Rohingya rebel fighter groups. The reaction of the Myanmar military was swift and indiscriminate: burning and destroying the villages of the Muslim minority. Because of their differing ethnicity and religion, this minority group was a stateless people during their existence in Myanmar.

In 2017, the former Serbian military commander, Ratko Mladic, was sentenced to life imprisonment for the crime of ethnic cleansing in Bosnia. Eight thousand Bosnian Muslim men and boys were slaughtered during the Yugoslavian civil war in the 1990s. In addition, about ten thousand civilians were killed in Sarajevo by mortar attack. The Western countries, including the United States, were involved in stopping this ethnic cleansing. The external intervention stopped the massacre and brought the leaders to justice. It is important for the world community to be vigilant in protecting the powerless who are not allowed voices of their own. Only the will for justice to prevail over injustice will foil any governmental attempt to harm minorities during a time of crisis.

NOTES

1. C. Harvey Gardiner, *Pawns in a Triangle of Hate: The Peruvian Japanese and the United States* (Seattle: University of Washington Press, 1981).
2. Jesse Tawil, "An Analysis of the Conditions of Life of Japanese Americans during World War II," accessed April 12, 2017, http://essaymixture.com/an-analysis-of-the-conditions-of-life-of-japanese/.
3. Lika C. Miyake, "Forsaken and Forgotten: The U.S. Internment of Japanese Peruvians during World War II," *Asian American Law Journal* 9 (January 2002), 167.
4. Ibid.
5. Ibid., 164. Peruvian Japanese comprised about 84 percent (1,771) of the total 2,118 Japanese Latin American internees held in America.
6. Ibid., 165.
7. C. Harvey Gardiner, *The Japanese and Peru 1873–1973* (Albuquerque: University of New Mexico Press, 1975), 68.
8. Jaime Gonzalez, "The Japanese-Peruvians Interned in the US during WWII," *BBC Mundo*, Los Angeles, accessed August 4, 2016, http://www.bbc.com/news/world-latin-america-31295270.
9. Miyake, "Forsaken and Forgotten," 167.
10. Jeffrey Lesser, *A Discontented Diaspora: Japanese Brazilians and the Meaning of Ethnic Militancy, 1960–1980* (Durham: Duke University Press, 2007), 8.
11. Miyake, "Forsaken and Forgotten," 164.
12. Ibid.
13. Ibid.
14. Seiichi Higashide, *Adios to Tears: The Memoirs of a Japanese-Peruvian Internee in U.S. Concentration Camp* (Seattle: University of Washington Press, 2000), 177.
15. Gardiner, *Pawns in a Triangle of Hate*, 19.
16. Gardiner, *The Japanese and Peru 1873–1973*, 88.
17. Gardiner, *Pawns in a Triangle of Hate*, 25–27.
18. Miyake, "Forsaken and Forgotten," 168.
19. Gary K. Reynolds. CRS Report for Congress, "U.S. Prisoners of War and Civilian American Citizens Captured and Interned by Japan in World War II: The Issue of Compensation by Japan." Updated July 27, 2001.
20. Densho Encyclopedia, "The Gripsholm WWII Exchanges," accessed September 15, 2016, http://encyclopedia.densho.org/The%20Gripsholm%20wwwII%20Exchanges/.
21. Ibid.
22. Ibid.

23. Gonzalez, "The Japanese-Peruvians interned in the US during WWII."
24. Harry S. Truman, "Proclamation 2662—Removal of Alien Enemies," 1945, accessed April 5, 2017, http://www.presidency.ucsb.edu/ws/?pid=87040.
25. Densho Encylopedia, "The Gripsholm WWII Exchanges."
26. Ibid.
27. Higashide, *Adios to Tears,* 178.
28. Stephen Mak, "Japanese Latin Americans," accessed August 28, 2015, http://encyclopedia.densho.org/print/Japanese%20Latin%20Americans/.
29. Eve Kushner, "Japanese-Peruvian-Reviled and Respected: The Paradoxical Place of Peru's Nikkei," in NACLA, accessed August 21, 2018, https://nacla.org/article/japanese-peruvian-reviled-and-respected-paradoxical-place-peru%27s-nikkei.
30. Higashide, *Adios to Tears,* 177.
31. Ibid., 179.
32. Ibid., 181–88.
33. Ibid., 223.
34. Giuseppina Wright, "WWII Secret: Italian-American Internment as Alien Enemies," accessed April 14, 2016, http://www.ejjournalncrp.org/wwii-secret-italian-americans-internment-as-alien-enemies/
35. Fallon and Jacobs, "Chronology—Suspicion, Arrest, and Internment," accessed April 14, 2016, https://www.foitimes.com/internment/chrono.html.
36. Military Wiki, "German-American Internment," accessed April 14, 2016, https://military.wikia.org/wiki/German-American_internment.
37. Marx, *The Eighteenth Brumaire of Louis Bonaparte*, 1.

Chapter Nine

An Empire Never Defeated

The Japanese in Brazil

Japan paid a heavy price for starting the Great East Asian War, the Pacific theater of World War II, against the United States. Besides the physical destructions of its cities and towns, the loss of human life was horrendous. About 4 percent of Japan's total population of seventy-two million perished during the span of less than four years, between December 7, 1941, and August 15, 1945. The casualties numbered about 2.7 million, including 2.1 million military personnel and 550,000 civilians.[1] Most of the casualties were Japanese in their prime years of their twenties and thirties. Only China, Germany, Poland, and the Soviet Union lost more human lives than Japan during the Second World War. Many Japanese soldiers and civilians died in foreign lands throughout much of East Asia, Southeast Asia, and Micronesia (Western Pacific islands). Tens of thousands of Japanese soldiers were buried in the sands of the west Pacific Ocean in their sunken battleships and airplanes. Moreover, Hiroshima and Nagasaki became the targets of the first two atomic bombs. Worse than that terrible devastation was the hellish carpet bombing on the capital city near the end of the war. On March 9 and 10, 1945, the US firebombing of Tokyo, a densely populated metropolitan area, resulted in around one hundred thousand deaths and destruction of sixteen square miles around the center of the capital.[2] It was the single deadliest air raid during the war.

Although Japan had provoked America by attacking Pearl Harbor, the United States was crucial in Japan's reconstruction in the post-war years. America ended its occupation of Japan in 1951, when the two countries signed the San Francisco Peace Treaty. In 1964, Japan demonstrated to the world its ability to rise again by hosting the Tokyo Summer Olympic games.

It was the first Olympic games ever held on the Asian continent. The painful memories of the Pacific War were rapidly fading in the minds of many Japanese in a booming Japan.

OUT OF THE JUNGLE

When a Japanese government representative signed the surrender document in the presence of General MacArthur and his staff on the battleship *USS Missouri*, a few Japanese soldiers still remained in a state of war. Unexpectedly, a generation later, the whole country was reminded of its role in World War II when a Japanese soldier in a tattered Imperial Army uniform appeared out of the Philippine jungle. He was discovered by a Japanese traveler who had heard the news of a Japanese straggler being spotted in the area. The traveler had searched for and found Hiroo Onoda[3] and convinced him that the war was indeed over. For thirty years, he had been hiding alone in the jungle. Despite hearing news related to the end of the war, he refused to believe it. He was convinced it was impossible that Japan could be defeated by the United States. In fact, Hiroo Onoda had been informed of the war's end by leaflets dropped from airplanes, yet he suspected that these leaflets were decoys and propaganda tools to capture less vigilant Japanese soldiers.

Hiroo Onoda, the former second lieutenant, insisted that he should be formally released from his military duty by his former unit commander. The emaciated Onoda stood at attention before his former commander, Major Yoshimi Taniguchi. This extraordinary scene took place on the island of Lubang, Philippines, on March 9, 1974. Onoda's former commander, then a civilian bookseller, read his military orders to discharge the former intelligence officer from his military duties. Following that ceremony, the fifty-four-year-old straggler in his ragged uniform and hat returned his rifle and sword he had kept all those years in the jungle. Finally, he left his assigned post in Lubang Island. Although he had killed villagers during his ventures for food, then-Philippine president Ferdinand Marcos granted him amnesty and Onoda was able to return to Japan. His homecoming was delayed by almost thirty years. The whole country was mesmerized by Hiroo Onoda's unbending loyalty and patriotism, but he was not alone. Two years earlier, Shoichi Yokoi[4] had been forced to surrender on Guam on January 24, 1972. Since he was born in the former Japanese colony of Taiwan (1895–1945), he chose to return to his native land. The very last Japanese soldier that held out was Teruo Nakamura,[5] who was also a Taiwanese-born Japanese. He had lived alone for almost thirty years in the deep jungle of Morotai Island, Indonesia. His existence was uncovered when a pilot happened to spot his small hut in a thick jungle grove. This led to his surrender on December 18, 1974. He had held out almost a year longer than Hiroo Onoda.

The unbelievable stories of former Japanese soldiers hiding alone for so long in tropical jungles demonstrated their absolute loyalty to the emperor and their belief in the invincibility of the Japanese empire. These highly disciplined Japanese soldiers chose the honor of death rather than a shameful surrender to an enemy. Both Onoda and Nakamura returned to Japan where they received a hero's welcome for the perseverance and long-suffering they had demonstrated for their country.

The idea of surrender did not exist in the Japanese military. In the long tradition of Samurai warriors, holding honor was one of the core virtues among Japanese soldiers. "Honor was bound up with fighting to the death. In a hopeless situation, a Japanese soldier should kill himself with his last hand grenade or charge weaponless against the enemy in a mass suicide attack. But he should not surrender," states Ruth Benedict, the author of *The Chrysanthemum and the Sword*. She continues to observe this indomitable spirit when she says: "Even if he were taken prisoner when he was wounded and unconscious, he could not hold up his head in Japan again; he was disgraced; he was dead to his former life."[6]

According to Benedict, Japanese soldiers would rather kill themselves than become prisoners of war who were considered "damaged goods." During the war, the ratio of captured to dead was 1:120 among Japanese troops in North Burma. In stark contrast, the ratio of captured to dead for the allied soldiers was 4:1 in Hollandia (present Jayapura), Indonesia.[7] These figures show that the overwhelming majority of Japanese soldiers chose death rather than capture, whereas most Western soldiers surrendered. To most Japanese soldiers, death was the ultimate expression of their fealty to the emperor. After being alone so long in the deep Philippine jungle, Onoda became uneasy about the public attention he was receiving in Japan. A year later, he moved to a small Japanese agricultural colony in Brazil where he began to raise cattle. He also married in Brazil. When a teenager murdered his parents in Japan, he returned to start an educational camp for troubled youth. He split his time between Japan and Brazil, spending three months a year in the latter and the remainder in Japan.

The stories of Japanese soldiers holding out in Southeast Asian jungles were somewhat overshadowed, however, by the story of some stubbornly nationalistic Japanese residents in Brazil. Many of them in Brazil refused to accept that Imperial Japan had been defeated in August of 1945. The only differences between the Japanese soldiers in the jungles and the Japanese residents in Brazil were the physical settings and number of people involved. The Japanese soldiers were alone in the tropical jungles, but their compatriots halfway across the world resided in cities or villages. If the Japanese residents in Brazil had chosen to find out what had really happened to Japan in 1945 with open minds, they could have easily found out the outcome of the war. In both cases, they were blinded by their conviction about the invincibility of their demi-god emperor and his empire.

Many years before Japanese soldiers began to emerge from the jungles, some Japanese residents in Brazil could not imagine that their Emperor had surrendered to a foreign power. It was absolutely contrary to their deeply ingrained belief in the Emperor and his empire, Nippon. Besides their blind faith, a number of social circumstances contributed to the denial of the Japanese defeat in the Great East Asian War. It happened in Sao Paulo, the largest metropolitan area in South America, and its surrounding areas.

THE JAPANESE COMMUNITY IN BRAZIL

The largest South American country, Brazil, is about the furthest place on earth from Japan. Until the middle part of the twentieth century, Brazil had received a large number of Japanese immigrants. As a result, the country became home to the largest Japanese overseas community in the Western hemisphere. For decades, the city of Sao Paulo and its surrounding areas were a major attraction for Japanese immigrants. Japanese immigration to Brazil started in 1908 and continued until the beginning of the Pacific War. Nearly 190,000 Japanese immigrated to the South American country during the period between 1908 and 1941.[8] On average, six thousand Japanese immigrated to the country annually during this migration period. Unlike early Chinese immigrants to the Americas, many Japanese came as families with the intention to return home someday.[9] About three-quarters of the Japanese immigration to Brazil took place between 1925 and 1935. In 1933, for instance, 24,494 Japanese immigrants made up more than a half (53.2%) of all immigration to Brazil that year.[10] Such an influx of Japanese made many Brazilians somewhat uneasy, and they suspected the rapid surge of Japanese immigration as an attempt to establish a Japanese territory in Brazil. It was looked upon "as an immigration for conquest and . . . each immigrant was a soldier in disguise. Brazil is a Manchuria in South America."[11]

The mention of Manchuria in connection with this rapidly growing Japanese population revealed the underlying fear of the host country. Japan had invaded the northeast region of China and established a puppet government, Manchukuo (1932–1945). In fact, the people of Manchuria had established China's last dynasty, the Qing (1644–1911), after defeating the last Han Dynasty, the Ming (1368–1644). Ironically, the first emperor of Manchukuo was Puyi, who was the last emperor of the Qing Dynasty. This ill-fated emperor was only three when he was put on the Qing throne and six (1908–1911) when that dynasty came to an end in 1911. Many Brazilians questioned the hidden motivation of the Japanese government in pushing for such a massive Japanese immigration to Brazil. They wondered if the crowded island nation of Japan might have territorial ambitions for a piece of land in Brazil. Besides Manchukuo, the Japanese colonial rule in Korea raised suspicion and fear on the part of the Brazilian government. Such concerns gradually led to controls and restrictions of Japanese residents by the Brazilian government in later years.

The majority of Japanese immigrants engaged in agriculture, and many of them belonged to rural farm colonies that varied in size. These close-knit colonies were quite conducive to retaining and preserving Japanese identity and culture. Many Japanese immigrants, if not all, maintained strong emotional ties with their country of origin. They were in Brazil mainly for economic reasons, not for any sentimental values attached to South America. Thus, integration and assimilation into Brazilian society and culture were not major concerns. At the same time, they felt that Japanese culture was superior to Brazilian culture. Such a perception made some Japanese residents reluctant to integrate into Brazilian society. Instead, they wanted to preserve Japanese identity and culture by running Japanese schools for their children.

The separation between the larger mainstream society and these early Japanese immigrant communities was more obvious in rural areas. Most first-generation immigrant adults remained highly nationalistic and patriotic to their homeland. Even before the Pacific War, Japanese residents in Brazil began to feel pressure from the Brazilian government in the 1920s and 1930s. Their rapid growth in population and relative isolation were causes for concern. Events occurring in the United States added pressure for the Brazilian government to do something. They saw political measures being enacted in the United States, beginning with the Chinese Exclusion Act of 1882. Anti-Asian sentiment continued to increase until it had finally culminated in the passage of the Oriental Exclusion Act in 1924. According to this law, no Asian country could send more than 105 immigrants per year to the United States. This was much more restrictive than the Chinese Exclusion Act, which maintained exemptions for certain professional categories such as diplomats, scholars, students, business people, and their family members.

In contrast, the US government was still open to extensive European immigration from Eastern and Southern European countries. Although the American public was uneasy about the social and religious backgrounds of these new European immigrants, they were at least Caucasians. Nonetheless, the US government wanted to control the number of European immigrants based on the proportion of each national group in America. The policy, known as the National Origin Act of 1924, was definitely in favor of Northern and Western Europeans over Eastern and Southern Europeans. But the proportional restriction placed on Eastern and Southern Europeans was never near the annual fixed quota of 105 immigrants from each Asian country. The anti-Asian immigration policies in the United States resulted in a sudden surge of Japanese immigration to Brazil. As the United States closed its borders to Japan, many Japanese turned to South America. Thus, America's exclusionary policy had a ripple effect on South American countries and soon others followed suit with similar legislation. Observing disturbing domestic and international developments, the Brazilian government took a number of actions to limit the political activities of its own internal immigrant communities.

In April of 1938, the Brazilian president, Getulio Vargas, issued decree 383, which forbade any public activities in foreign languages. The prohibition applied to a wide range of ethnic activities such as public speeches in foreign languages, foreign language radio broadcasts, foreign language lessons, and newspaper and magazine publications other than in Portuguese. Although the decree restricted publications in any language other than Portuguese, the Brazilian government allowed exemptions by making a difficult provision. A foreign-language newspaper or magazine would be permitted with a bilingual format by adding a Portuguese version.[12] The provision, however, was a mere cosmetic gesture as such a format would be prohibitively expensive and cumbersome to produce for a limited ethnic community readership. This language policy deliberately targeted German and Japanese immigrant communities, as the Japanese alliance with Germany and Italy had roused the suspicions of the Brazilian government. Eventually, the Brazilian government closed 187 Japanese schools for around ten thousand students.[13]

On the surface, such actions were presented as a program to homogenize Brazilian society, and the program was known as the "Brasilidate" campaign.[14] Since Japanese culture was so far removed from Judeo Christian European civilization, which Brazil so eagerly sought to emulate, the Japanese community was the main target of the homogenization campaign for its size and increasing political and economic clout. It was an attempt to diminish diverse foreign influences in Brazil. From the moment Brazil opened its doors to immigration, Asian immigrants had been second choice. When European response to Brazil's calls for immigration had been lackluster, it had no other choice but to open its doors to Asians, particularly the Japanese. If the Brazilian government could have populated its vast land with European settlers, it would not have welcomed the Japanese.

WARTIME MEASURES

Unlike most other Latin American countries, the Brazilian government did not cooperate with the United States in deporting suspected Japanese residents following the Pearl Harbor attack. Yet it took a number of cautionary wartime measures toward the nationals of the three Axis nations. Among these three, the Japanese residents stood out for being nationals from the nation that had attacked the United States, a leading member of the Organization of American States (OAS). The sensationalized surprise attack triggered negative public reactions. Besides, the relatively isolated existence of the many Japanese communities and the obvious racial differences increased the profile of the Japanese as an alien people of an enemy nation. These wartime governmental measures upset many Japanese residents in Brazil, as they began to feel an overt hostility.

Furthermore, most local Japanese news media no longer existed because of the policy for ethnic publications in foreign languages. The majority of Japanese immigrants had no access to sources of reliable information. They had lost the means of holding their community together through print and radio media. Consequently, many became disoriented during the war. This communication void exacerbated the anxiety that many Japanese residents felt as any print news that originated in Japan was also blocked due to the language policy.[15] The Japanese community's perception of Brazil's hostility toward them and an information void provided room for generating misinformation, and some nationalistic Japanese groups turned the lack of reliable information into pro-Japanese propaganda.

When the Pacific War broke out in December 1941, Brazil sided with the United States like most other nations in the Western hemisphere. Brazil followed the United States by declaring war on Germany and Italy in August of 1942. The nation had severed its diplomatic relations with Japan earlier that year, in January, but it did not declare war on Japan until three months before the end of the war. Officially, Japan became a hostile enemy nation only in June of 1945. Brazil's change of position toward Japan came only after Germany's surrender to the allied forces one month earlier. Brazil's geography might have something to do for its differing reaction to the Axis nations during the Second World War. Perhaps the South Atlantic-facing Brazil felt only a remote and indirect threat from Japan on the western end of the Pacific Ocean. On the other hand, it might have felt immediately threatened from the North Atlantic nation Germany and its weak ally Italy. Nevertheless, these domestic wartime controls and restrictions applied to all residents of the Axis nations alike, and the government banned any activity favorable or beneficial to the war efforts of Axis nations.

As the war began, both the Japanese Embassy in Rio de Janeiro and the Consulate General in Sao Paulo closed their doors. The departure of Japan's diplomats left a great psychological void in the Japanese communities of Brazil. Before, the Japanese diplomats had provided valuable guidance and assistance. Their physical presence was significant to the Japanese residents' identity and morale. All of a sudden, many Japanese residents in Brazil lost all contact with their country of origin. Communication, interactions, and transactions with Japan through the diplomatic channels ended. Furthermore, Brazil's wartime control and restrictions were the source of discontent and anxiety among many Japanese residents who were blocked from access to reliable information. They were kept in the dark as to what was happening in the war.

At the same time, various forms of economic sanctions affected their livelihood. Not long after the Pearl Harbor attack, about three hundred Japanese families were evicted from Sao Paulo and about one thousand were removed from the Santos harbor and its vicinity. Santos, located about 45 miles (75 km) to the southeast of Sao Paulo, was a major harbor serving the Greater San Paulo metropolitan area.[16] The strategic importance of the harbor to Brazil's largest urban center led to the evacuation of the Japanese residents. Although the probability of a successful Japanese invasion of Brazil was not in the realm of possibility, the Santos harbor could serve as a launching pad by the Japanese navy in the event of a Japanese invasion. Most Japanese residents in Brazil were concentrated in Sao Paulo and surrounding agricultural areas.

Two events led to the removal of the Japanese residents in the Santos harbor area by the Brazilian government. One happened in Japan and the other in Brazil. In reaction to the Brazilian government's closure of the Japanese embassy in Rio de Janeiro and the Consulate General in Sao Paulo, the Japanese government put Brazilian diplomats in Japan under house arrest. The report of the treatment of Brazilian diplomats in Japan angered the public in Brazil. It was a clear violation of international law regarding the immunity of foreign diplomats. The second domestic incident was far more volatile. A Brazilian government informer infiltrated the Japanese community and discovered a secret plot against Brazil. According to the alleged plot, Japan would use twenty-five thousand soldiers to occupy Sao Paulo with the help of Japanese residents who would be disguised as farmers. Since Sao Paulo and its vicinity had the largest concentration of Japanese residents, this plot sounded somewhat plausible. According to the allegation, the invading Japanese army would destroy key military facilities near Santos' strategic harbor. Then Japan would eventually establish its own territory in the Amazon region. They would call the newly established territory New Japan.[17]

Considering Japanese imperial actions in other Asian countries at the time, this secret plot did not sound so far-fetched. This alleged discovery reinforced Brazilian suspicion about the territorial ambitions of the Japanese government. However, the alleged plot was far-fetched, at best. If Japan intended to invade Brazil, it would face a logistical nightmare. First of all, the Panama Canal, under US administration, would be inaccessible. Reaching any major Brazilian harbor would be a tremendous naval feat as the fleet would have to sail around the tip of South America. The transport of twenty-five thousand soldiers, including supplies such as water, food, and weapons, would require a huge naval operation. Moreover, the logical landing spot in Brazil had to be the Santos harbor. The invading Japanese army would have to reach Sao Paulo to collaborate with the Japanese residents there. Whether the so-called invasion plan was real or a fantastical fabrication did not matter. The news was sensational enough to agitate the Brazilian public. This reinforced Brazilian perception of "immigration for conquest" and each immigrant as a soldier in disguise. Congressman Xavier de Oliveira declared that "Brazil is Manchuria in South America."[18]

The Brazilian government began to apply wartime economic controls and restrictions on Japanese residents. These government measures included freezing Japanese assets, limiting the monthly amount of cash withdrawals from banks, a refusal to supply industrial necessities like oil, machines, and parts to Japanese farmers and shop-owners, and the cancellation of property lease agreements, and so forth.[19] Such harsh economic measures scared and angered Japanese residents. They could not understand the actions of the Brazilian government, which was a third party to the Pacific War. Their wartime troubles were not limited to tangible economic activities. The hostile reaction of Brazilians to Japanese residents was often ugly and violent. Some Japanese were robbed, tortured, raped, beaten, and even shot to death. Although Brazil was not engaged in any military action against Japan during much of the war, the Brazilian people treated the Japanese residents as if they were enemy aliens. This vigilantism was fueled by similar actions against Japanese residents in the United States, Peru, and Panama, to name a few. The spillover effects of hostile acts in other countries were unmistakable in affecting people's attitude and actions toward the Japanese residents in Brazil. The Brazilian people knew about the wholesale evacuation of Japanese residents in the United States and the forced deportation of Japanese to the United States by some Latin American countries.

JAPANESE REACTIONS DURING THE WAR

Reactions to the hostility they were facing were varied among the Japanese residents in Brazil. Many were fatalistic about the situation, and they became stoic in bearing the hatred and hardships. Others were defiant, yet they never intended to cause any harm to the Brazilian people. Instead, they tried to do something for Japan and its war efforts. Pro-Japan groups began to emerge in Brazil, and their members were fed with upbeat news on alleged Japanese military victory after victory on distant sea and land battlefields. Buoyed by the impressive military operation at Pearl Harbor, many nationalistic Japanese came to believe that Imperial Japan would prevail in the war. Such conviction was not merely wishful thinking. Throughout much of their primary and secondary education in Japan, they had been taught about the invincibility of the divine Emperor and the superiority of Japan.

On the other hand, there were open-minded Japanese residents who were relatively well informed of world affairs, especially of the industrial capability of the United States. They were the ones who were better educated and more integrated with Brazilian society because they lived in urban areas. They anticipated the inevitability of Japan's military defeat at the end. Such views grew stronger after the Battle of Midway in June 1942, a decisive US victory that caused heavy losses to Japan's naval capability. In the four-day sea battle, Japan lost four aircraft carriers, one heavy cruiser, nearly three hundred aircrafts, and about three thousand soldiers. In comparison, the US navy lost one aircraft carrier, one cruiser, 145 aircrafts, and about 360 soldiers.[20] In the ensuing sea battles in the South Pacific, the outcomes were definitively in favor of the United States.

As the Pacific War progressed, the Japanese community in Brazil was split on the outcome of the war. Some, particularly former Japanese Imperial Army soldiers and officers, had almost a blind faith in Japan's eventual victory. Others were skeptical about Japan's military strength against the mighty American military power. Those who believed in Japan's victory were called *kachigumi* (victory faction) or *kyokoha* (hardheaded school), while those who doubted Japan's military power were called the *makegumi* (defeat faction).[21] In the Brazilian Japanese community, the victory faction was more vociferous and active while the defeat faction remained somewhat cautious and circumspect. An open expression of doubt regarding Japan's military capability could easily trigger angry reactions from the hardheaded Japanese. The defeat faction was not a popular stance in their closed, patriotic ethnic communities.

When the Japanese emperor broadcasted his surrender message on August 15, 1945, two reactions emerged in Brazil. In that faraway South American country, none of the Japanese residents could hear the actual voice of the emperor in his surrender broadcast. They had to rely on second-hand news reports. Japanese residents in the defeat faction accepted the surrender at face value as they had anticipated Japan's eventual downfall. The victory faction, however, refused to accept the fact that Japan had lost the war. They treated the news of Japan's surrender as mere deception or propaganda by the enemy. They argued that a superior Japan under the divine guidance of the Emperor could not lose the war. It was an unshakable conviction based on the belief that their Emperor was divine: "When Japanese subjects [in Brazil] learned of Japan's unconditional surrender through news agencies, their reaction was one of disbelief, and the news was considered allied propaganda."[22]

Almost religious belief in the Emperor was a relatively new phenomenon. The phenomenon began during the height of the militaristic rule that led Japan into the Great East Asia War (Pacific War). The intense Emperor worship campaign was a means to mobilize the Japanese people in the war effort. Its goal was to ensure that all patriotic Japanese would submit to the will of the Emperor to the extent of sacrificing themselves for this demigod. Various military suicide commando units, including the *kamikaze* pilots, exemplified this new idea. In fewer than ten months before the end of the war, almost four thousand Japanese *kamikaze* pilots took off for their final missions for the empire. With about a 20 percent success rate in diving their single-engine airplanes into US ships, they sunk forty-seven US navy ships[23] exemplifying human sacrifices for the emperor. Emperor worship ended officially on January 1, 1946, when Emperor Hirohito denied his divinity in his rescript.[24] The demythologization of the Japanese emperor was carried out on the order of the Allied Forces Occupation Administration. In fact, the emperor's naked voice in his surrender declaration on radio conveyed the message to his people that he was a mere mortal human being like anyone else. The Japanese people heard the emperor's human voice for the first time on radio. Even during the heavy Tokyo air raids toward the end of the war, the American pilots were instructed not to bomb the palace for fear of a fanatical reaction by the Japanese people.

SHINDO RENMEI

Shindo Renmei was a secret Japanese organization in Brazil. Literally, it meant "League of the Way of the Emperor's Subjects."[25] The members of this league had an absolute conviction in the invincibility of the Japanese emperor, and the proper way of showing fealty was to be completely loyal to his empire. In Brazil, Japanese residents with such an absolute faith in the emperor existed even before the Pacific War. It was a legacy of their public education and upbringing in Japan, and the war reinforced their belief. The Shindo Renmei was formed toward the end of the war, in 1944. Because of the Brazilian government's control and surveillance of the activities of enemy aliens during the war, the league operated as an underground entity. Brazilian authorities uncovered the secret organization in 1946, after the war.[26] This pro-Japanese league employed violence not only in Brazil but also in some other South American countries. Members often assaulted fellow Japanese residents who acknowledged the defeat of Japan in the Pacific War. They remained active for about three years after the war, until 1947. At one time, Shindo Renmei claimed to have over one hundred thousand members and eighty branches in the Greater Sao Paulo area and beyond. However, the official estimate varied on the lower end from 30,000 to 50,000 up to 100,000 on the higher end. For instance, the Sao Paulo Police Department suspected that more than thirty thousand Japanese residents were connected with Shindo Renmei. Regardless of estimated size of membership, their influence reached almost 90 percent of Japanese residents in Brazil.[27]

During the war, Shindo Renmei members engaged in a wide range of pro-Japanese activities. The most common tactic was the spreading of misinformation about the outcome of battles to fellow Japanese residents. Their messages conveyed that Japan was winning the war. Since the Brazilian government prohibited any print or broadcast media in the Japanese language unless it was bilingual, many Japanese in Brazil had no way to check the truthfulness of this fabricated propaganda. This distortion of reality was worse in more isolated, rural Japanese colonies. To many, news of Japanese victories was morale-boosting in the midst of war-time depression and restrictions in Brazil.

Those in isolated rural areas had only one channel for news in Japanese: short-wave radio messages originating from Japan. The reception of short-wave radio broadcasts from the other end of the earth was often nothing but a buzzing noise. Some short-wave radio operators in Japan conveyed the reality of the Pacific War, including news about the defeats of the Imperial Army. To this short-wave radio reception problem and the less than encouraging war news, the Shindo Renmei members would say that "only the true Japanese with Japanese spirit can hear the correct message from Japan."[28]

Much of the misinformation the Shindo Renmei League fabricated was ludicrous. One of the most ridiculous news items was the imprisonment of General Douglas MacArthur, the Commander of the Allied Forces in the Far East. Similar absurd stories included the bowing of American President Truman to Emperor Hirohito, the landing of an invading Japanese army in San Francisco, the marching of the Japanese army to New York City, and the like.[29] Many nationalistic Japanese in Brazil, especially those in isolated rural areas, embraced these stories in the absence of reliable sources. The League members took advantage of a news vacuum in many Japanese communities. Their very limited knowledge of Portuguese was another contributing factor to the vulnerability of many Japanese immigrants to such fake news. No matter how absurd the fabricated news was, they had no means to verify the authenticity of the news they were receiving from the League members.

During the Pacific War, the only occurrence that might resemble a Japanese landing in San Francisco or the marching to New York happened in the remote Aleutian island off Alaska proper. The Japanese army managed to occupy Attu Island for a year, between June 1942 and July 1943. Initially, the Japanese hoped to use the island as a launching pad for Japanese warplanes to attack American military facilities in Alaska and the mainland. After three weeks of intense fighting, including hand-to-hand combat, the US Army retook Attu with considerable casualties on both sides.[30] The Aleutian Campaign was just a one-time, brief Japanese occupation of a small piece of American territory in Alaska.

To spread false information of alleged Japanese military victories, the secret organization published their own newspaper in Japanese. This underground newspaper flouted the Brazilian law regarding foreign language publications. Those who had no access to other reliable sources of information tended to believe what they read in the Shindo Renmei newspaper. To some, the made-up stories reinforced their belief in the invincibility of the emperor and Japan. The same organization operated clandestine radio broadcasts with pro-Japanese propaganda.

At the same time, some Shindo Renmei members engaged in deceiving their fellow Japanese residents in a number of different ways. Some deceptions were more preposterous than others. For example, the organization promoted the idea of re-immigration of patriotic Japanese in Brazil to new Japanese colonies in the Philippines and Java in Indonesia. They sold pieces of land that did not exist in these newly conquered Southeast Asian countries.[31] Some disgruntled Japanese residents, nonetheless, were interested in such bogus land deals in Asia. It was an expression of frustration and anger among the Japanese in Brazil during the war.

More aggressive Shindo Renmei members carried out acts of sabotage to help Japan's war effort. Although Brazil was very far away from Japan and the distant Pacific battlefields, the league members tried to stop the creation of certain products that could be used by the United States and its allied forces against Japan. In order to prevent the production of silk that could be used for military parachutes, they burned down silkworm houses. By then, however, military parachutes were made of more durable synthetic fabric, nylon. Peppermint farms were another target. The fanatic Shindo Renmei members tried to destroy these farms as extract of the plant was used in explosives.[32] If Japanese farmers in Brazil had grown other farm products that could have been used for war materials against Japan, the list of sabotage targets would have been longer.

Far more than anything else, what the Shindo Renmei members could not tolerate was the notion of Japan's defeat among the Japanese residents in Brazil. They were furious at any Japanese who questioned the ability of the Japanese army. Any sign of skepticism or doubt of Japanese military strength attracted the attention of the league members. When the Pacific War ended in August of 1945, Shindo Renmei began to target those who accepted Japan's surrender to the United States as a fact. To league members, this defeatist attitude was considered a dishonor and a betrayal to the emperor. To them, it was an unforgivable sin. At the height of pro-Japanese activities, league members marked suspected defeatist houses with handwritten signs that read: "An enemy of the nation."[33] This was to intimidate the defeatist family members and, at the same time, warn others who might harbor any idea that Japan was defeated. Once a house was designated as an enemy of the nation by the league, they would be subject to ridicule and ostracism.

Furthermore, some aggressive Shindo Renmei members formed assassination units called *tokkotai*,[34] which meant death squad in Japanese. Each unit was made of fanatic young Japanese residents. They compiled names of defeatists who had acknowledged the defeat of Japan in the war then sent each a warning letter. In this letter, the league suggested that the defeatists should commit suicide following the ritual of *seppuku*,[35] the traditional Japanese method of suicide by disembowelment. It was considered an honorable way of ending one's life in the face of shame or dishonor. In the letter they sent to the members of the defeatist group suggested to have their throat washed for having a dirty heart. It implied that the recipient of the letter should kill himself or herself, but nobody paid much attention to the threatening suggestions.

In September of 1946, some extreme *tokkotai* members began to carry out physical attacks on the defeatists, more than a year after the end of the Pacific War. By then, the whole world knew that Japan had lost the war. Yet, the *tokkotai* members killed fellow Japanese residents in Brazil simply because the victims had accepted Japan's surrender the previous year. Altogether, twenty-three Japanese residents lost their lives by the extremists. In addition, as many as 147 Japanese were wounded for the same reason,[36] some of the injured no doubt having survived assassination attempts. League members also committed nine cases of arson on the property of those they deemed as defeatist. In the end, a total of fourteen *tokkotai* members were convicted of murdering fellow Japanese residents in Brazil.[37] This fanatic, blind faith among diehard victorists lingered many years after the war, up to the 1970s. It took a generation to finally accept the defeat of Japan in the Second World War.

The few league members in Brazil who still clung to the idea of Japan's invincibility argued as follows: the simple fact that the emperor and his subjects continued to carry on their prosperous lives in a post-war Japan provided undeniable evidence of Japanese victory. In other words, Japan was not defeated by a foreign army because they earnestly believed that all Japanese, including the emperor, would have committed suicide if the country had really lost the war. No honorable Japanese would continue to carry on living in the face of such a shameful defeat to the United States.

Such a lingering attitude was reflected in many forms. In 1950, a Japanese national swimming team, including an Olympic gold medalist, visited Brazil. In an interview with the news media, the visiting members expressed shock that some Japanese residents in Brazil continued to deny the defeat of Japan in the Pacific War. Quite disturbed by the swim team's reaction, Shindo Renmei tried to cover the truth by saying that "the swimmers were Koreans masquerading as Japanese."[38] Why did they blame Koreans? The ultra nationalistic Japanese in Brazil hated and distrusted Koreans from their former colony of thirty-six years. Koreans had resisted colonial rule and fought hard to regain their freedom and independence. Many Koreans had engaged in freedom fighting with sabotage and the assassinations of Japanese leaders.

When Japanese residents in Brazil began to visit a booming post-war Japan, some of them took the prosperity of their homeland as evidence that

Japan had never been defeated in the war. In 1972, an elderly Japanese man by the name of Ryoki Hamahiga visited home after fifty years of having lived in Brazil: "He was so completely convinced of Japan's victory in the war that everything he saw in Japan—the new prosperity, the emperor still living in the Imperial Palace, and so on—appeared to him as proof of Japan's victory."[39] Some old nationalistic Japanese immigrants in Brazil assumed that no right-minded Japanese could have lived in a defeated Japan without guilt and shame. To them, authentic Japanese with a true Japanese spirit would have committed suicide rather than bearing the shame of defeat.

If they had seen the picture of a Japanese cabinet member signing the surrender document while General MacArthur and his staff watched on the *USS Missouri,* many would have accepted Japan's defeat. But the zealous Shindo Renmei members could have still denied Japan's surrender by saying that the picture had been fabricated by the United States in order to mislead. Even if they had heard the radio broadcast of the emperor's surrender speech on August 15, 1945, they could have still denied Japan's defeat by saying that the broadcast was a ploy of the United States to deceive the Japanese people. In fact, some league members fabricated a picture to mislead Japanese residents in Brazil. In it, President Truman and General McArthur are bowing to Japanese officials as a sign of surrender aboard the *Battleship Missouri.* Since both were in a deep bowing position, their faces were not visible. Anyone who was familiar with the American president and the general could have recognized that the figures in this picture were not authentic. Not many Japanese in Brazil, particularly those in isolated rural farm areas, could discern the deception. And many accepted the Japanese caption below the picture as fact. The picture reinforced their belief that Japan had won the war.[40]

As many Japanese residents in Brazil were living in an information void because of the prohibition of publications or radio broadcasts in Japanese, they tended to believe what the Shindo Renmei's clandestine underground propaganda machine produced. In addition, many Japanese in Brazil lived in communities isolated or even insulated from the outside world. They had no way of checking the authenticity of the information they received from Shindo Renmei. The league's violent acts targeted only Japanese defeatists, never engaging in hostile acts against either the Brazilian government or its people. Their secret activities, violent or nonviolent, were confined to close-knit Japanese communities. That was one reason why the organization's activities could avoid the censure of Brazilian authorities for some time. Following their crimes against their fellow countrymen, the *tokkotai* members usually surrendered to the police. They insisted that they had attacked the defeatists out of a duty to their fatherland and in honor of their emperor.

THE POST-WAR TRAUMA

On April 19, 1946, the governor of Sao Paulo, Macedo Soares, gathered 436 Shindo Renmei members at his residence. The invitees were the leaders of the league and its branch representatives, mainly from the Greater San Paulo area. Because of their continuous denial of Japan's defeat in the war, the governor tried to persuade them to accept its outcome. As the governor asked them to sign their names on the attendance book, some of the league members demanded that the governor not use humiliating expressions such as "Japanese surrender," "unconditional surrender," and the like.[41] The governor was simply referring to the end of the war, and was quite upset by the challenges posed by the stubborn league members.

Soon after the meeting, he ordered the state police to arrest hardcore members of Shindo Renmei. A total of 172 Japanese were arrested and sent to a notorious penal island. These prisoners included hardcore *tokkodai* members who were involved in assassinating the defeatists. During interrogation, some Brazilian officers asked the arrested league members to step or spit on the portrait of the emperor[42] or the Japanese flag. Compliance with the order would be considered a sign of reneging on their loyalty to the emperor and Japan. Some of the league members were defiant and refused to do so.

The league members who had been rounded up were detained for three years in a prison on Anchieta Island.[43] The Brazilian penal island was often compared to the notorious Alcatraz Island in San Francisco Bay for its danger and severity. Due to strong ocean currents around the island, no prisoner was successful in an escape attempt. Like Alcatraz, Anchieta was for hardcore, violent criminals. In the prison, former Shindo Renmei leaders were subjected to torture and harassment by other inmates. They suffered harsh treatment and ordeals in one of the toughest prisons in Brazil, including passing naked through the infamous corridor of death. In the process, some were beaten and others died. Except for those who were involved in killing and harming fellow Japanese who had acknowledged the defeat of Japan, the majority of the Japanese detainees had not committed any crimes against people or property.

Although the league members were model prisoners for their good behavior, their imprisonment of three years caused many to suffer PTSD (post-traumatic stress disorder). This dark chapter of the post-war trauma in the Japanese Brazilian community remained sealed until 2000. Family members and close friends of the imprisoned league members remained silent on the suffering of the imprisoned for many years. Then, three artistic works brought this post-war tragedy to light: a nonfiction book titled *Dirty Hearts* published in 2000 and two documentary films, *Dirty Hearts* and *A Dark Day*, both of which premiered in 2012.[44]

Many young Japanese and the larger Brazilian community had not known of the imprisonment of Shindo Renmei league members. Some former detainees and their children revealed the suffering they had endured on Anchieta Island. In response, the Brazilian government established the National Truth Commission to investigate the incident.[45] Based on its findings, the commission recommended an official apology to the surviving members of the Anchieta imprisonment and their descendants. The governments of the United States and Canada had already made their official apology to wartime Japanese internees and had offered monetary compensation, although the amount was far from adequate. A similar official apology came from the government of Brazil twenty-five years after that of their North American counterparts.

As a result of this revelation, the Japanese community in Brazil demanded its government to redress their economic losses during and after the war. They pointed out the fact that the Brazilian Central Bank had kept records of confiscated Japanese property. The Brazilian government also closed the infamous prison on Anchieta Island in 1955. This decision came following a massive inmate riot in 1952 that claimed as many as 118 lives, including eight prison officers. The Japanese inmates were spared as they had been released four years before the prison riot. Nonetheless, the riot and its consequence testified as to the conditions of the island prison that the Japanese had to bear with for three years.

Today the only reminder of the Japanese imprisonment on the island is a sign by a ground well pipe for drinking that reads *Bica Shindo Renmei*.[46] It means Shindo Renmei spout, a reminder of the sequential tragedy in the postwar Japanese community in Brazil. It was a rather tragic comedy performed by some fanatic Japanese misguided by their blind faith in the emperor and his empire. Perhaps the remoteness of Brazil from Japan could be the root cause of the tragedy, as no one in Japan denied the outcome of the war.

REFLECTIONS

The denial of the Japanese defeat to the United States among many Japanese residents in Brazil was bizarre, to say the least. Although Japanese residents in Brazil faced some difficult wartime circumstances, the history of Japan might offer some clues about their unusual behavior. First of all, twice in the thirteenth century, the Mongol-ruled Yuan Dynasty of China under Kublai Khan attempted to invade Japan to make the island nation its vassal. In spite of the massive number of Mongolian, Chinese, and Korean soldiers on many vessels, the invading army was defeated in 1274 and 1281, respectively. Each time, Japan was protected by a typhoon (hurricane). The Japanese called these typhoons divine winds, or *kamikaze*.[47] Since that time, most Japanese believed that their island nation was under special divine protection, and this became a national belief. Second, the Japanese concept of a divine nation was related to their emperor. The Japanese viewed their emperor as a descendant of Ameratsu (Sun Goddess). Yet for almost a thousand years, the country had been ruled by shoguns who were military dictators. The emperor was a mere figurehead until the time of the Meiji Reform in 1868.

Among the many changes introduced, one reform restored the role of the emperor as the supreme ruler of the nation. Soon after, certain Shinto leaders began to emphasize the divine nature of the Japanese emperor.[48] This emphasis led to the deification of the emperor and even to emperor worship, with many Japanese calling their emperor the "Celestial Emperor." In the pre-war years, emperor-worship became mandatory in Japan's colony of Korea. This requirement promoted undivided patriotism and loyalty in the emperor's subjects. The military leaders needed a strong, charismatic and central figure to hold the people together. The deity of the emperor ended when Hirohito denied his divinity on January 1, 1946.[49] Until then, the Japanese had believed that their empire, under a divine ruler, was invincible. Japan's victory in the two wars with much larger, neighboring nations, China and Russia in 1895 and 1905, confirmed this belief.

Following the end of Pacific War, the American Occupation Administration rewrote the Japanese constitution according to its image of democracy. Among many other prohibitions, the new Japanese constitution prohibited any offensive military ventures, and the modest military establishment was only for self-defense in case of a foreign attack. The one-time aggressive militaristic nation was forced to become a pacifist nation. Its neighboring Asian nations in the Pacific region welcomed the altered passivity of Japan.

In the twenty-first century, however, the remarkable rise of China both in economic and military terms has made Japan and the United States uneasy. In the face of an imagined Chinese threat, the United States has not discouraged the rearmament of Japan. America includes Japan as a vital part of the "diamond strategy" against an expanding China. When India, Japan, Australia, and the United States (Quad) are linked, a huge diamond shape appears. The alliance against China and its neighbor Russia covers both Pacific and Indian oceans that serve as major sea lanes for global trade. At the same time, China has never forgotten its numerous humiliations by Japan during the one hundred–year period between the Opium War and the Pacific War: the Sino-Japan War (1895), the colonization of Taiwan (1895–1945), the establishment of the Empire of Manchu (1932–1945), and Japan's invasion of China during the Second Sino-Japan War (1937–1945). The massacre of Nanjing by Japanese soldiers has remained as a constant reminder of Japanese brutality.

There are signs and movements to make Japan an offensive military power by changing the constitution. Prime Minister Abe Shinzo and his supporters did not try to hide their intent to make Japan a regional military power, if not a global power. This time, Japanese citizens in a more Westernized, open, secular society are well educated and informed. Convincing them of a military build-up for offensive purposes will be challenging.

The myth of the divine islands and the divine ruler has become a mere one-time myth to the highly educated Japanese people. And the collective memory of the human tragedy wrought by the Great East Asia War (Pacific War), especially in Hiroshima and Nagasaki, is still an unfading memory in the minds of many Japanese.

NOTES

1. John Misachi, "World War II Casualties by Country," in World Facts, accessed August 24, 2020, https://www.worldatlas.com/articles/wwii-casualties-by-country.html.
2. History, "Firebombing of Tokyo," accessed June 17, 2018, https://www.history.com/this-day-in-history/firebombing-of-tokyo.
3. Robert D. McFadden, "Hiroo Onoda, Soldier who Hid in Jungle for decades, Dies at 91," *New York Times*, accessed August 27, 2020, https://www.nytimes.com/2014/01/18/word/asia/hiroo-onoda-imperial-japanese-army-officer-dies-at-91.html.
4. Mike Lanchin, "Shoichi Yokoi, the Japanese Soldier who held out in Guam," in *BBC Magazine*, accessed August 4, 2015, https://www.bbc.com/news/magazine-16681636.
5. Timenote, "Teruno Nakamura," accessed August 4, 2019, https://timenote.info/en/Teruno_Nakamura.
6. Ruth Benedict, *The Chrysanthemum and the Sword: Pattern of Japanese Culture* (Tokyo: Charles E. Turtle Co., 1954), 38.
7. Ibid., 38–39.
8. Daniel M. Masterson with Sayaka Funada-Klassen, *The Japanese in Latin America* (Chicago: University of Illinois Press, 2004), 113.
9. Kozy K. Amemiya, "Being 'Japanese' in Brazil and Okinawa," *Japan Policy Research Institute, JPRI*, Occasional Paper No. 13, May 1998, 2–3, accessed August 12, 2015, http://www.jpri.org/publications/occasionalpapers/op13.html.
10. Ibid.
11. Ibid.
12. Ibid., 6.
13. Ibid., 2.
14. Jeffrey Lesser, "In Search of the Hyphen: Nikkei and the Struggle over Brazilian National Idenity," in *New Worlds, New Lives: Globalization and People of Japanese Descent in the Americas and from Latin America in Japan*, ed. Lane Ryo Hirabayashi, Akemi Kikumura-Yano, and James A. Hirabayashi, 37–58 (Palo Alto: Stanford University Press, 2002), 46.
15. Jeffrey Lesser, *Negotiating National Identity: Immigrants, Minorities, and Struggle for Ethnicity in Brazil* (Durham: Duke University Press, 1999), 132.
16. Amemiya, "Being 'Japanese' in Brazil and Okinawa," 4.
17. Lesser, "In Search of the Hyphen," 47.
18. Amemiya, "Being 'Japanese' in Brazil and Okinawa," 3.
19. Ibid., 4.
20. History, "Battle of Midway," accessed August 29, 2020, https://www.history.com/topics/world-war-ii/battle-of-midway.
21. Katsuo Higuchi, "SHINDO RENMEI, a Dark Chapter in the History of Japanese Immigration in Brazil," *Discover Nikkei*, accessed August 30, 2020, https://www.discovernikkei.org/en/jopurnal/2018/11/7/shindo-renmei.

22. Eloisa M. Prada Queiroz Guimaraes, "The Role Played by the Shinto Remmei Trial in Japanese Immigration to Sao Paulo," in *Asiatic Migrations in Latin America*, ed. Luz M. Martinez Montiel (Mexico: El Colegio De Mexico, 1981), 117.
23. Bill Gordon, "47 Ships Sunk by Kamikaze Aircraft," accessed August 7, 2015, https://wgordon.web.wesleyan.edu/kamikaze/background/ships-sunk/index.htm.
24. BBC, "Divinity of Emperor," accessed January 31, 2018, http://www.bbc.co.uk/religion/religions/shinto/history/emperor_1.shtml.
25. Masterson, *The Japanese in Latin America*, 134–39.
26. Ibid., 137.
27. Amemiya, "Being 'Japanese' in Brazil and Okinawa," 5.
28. Ibid.
29. Kaori Shiraishi, "The Kachigumi/Makegumi Conflict in Brazil: Its Social and Psychological Influence on the Japanese Community" (BA thesis, Sophia University in Tokyo, 2015), 42.
30. History, "Battle of Attu," accessed January 27, 2020, https://www.history.com/topics/world-war-ii/battle-of-attu.
31. Amemiya, "Being 'Japanese' in Brazil and Okinawa," 5.
32. Ibid., 4.
33. Shiraishi, "The Kachigumi/Makegumi Conflict in Brazil," 42.
34. Lesser, "In Search of the Hyphen," 48.
35. The same ritual is also known as hara-kiri, which was practiced among ancient samurai warriors in Japan.
36. Katsuo Higuchi, "SHINDO RENMEI, a Dark Chapter in the History of Japanese Immigration in Brazil."
37. Ibid.
38. Lesser, "In Search of the Hyphen," 49.
39. Queiroz Guimaraes, "The Role Played by the Shinto Remmei Trial in Japanese Immigration to Sao Paulo," in *Asiatic Migrations in Latin America*. ed. Luz M. Martinez Montiel, 113–23 (Mexico: El Colegio De Mexico, 1981), 119.
40. Shiraishi, "The Kachigumi/Makegumi Conflict in Brazil," 39.
41. Black Women of Brazil, "Brazil's Truth Commission Apologizes for Persecution and Torture of Japanese Immigrants during World War II," accessed April 18, 2017, https://blackwomenofbrazil.co/2013/10/18/brazil-truth-comission.
42. Jonathan Watts, "Brazil's Japanese Community Gets Apology for Abuse," in *The Guardian*, accessed April 9, 2017, https://www.theguardian.com/world/2013/oct/11/brazil-japanese-community-apology-abuse.
43. Masayuki Fukaswa, "Prison Island Anchieta: The Site of Numerous Tragedies-'Winning or Losing Feud' Resulted in Imprisonment of 170 People," in *Discover Nikkei*, accessed April 19, 2017, http://www.discovernikkei.org/en/journal/2015/1/19/anchieta.
44. Ibid.
45. Black Women of Brazil, "Brazil's Truth Commission apologizes."
46. Fukasawa, "Prison Island Anchieta."
47. Encyclopedia Britannica, "Kamikaze of 1274 and 1284," accessed October 20, 2020, https://www.britannica.com/event/kamikaze-of-1274-and-1281.
48. BBC, "Divinity of Emperor."
49. Ibid.

Chapter Ten

Japanese War Brides Following GI Husbands

The American military occupation of post-war Japan had lasted for almost seven years. It came to an end when the San Francisco Peace Treaty was signed in September of 1951 and the occupation administration was dissolved in April of 1952. During the seven-year occupation, millions of American soldiers were stationed in Japan for varying amounts of time, ranging from a few months to a few years. Toward the end of the occupation, a major war broke out in neighboring Korea in June of 1950. It was the first hot war in the age of the cold war. As Korea was very near to Japan, thousands of American soldiers went to the Korean battlefields via Japan. Also, many American soldiers fighting in Korea spent their vacations and holidays in Japan. Even after a ceasefire in the Korean War in July 1953, Japan continued to serve as a supply base for American troops stationed in Korea. The two major wars, the Pacific War (1941–1945) and the Korean War (1950–1953), and the maintenance of sizable US military bases both in Japan and Korea, created ample opportunities for interaction between young American soldiers and Japanese civilians, especially young women.

In the immediate post–World War II years, the gap in living standard between America and war-devastated Japan was quite considerable by any measure. This gap made America soldiers attractive to many young Japanese women. Life in post-war Japan was misery itself. Nearly four years of war against the United States and her allies had destroyed the infrastructure of Japan and its ability to take care of people's basic needs. Furthermore, the spirit of many Japanese was broken. One of the initial decrees by the Supreme Commander of the Allied Forces, General Douglas MacArthur, was to prohibit Allied Forces personnel from consuming scarce Japanese food. In the first six months following the end of the war, 1,291 Japanese were reported to have died of malnutrition in Tokyo alone. In 1946, more than 250 bodies were found in the streets of the capital city in the month of April.[1] The scenes in the heavily bombed capital were apocalyptic.

On top of many problems facing Japanese nationals, thousands of returning Japanese from former colonies in Asia or occupied areas worsened food shortages. Moreover, returning Japanese soldiers from various battlefields in East Asia, Southeast Asia, and the South Pacific islands aggravated the already dire socioeconomic situation. Many of these former soldiers were wounded not only physically, but also mentally. They had witnessed horrific human tragedies in the living hell of battlefields and had lost fellow soldiers in showers of bullets and bombs. Many hiding in the trenches and caves had witnessed comrades instantly consumed by the chemical flame known as napalm used by the US Army. They had seen fellow soldiers buried in the sunken battleships at the bottom of the South Pacific. Wartime hostilities were still lingering in the hearts of both sides. The victors and the losers alike could not easily erase their hatred toward their former enemies. Both civilians and soldiers had witnessed the cruelty of military destruction on the battlefields and in massive air raids.

To avoid tense confrontation, General MacArthur ordered American personnel not to assault the Japanese people in any manner. The occupation administration was very strict on American mistreatment of the Japanese: "any soldier who so much as slapped a Japanese would get five years in prison; rapists faced the death penalty."[2] To prevent any hostile actions between the occupation soldiers and Japanese civilians, the GIs were not allowed to ride Japanese trains unless the railroad authority provided attached cars exclusively for American soldiers.

As serious as the physical damage to people and property might have been, the spirit of post-war Japan was badly shaken. The national belief in the sacrosanct emperor and the motherland had been shattered. Before the war, the Japanese had literally worshiped their demi-god emperor. Japan's military defeat defied the people's faith in the emperor and his invincible empire. Many Japanese began to question the value of patriotism and the sacrifice they had made for their country. As the foundation of national belief crumbled, traditional behavioral norms that had held the Japanese people together for so long began to lose their grip. The trauma of the war turned many Japanese into self-centered, live-for-the-moment sensualists. This change especially affected the young who in the post-war years wanted to pursue pleasure and were not overly concerned about national issues.

The visible presence of Americans opened up opportunities for Japanese to escape from their war-caused depression. American soldiers and civilians presented a somewhat different life perspective and lifestyle. Whenever the Japanese entered the realm of American life, they sensed a difference. Optimism, light-heartedness, openness, kindness, pleasure-seeking, and the like provided a stark contrast with the tendency to be formal, serious, submissive, and stoic Japanese personality. Many Japanese found the outlook and lifestyle of Americans enticing.

American soldiers stationed in Japan wanted to have a good time. With no more anxiety about the war, the relaxed, young Americans wanted to have some peacetime normalcy in their lives. Naturally, they sought the company of women. From the beginning, however, the military occupation administration prohibited soldiers from fraternizing with Japanese women. American soldiers, however, had plenty of close encounters with Japanese women who worked for the US Army as civilians. The army PX, cafeteria, administration offices, and other services depended upon the help of local Japanese. In addition, all sorts of entertainment businesses sprung up near US Army bases, targeting American soldiers. These included brothels, dance halls, theaters, and cafes, among others. Many casual interactions between American soldiers and Japanese women at these places developed into close relationships. At the same time, some fun-seeking Japanese women ventured out to have a good time with American soldiers. In spite of military restraints and cultural differences, thousands of Japanese women developed close relationships with American soldiers and married them, becoming so-called war brides.[3]

During the Second World War, both in Europe and Asia, women of many different nationalities married American soldiers and followed their husbands when the soldiers returned home. Besides Japanese women, British, German, French, Australian, Chinese, and Filipino women married American GIs. An attraction these women had for American soldiers included the fact that their mighty, powerful country was untouched by the destructive effects of war. To these women, an unscathed America meant peace and prosperity and was a direct contrast to their war-torn homes. Thus, American soldiers were more popular than their peers from other allied nations. After all, America was a large, mighty country that contributed heavily to the defeat of the Axis nations on both fronts.

JAPANESE WAR BRIDES

The war had indiscriminately flattened both rich and poor families alike, and in post-war Japan almost everyone was desperate. Some of the Japanese war brides were from well-to-do families that provided a good upbringing and quality education. The women from a higher social class tended to be more ambitious in fulfilling their personal goals by marrying Americans. They hoped their husbands would help them in achieving their life goals in the United States; however, these men often had different expectations toward their Japanese wives: "Many of the men were looking for the docile Asian women that American stereotypes had led them to expect, while many of the women were looking for men who would allow them to leave that role."[4] Different perspectives about the place of a woman in the family and society caused marital tension and conflict, which would lead to the end of many marriages later in America.

Many Japanese war brides experienced severe war-time poverty.[5] In war-devastated Japan, physical survival was a far more urgent concern among the poor. Some desperate women were forced to serve as sex workers or in entertainment jobs in order to support themselves. Often, this type of work opened up opportunities to get acquainted with American soldiers. In the families that had lost husbands or sons in the war, young daughters had to support their parents and siblings by working at or around American military bases. However, the general public mood in Japan during the 1940s and 1950s was against interracial marriage.

In the homogeneous island nation in terms of people and culture, foreigners stood out as outsiders. Moreover, many Japanese could not take the idea of their women marrying soldiers from a former enemy nation. The lingering feelings of wartime hostility toward America were still vivid. It was not uncommon for some Japanese parents to disown their daughters for even thinking of marrying American soldiers. In particular, it was very painful for returning Japanese soldiers to witness scenes of Japanese women dating those who had been their former enemies.[6] They imagined that some of the American soldiers who now embraced Japanese women could have been the ones who had bayoneted their fellow comrades in hand-to-hand combat. The smaller Japanese soldiers had often been losers in such close encounters with the taller and stronger American soldiers. Some of the Americans holding the hands of Japanese women could have been the handlers of the deadly flame-throwers that had consumed their fellow soldiers instantly. They could not muffle the screams of their burning comrades in the caves. Some of these Americans could have been crew members of the bombers that had dropped hundreds of heavy bombs on Tokyo and had destroyed their houses and instantaneously killed their parents or siblings. Some of the Americans walking on the street with Japanese women could have been sailors from US ships that had sunk their battleships.

When some former Japanese soldiers witnessed firsthand interracial dating between American soldiers and Japanese women, they felt betrayed by their own people and wept because their nation had been brought so low. A weeping former soldier told a Japanese girl dating an American soldier that: "he [had] fought his heart out for Japan, and now he was returning to find that the people [had] not [been] worth his effort."[7] Some of the returning soldiers felt compelled to run after the interracial couples to separate them, an urge that was only constrained by civilian friends.

In defeated post-war Japan, many rejected the old norms, and the authority of the old over the young was ignored. Young Japanese became cynical and skeptical about any established authority. Old-fashioned family members were more likely to be against the idea of intermarriage, yet many self-liberated, rebellious young women sought individual freedom and pleasure. Some of the women entered into interracial relationships initially for economic reasons but were willing to step into the unknown territory of loving a foreigner. One strong motivation stemmed from their curiosity about Western romances as portrayed in many Hollywood movies they had watched before.

The US military commissary, the PX, played a significant role in enticing Japanese women to American soldiers. The goods that American soldiers could obtain from the PX were eye opening. Face creams, shoes, nylon stocking, canned foods, chocolates, sweet candies, gum, toothpaste, and the like were almost things of another world in a time of such severe shortage. American consumer goods seemed to be far better, and many Japanese women were fascinated by the white men and their goods. To them, America was not only powerful but also rich, and most American soldiers seemed to be charming. The tall, fair-skinned young Americans were like the Hollywood actors they had so adored in the pre-war years. Every time they had watched Hollywood movies during peacetime, they had fantasized about the handsome, easy-going, smiling American actors. In comparison, the smaller Japanese men looked a bit stiff and serious. The women also noticed that the American treatment of women was gentle and sweet during dates. With their lady-first attitude, American soldiers made Japanese women feel special, especially with their unrestrained expressions of affection. They had seen such dreamy romantic scenes only on movie screens. Now, they were experiencing it in real life, and it seemed surreal.

In the meantime, an average Japanese woman's prospect of finding a reasonably decent Japanese man was rather grim during the post-war years. Countless young men in their prime years had died on overseas battlefields. Many who had survived the war suffered from all sorts of battlefield trauma. Due to the loss of a large number of young Japanese men, the sex ratio in the age cohort of the twenties, thirties, and forties was skewed, with a much larger percentage of females. According to a Japanese census, its population was reduced by more than one million between 1940 and 1945.[8] It is safe to assume that much of the population loss took place in the segment of the young male category. This statistic was confirmed by a 1950 population pyramid that showed the uneven distribution of both sex and age in Japan's population. This population pyramid clearly displayed a female surplus from the ages of twenty-two to forty-three.[9] Unquestionably, it was difficult for a Japanese woman in her twenties to find a suitable Japanese man for marriage. Aside from the shortage of suitable future husbands for single Japanese women, many returning Japanese soldiers had to deal with severe psychological wounds. The horrible battle scenes kept haunting them day and night. It took a long time, if ever, to recover from their nightmarish traumas. Nevertheless, many Japanese parents had a hard time allowing their daughters to marry American soldiers and follow them home to America. More than anything else, the distance between Japan and America was just too great.[10] The faraway country lay beyond a big ocean. Like all parents, the Japanese wanted their daughters to live close by for easy visitation and providing help. They wanted to have the joy of watching their grandchildren grow. To them, a marriage to an American soldier meant the end of physical contact with their daughters. In the days of international travel by ship, America appeared to be too far away and too expensive to visit let alone language and cultural unfamiliarity.

There was one exception that overcame the sense of both physical and psychological distance, however: Japanese American soldiers who served in the occupied motherland mainly as interpreters or intelligence officers. Even before the war, many second-generation Japanese Americans (*Nisei*) went to Japan for their high school education. While staying with their relatives, they learned the language and customs of Japan. They also had their eyes on potential lifelong partners before they returned to the states for a college education. They were known as *kibei*. In spite of their forced internment at relocation camps at the beginning of the war, some young Japanese Americans volunteered for military service in the US Army. Some of them were assigned to Japan during the American occupation.[11] The parents of girls dating *Nisei* American soldiers had far fewer reservations about their daughters' futures in America. Racial prejudice, either out of fear or wartime resentment toward Americans, was one of the major causes in opposing interracial dating or marriage.

AMERICAN LEGAL BARRIERS

The objection of family members and the resentment of the public toward intermarriage was difficult but not insurmountable. These were more or less emotional reactions to unfamiliar arrangements under unusual post-war circumstances. Family or public objections to intermarriage could be eventually overturned, and many initial hard feelings melted during the course of time. Most parents, if not all, changed their minds and accepted their daughters' marriages and their mixed-blood grandchildren. Far more formidable objections to American-Japanese intermarriage were waiting in the laws of the United States. Legal challenges to intermarriage existed both at the federal and state level. More than two decades before the Pacific War, the US Congress had passed the Oriental Exclusion Act of 1924. According to this act, only 105 immigrants per year from each Asian nation would be permitted to the United States for permanent residency. Unless the US Congress made a provision for the admission of hundreds of Japanese war brides, the union of American GIs and Japanese women could not be materialized in the United States.

Realizing the extent of American-Japanese intermarriage, President Truman signed the Soldier Brides Act in 1947. It read as follow: "The Alien spouse of an American citizen by marriage occurring before 30 days after the enactment of this Act [July 22, 1947], shall not be considered as inadmissible because of race, if otherwise admissible under this Act."[12] In other words, Japanese spouses would be eligible for admission into the United States. As a result, many hundreds of Japanese women could follow their American GI husbands or fiancées to America.[13] In this regard, they were treated like European war brides and their children who could enter the United States without legal restrictions. The label of ineligible alien race for naturalization was removed from Japanese women because of their marriages with American servicemen.[14] The special legal provision, however, became unnecessary when the US Congress repealed the Oriental Exclusion Act in 1952. The legal prohibition of Asian immigrants becoming naturalized US citizens also came to an end. The act, also known as the McCarran-Walter Act, opened the door for Japanese war brides. In 1952 alone, 4,220 entered the United States, and in the following year, two thousand more accompanied their men to the United States.[15] By the end of 1952, more than ten thousand Japanese women had married American soldiers. A little over two-thirds of these women, or 75 percent, married Caucasian Americans while the remainder married Japanese American or African American soldiers.[16]

Besides the barrier of federal immigration laws that existed until 1952, many states in America, including California, had laws prohibiting interracial marriage. Such laws existed until 1967 when the US Supreme Court ruled them as unconstitutional in the case of *Loving vs. Virginia*. Most Southern states, nevertheless, held onto their anti-miscegenation laws in the years following the US Supreme Court decision. This was the sociocultural atmosphere of the United States when the Japanese war brides arrived in the land of their husbands.

The United States had had wars with other nations in the Americas and Europe, but it had never declared all-out war with an Asian nation until Japan had challenged it by attacking Pearl Harbor. For this reason, the Japanese were regarded as "the most alien enemy the US had ever faced."[17] This Asian nation was quite different from other enemies that the United States had encountered in the past. For this reason, among others, the US occupation administration tried hard to discourage fraternity between American soldiers and Japanese women. Thus, any American soldier who showed interest in marrying a Japanese woman had to go through a great deal of bureaucratic red tape. First of all, unit commanders used all sorts of imaginable tactics to dissuade soldiers who had fallen in love with Japanese women. One high-ranking officer accused a soldier named Bill for "being disloyal and reprimanded him for even entertaining the thought of marrying a former enemy national and threatened that he would do everything in his power to see that Bill would be transferred out of Japan forthwith."[18]

Sometimes, unit commanders showed their concern for the long-term effects of intermarriage in America. Their advices sounded personal and genuine: "We don't want officers with yellow wives. Where would you live in America? None of our friends will want you hanging around with a yellow wife. What about your children? You can't send half-Jap boys to the [West] Point."[19] If soldiers did not yield to the pressure of their commanders, they would often be transferred to other locations in Japan. Sometimes, the non-compliant soldiers were transferred to Europe or the United States. When the Korean War started in June of 1950, some stubborn, unyielding soldiers were sent to the front lines. In such cases, most relationships would end. Death, injury, or the stresses of the battlefield left hardly any room for personal affection.

A softer approach at dissuasion was to use a military chaplain in the hopes of changing a soldier's mind. The chaplains usually offered counter opinions against the idea of intermarriage, either on religious or cultural grounds, but it seldom worked. Another tactic was to make the paperwork for marriage approval unnecessarily complicated and prolonged. Often, soldiers were assigned to different bases in the middle of applying for marriage approval. In this case, only a few, really committed soldiers overcame the many hurdles to seeing their marriage aspirations achieved. If a soldier was transferred to another country, including the United States, often that was the end of their relationship.

Yet another tactic to make the official approval of interracial marriage more difficult was to require soldiers to prove their ability to provide support for their future wives "in the event [they] should [die]."[20] It was indeed cruel to demand a transferring soldier to come up with support plans for his future spouse in the event of his death. As a result of the many intentional bureaucratic hurdles and requirements, "military [personnel] waited an average of 5.6 months to obtain approval for marriage: civilians obtained permission in an average of one week."[21] This wait would become far more challenging, often almost impossible, if GIs were transferred to other regions in Japan or to another country.

In the course of time, the early, stern attitude of the military leadership toward intermarriage softened somewhat. The US government was willing to accommodate the needs of its soldiers by changing the rules and regulations. By 1965, about fifty thousand American soldiers had brought their Japanese wives home to America. This was about 3 percent of approximately two million US servicemen who had served in Japan for varying amounts of time over the twenty-year period from 1945 to 1965.[22]

Once a couple had obtained approval for their marriage, the preparation for a new life in America began for the Japanese bride. Because of the cultural differences between Japan and the United States, many Japanese cities with a sizable US military base ran what they called War Bride Schools. Local Japanese YMCAs (Young Men Christian Association) or YWCAs (Young Women Christian Association) were common sponsors running these schools, where Japanese women learned basic everyday English, American etiquette, bed making, cooking, house cleaning, and so forth. Throughout Japan, there were more than 150 war bride schools that helped to prepare the future wives of American soldiers.

The Japanese women at these preparation schools, for instance, were advised to avoid excessive bowing when meeting their husband's family members and friends. Since Japanese women had no idea about American currency, they learned that a cent is a copper coin called a penny. On some minute details such as whipping cream, they were instructed to use a beater instead of chopsticks.[23] The Japanese war brides also learned that there were different styles of Western dancing other than jitterbugging in America. Some customs were far more complicated and confusing: "Salad is served before the meat course on the West Coast, with it in the Middle West, and afterward in the East."[24] At the same time, these war brides learned that they should expect some animosity in America. Racial discrimination and segregation of public facilities along color lines was a fact of life in many parts of America.

THOSE WHO LEFT AND THOSE WHO REMAINED

American GIs began to bring their Japanese war brides home in 1947. In the first year, nineteen Japanese women followed their American husbands to the United States. The real surge occurred in 1952, when 4,220 Japanese women made the journey. After that, no less than two thousand Japanese war brides went to America every year until 1965. The peak years came in 1957 and 1958, when 5,003 and 5,027 Japanese women established homes with their American husbands. Over a twenty-year period, between 1947 and 1965, a total of 48,912 Japanese war brides left their native land for their husbands' country.[25]

On the other hand, there was a dark side of the Japanese war bride story. Far more Japanese women were forgotten or abandoned in the shadow of the war bride drama. According to one estimate, twice as many as those who went to America were left in Japan by their American lovers or husbands: "Possibly as many as 100,000 'Madam Butterflies' were left behind like the ill-fated Cio-Cio San in Puccini's opera."[26] Broken promises and broken marriages left bitter memories for many unfortunate Japanese, and their mixed-blood children abandoned by American fathers constituted another group of victims in the post-war Japan. In a land of homogeneity, the children of intermarriages were discriminated against and marginalized. They became perpetual foreigners (*ganji*) in their own native land. They were constant reminders of a bitter war lost and a foreign occupation for the first time in the long history of the island nation.

In occupied Japan, some American soldiers entered into marital relations without serious thought and commitment. Often, their marriages were short-term, temporary unions based upon pleasure and convenience. Far away from home, loneliness in a foreign country pushed some soldiers to look for companions. Their love was a spontaneous impulse without much consideration for the long-term consequences of such actions. When they left Japan on a transfer or discharge, many lost their initial passion and drive to continue their relationship. It would take extraordinary effort for soldiers outside Japan to continue pursuing their relationships with Japanese fiancés or wives.

In some unfortunate cases, soldiers were taken to the Korean front line where they died or were wounded. The US military authority was not so willing to help Japanese wives who were separated from transferred husbands. If their husbands died on Korean battlefields, the wives would lose every right as a spouse of a US soldier killed in action: "If a soldier who married prior to being sent to Korea got killed in action, the petition he filed to allow his wife to enter the U.S. was revoked."[27] Japanese wives of American soldiers were not a high priority group in the event of such unexpected misfortune. From the beginning, the military authority was adamant, then eventually reluctant, about American soldiers' engaging in romantic relationships with Japanese women.

DOUBLE REJECTION

Like many transplanted foreigners to the United States, Japanese war brides faced many challenges. In spite of their preparation at war bride schools in Japan, the adjustment to a new home in America was far more challenging than they had anticipated. Communication difficulties, cultural unfamiliarity, rejection, and loneliness were the most common problems facing these war brides. On top of that, former American soldiers seemed to have a different perspective and attitude to their wives once in America. Their views of Japanese women changed as they compared their wives with American women. In Japan, they had only seen Japanese women. Consequently, language problems and cultural differences had not mattered much. Often, hand gestures and facial expression were the only means of communication, yet they had felt affection toward each other. For instance, one GI named Frank proposed nonverbally: "They dated, although she spoke no English and he didn't understand Japanese. Frank proposed in January 1946 by pointing to Sachiko's heart and then to his own."[28]

In America, the same Japanese women looked quite different. In Japan, American soldiers had compared their lovers or wives with other Japanese women. However, in America, they could not help but compare their wives with American women. Aside from language and cultural clumsiness, most Japanese women looked much shorter and smaller. The taller, fair-skinned, and culturally relaxed American women offered the returning soldiers a different feeling and ambience. Unless they had deep affection and strong commitment for their Japanese wives, it was not easy to bear the social stigma of having a foreigner as a wife.

Their married lives began in the very racially conscious America of the 1950s and 1960s. Both inside and outside their homes, there were numerous points of pressure and tension. In fact, many commanders and chaplains in Japan warned the soldiers that they might change their minds once they returned to America: "You think you want to marry her now, but that's because there are no round-eyed chicks around."[29] The ease of communication and physical attraction of American women was the cause of much trouble for Japanese-American couples. By then, many former soldiers suddenly realized the almost irreconcilable incompatibility with their Japanese wives.

At the same time, many Japanese wives saw different aspects of their husbands as civilians. Often discharged soldiers could not find jobs, and they had a hard time supporting their families. These now unemployed men sometimes acquired bad habits such as excessive drinking, neglect, and spousal abuse. Moreover, not many American parents were ready to welcome Japanese daughters-in-law. Post-war America was still in the thick of racial prejudice and discrimination, especially in the South. Members of minorities, either black or brown, were considered second-class members of American society. Many whites engaged in open or covert racial discrimination toward non-whites.

In addition, the Japanese-provoked Pacific War still lingered in the minds of many Americans. Even some close family members of American soldiers were uneasy about the presence of a person from their former enemy nation in their midst. This sentiment was only magnified outside the family. Often Japanese war brides had to face unpleasant situations by themselves as they had no one to turn to for support.

Even some Japanese Americans had negative views of war brides from Japan. The longtime Japanese residents were often cold and indifferent, if not hostile, toward these war brides. They were fed negative stereotypes of these women by newspapers and magazines originally published in Japan. The print media in Japan portrayed most Japanese wives of American soldiers as morally loose women. The image that tended to be associated with war brides was of prostitutes serving foreign soldiers. While some were, the majority were not. In fact, the occupation authority made it impossible for Japanese prostitutes to marry American soldiers through a strict certificate system: "A woman registered as a prostitute forfeited any possibility of ever marrying a GI, for her record eliminated her as a candidate for marriage."[30]

Some Japanese Americans had developed racist feelings toward African Americans. Being minorities in a white dominant society, both groups were in the same boat, yet Japanese residents had a hard time relating to the war brides of African American soldiers. The cold stares from fellow Japanese made newly arrived war brides feel awful. Thus, many Japanese war brides faced double resentment from the general American public and from their own community. Rejection by the Japanese American community, however, was far more painful and bitter as the war brides had expected some understanding and moral support.

TRIPLE REJECTION

According to one estimate, about 10 percent of intermarriages between American soldiers and Japanese women involved African American soldiers.[31] If that is true, approximately five thousand Japanese women married black GIs. To most people in Japan, Japanese-African American intermarriage was far less acceptable than Japanese-Caucasian marriage. For instance, a Japanese father expressed his profound shame when his daughter told him that she wanted to marry a black soldier: "You, a member of a respectable family, wish to marry a man of such blackness! How shall we apologize to our ancestors?"[32] Many Japanese saw blacks for the first time when US troops landed on their islands at the end of the Pacific War in August 1945.

The history of blacks in Japan, however, went back to the time of the early European arrivals in the second half of the sixteenth century, about four hundred years before the Pacific War. Portuguese merchants brought black slaves when they came to Japan during trade visits. Only a limited number of Japanese merchants in the trade harbors ever saw any blacks, because foreigners were confined to foreign guest houses. When Japan closed its doors to the outside world for almost 250 years during the Tokugawa period, only a small number of Dutch merchants were permitted to trade with Japan through the southern harbor city of Nagasaki. Thus, the sight of African Americans following the war was completely foreign to most Japanese.

The Japanese resentment toward African American GIs reflected a double negative: first, they were soldiers of a former enemy nation, and second, they were racially inferior. In general, the Japanese viewed themselves as white not only in socioeconomic terms but also in a biological sense. Even among Asians, they wanted to be differentiated from Chinese and Korean, let alone the swarthy Southeast Asians of the tropical regions. Such an attitude of superiority might have derived from the pace and extent of their industrialization (or Westernization) after the Meiji Reform: "[T]he Japanese never thought of themselves as yellow, and in fact considered themselves white."[33] Furthermore, the color white symbolized purity to the clean-conscious Japanese.[34] The color black, on the other hand, symbolized darkness and impurity.

Following the Pacific War, most Japanese admitted and accepted the superiority of America, particularly in military technology, and they were willing to play the role of the defeated. However, they had difficulty in associating black soldiers with a superior America. They were not comfortable submitting themselves to the authority of African American GIs. A few encounters between African American soldiers and the Japanese showed the depth of racial prejudice in post-war Japan. When an African American person entered a public bath, many Japanese ran away. They thought that his black skin would dirty the water like charcoal. Also, some Japanese barber shops and hair salons refused to serve black people for the reason of their skin color and curly hair. Their avoidance of African Americans was more than an unfamiliarity with their hair. Simply, they felt uneasy serving people of color.

In particular, the children of mixed marriages between Japanese mothers and African American fathers were worse off than any other group. They were the least wanted and most shunned people in post-war Japan. As a result, many half-black children did not get proper care from adults. According to one report, only half of Japanese African American babies reached the age of five in Japan.[35] Such a high mortality rate was mainly due to neglect and abandonment by their mothers. Inadequate nutrition and lack of proper medical attention, among other conditions, could have contributed to the high rate of premature death among these least wanted babies in Japan.

Not knowing what to do with half-African American youth, there was an attempt to send them to Brazil, a multiracial South American country where blacks of different mixes comprised almost half of the national population. Another plus for this plan was that Brazil had the largest overseas Japanese community, approaching almost two million during the 1950s and 1960s. A dozen African American Japanese youth were sent to Brazil, but the Brazilian government soon stopped this attempted relocation.[36] In order to survive in the hostile environment of their birth nation, some youth formed gangs and engaged in criminal activity. Their bitterness at being outcast members of Japanese society led to anti-social behavior.

BLACK-JAPANESE COUPLES IN A RACIST AMERICA

The Japanese wives of African American soldiers discovered that Americans were not so different from their countrymen in their attitude toward blacks. In the 1950s and 1960s, racial discrimination was widespread in the United States. In Japan, racial prejudice and discrimination was a matter of personal feeling and action. However, in some parts of America, racial discrimination was institutionalized in officially imposed rules and regulations. Most states in the South enforced Jim Crow laws by coercing racial segregation in public areas. Even many open-minded whites were forced to discriminate against African Americans, regardless of their personal convictions and attitudes toward race. As law-abiding citizens, they had no choice but to comply with the segregation laws of the day. Only a courageous few defied the laws at the risk of fines or imprisonment. This systemic racial discrimination hit hard the Japanese wives of African American GIs. It was beyond their wildest imagination.

A Japanese wife in Seattle followed her African American husband who had moved to a southern state a few months earlier. Without knowing the state's strict racial segregation practices, she checked into a hotel for whites only. She was shocked when her African American husband could not visit her at the hotel, so she had to move to another hotel to stay with him. In a similar situation, another African American husband had to sleep in his car in order to not disturb his wife. In some hotels, a mixed couple could check in together, but they were assigned separate rooms in different parts of the same hotel.

In many Southern cities, Japanese wives did not know where to sit in segregated buses. The public buses were divided into two, the front section for white passengers and the back section for blacks. Not knowing where they belonged, some Japanese wives sat in the middle section of these segregated buses. Since their African American husbands had not told them the shameful enforcement of racial segregation in America, most Japanese wives were shocked and disturbed. Moreover, some war brides took these painful experiences as a foreboding of their fate in America. When puzzled Japanese wives asked about the strange practices of racial segregation, their husbands told them that the whites had always treated them like that. What bewildered these wives were their husbands' attitudes in accepting racial segregation as a fact of life. For this reason, many came to respect the courage of Rosa Parks, a seamstress from Montgomery, Alabama, when she refused to concede her seat in the front section for a white passenger. This simple act helped trigger the American Civil Rights Movement led by the Reverend Martin Luther King, Jr., a Baptist minister from the same city.

When it came to mixed children, the situation was far more hurtful and unbearable to many Japanese mothers. For instance, in a movie theater, the wife of a former African American GI and her children sat in the balcony while the black father had to find a seat in a section of the theater exclusively for colored people. In Maryland, a Japanese mother with her dark-skinned children went to a general store, where a man inside swore at her. The mother did not quite understand what he was saying although a lady in the store told her in very deliberate language: "The man never serves niggers." When the Japanese woman tried to tell the lady that her children were not negro, she did not bother listening.[37] Of course, the Japanese mother did not know anything about the one-drop rule observed in many states. If a person contained even a single drop of black blood, that person would be legally considered black. Her children were half-black, and the store clerk made it very clear that he would not serve them.

What really angered and saddened many Japanese war brides with African American husbands was the attitude of fellow war brides who had married white GIs. Even Japanese war bride communities mirrored the race relations of the larger American society. They were split along the color line of their husbands. A Japanese woman who had married an African American soldier noticed the following: "It seems that Japanese girls who married white soldiers get very high hat when they come to America and drew a color line on us and our husbands."[38] They did not want to mingle with their compatriots who had married African Americans. As a result, the Japanese wives of former African American soldiers were the loneliest group in the entire Japanese American community. They had no support group other than women in a similar situation, a group which was much smaller than those of white-Japanese couples.

Another source of resentment toward the Japanese wives of African American soldiers were black women in America. Rather than maintaining a cold distance, many African American women were overtly hostile to Japanese war brides. In their eyes, the Japanese women had snatched potential husbands. Even in Japan, female military or civilian African American workers were angry at black GIs who passed them over to date Japanese women. The chances were much better for African American men to marry non-black women, including whites, rather than the other way around.[39] A common intermarriage in America at the time was between white women and black men. This tendency considerably reduced the pool of black bachelors as far as black, single women were concerned. The sex imbalance in the African American community, especially in the cohort of those in their prime marriageable years, was more prominent than in other racial communities. Other factors that adversely affected the availability of young black men eligible for marriage to young black women were high rates of homicide, incarceration, and military service.

Often Japanese women noticed that black women at their work were nice to them until they found out that they were married to black men. From that moment, the black women changed noticeably in words and deeds toward their Japanese coworkers.[40] The resentment and hostility of some black women was quite unbearable to many of the Japanese war brides. They had experienced racial discrimination with their black husbands in mainstream society, and it was far more painful to realize that some in their husbands' community did not accept them, even rejected them. This triple rejection left many Japanese war brides with no group to turn to for emotional support. The only source of encouragement and support for Japanese wives were their black husbands and other Japanese women in similar situations.

Even strong emotional bonds between a wife and a husband were often not enough without a stable economic condition. Not many former black soldiers met the two conditions for a happy marriage. A considerable proportion of discharged former soldiers had a hard time finding jobs that would provide a steady income and fringe benefits. Often, economic instability led to mental strains in many marriages. According to one report: "Two thirds separated or divorced within three years of arrival."[41] Japanese war brides had followed their GI husbands with their own American dreams. However, the reality of life in the land of dreams was far more challenging than they had anticipated. Many Japanese war brides had their American dreams shattered, and they did not have any options available in the land of opportunity.

HALF-BLACK JAPANESE CHILDREN IN AMERICA

Disappointed by being neglected or abandoned, many Japanese wives of African American soldiers often found comfort and hope in their children. Although some of the children were born in Japan and had grown up there, they could not be Japanese citizens as their fathers were American citizens. That was the Japanese law. Viewed as unmistakably foreign, they became "unwelcome aliens in the land of their birth"[42] and they encountered many unpleasant experiences in Japan. Some of these children experienced rejection from their own mothers, other family members, and relatives. Either because of the difference in their physical appearance or their non-citizen legal status, they viewed themselves as marginalized outsiders. They were often treated as if they should not have been born in the first place. The situation turned worse when their fathers returned to America and they were left without any support. In this case, struggling alone was a real possibility. When half-black children left Japan for America following their fathers, they thought that they would be accepted in their father's country. Unlike the homogeneous society of Japan, they anticipated that multiracial America would be far more open and tolerant to different people. Furthermore, blacks were the largest racial minority group, comprising more than 10 percent of the US population in the 1950s and 1960s. Instead, they came across many unpleasant situations from all sides. To many half-black children, this was more than just culture shock.

Some Japanese Americans, for example, did not accept half-black Japanese as authentic Japanese. In fact, the Japanese-born half blacks were far more Japanese, as they spoke the language fluently and were well versed in Japanese culture. Nevertheless, to Japanese Americans, the black Japanese were not sufficiently Japanese. Their dark skin seemed to overshadow everything they had internalized and acquired by being born in Japan. They were regarded as Africans, not Japanese. At the same time, some American blacks did not consider the half blacks from Japan as authentic blacks either. They did not look sufficiently black enough because of some of their Asiatic physical traits. The half-Japanese blacks did not quite fit in with the American black physique and psyche.

On the other hand, the larger white community regarded them as black and treated them accordingly. In some communities in parts of California, half-black youth from Japan had confrontations with different youth groups. In the morning, they fought with youth who called them "Japs" and, in the afternoon, with those who called them "niggers." Yet they felt neither Japanese nor black. They felt as if they stood in the middle of nowhere as far as their identity was concerned. Most Japanese mothers tried to instill a Japanese identity in their children by teaching them the Japanese language and customs. The influence of Japanese mothers was more evident upon their children in the families where fathers were often absent and contributed less.

Half-black Japanese girls faced a similar situation in America. When one girl decided to run for the black homecoming queen in her high school, other black girls strongly objected to the idea. They argued that she was not black enough to be a black queen. When the half-black Japanese girl did not listen, the other girls threatened her with physical violence. The brave girl did not yield to their threats and was selected homecoming queen.[43] Like any biracial children, half-black Japanese children in America went through a great deal of soul searching to forge an identity. If they tried to identify with both parents, they would "encounter torn loyalties. Unable to identify with both, however, a resentment [was] created toward one or both parents."[44] Some studies have shown that "black offspring showed a closer resemblance to the Japanese parents than to the father."[45]

Perhaps the tendency to identify with the country of their mothers might have something to do with the following factors. First of all, the black community in America was often presented to them as a community of hardship and trouble because of its many socioeconomic disadvantages. By and large, this structural problem originated from the time of slavery. In their own life experiences, either within the black community or outside of it, they felt marginalized, and news media reports and personal observations often confirmed these perceptions. Second, mothers usually raised children in the instance of separation or divorce, and black-Japanese couples were no exception. In fact, the probability of children being raised by mothers was much greater because of the high incidence of abandonment by black fathers. Since most Japanese mothers were not fully assimilated into mainstream American society due to a lack of English ability and cultural differences, they remained Japanese in their identity and life practices. This tendency had trickle-down effects on their children. Consequently, half-black Japanese children tended to identify with the country and culture of their mothers. Finally, Japan became a source of pride to these ostracized children for its economic and technological achievements. The international status of Japan as an advanced nation on par with other Western nations provided a sense of pride to its people. For instance, Japan has been the only non-Western member nation in the group of seven advanced nations (G7).

Some half-black Japanese children wanted to return to Japan where they felt at home with the language and culture. In Japan, they could deal with one mainstream community, whereas in America they had to interact with three distinctive ethnic communities: the Japanese American community, the black community, and the larger white community. Often the three groups were at odds with each other. And the post-war booming Japanese economy did offer better opportunities.

Like many other marriages, some Japanese war brides were happily married and realized their American dreams. However, far more couples struggled, and their marriages ended in divorce. From the beginning, Japanese women and American GIs had many obstacles to overcome. More than anything else, communication problems and a cultural gap were quite formidable, so only strong commitment and patient understanding were able to hold these interracial couples together. The combination of a Japanese woman's desire for survival in war-devastated Japan and an American soldier's loneliness in a foreign country could take their marriages only so far.

Their many incompatibilities became more prominent when they moved to America. Some couples overcame the myriad challenges they faced while many others broke apart. The prevalent racial prejudices both in Japan and America posed serious problems to these interracial couples. The tragedy of the Pacific War had brought these people together in an occupied land; many ended in personal tragedy in the dreamland of America.

REFLECTIONS

Approximately fifty thousand Japanese war brides were part of a much larger contingent of World War II American war brides. The total number of World War II war brides is estimated to have been around one million from over sixty nations around the world.[46] The majority of them came from Europe, especially Great Britain, Germany, and France. Other than personal attraction, the main consideration of these foreign women marrying American soldiers was the same: the peace and prosperity to be found in the United States.

The first US census taken after World War II indicated 141,768 people of Japanese ancestry in 1950. A decade later, the US census showed more than a threefold increase, with a total of 464,332. Aside from the post-war baby boom in America, the coming of Japanese war brides and their children, either born in Japan or America, may have partially contributed to this remarkable growth. As of the 2010 census, about 1.3 million people identified themselves as residents or citizens of Japanese ancestry.

Since the end of the Pacific War, the United States has maintained about fifty thousand American troops in Japan. In addition, another fifty thousand American civilians reside in the country. They include the family members of military personnel and civilian workers. Today, many young Japanese women of the third largest economy in the world are not attracted to the idea of living in America with American husbands. The rush of Japanese war brides was a one-time phenomenon in a war-devastated Japan where many women wanted to increase their social standing through marriage. Contemporary Japanese women regard the levels of education and occupation as important considerations for marriage. Many American soldiers in Japan today may not meet the high expectations of Japanese women. Moreover, the majority of Japanese are content with their country which has become peaceful and prosperous, although it is a known secret that some curious Japanese women entertain American soldiers at their own expense.

Not long after the rush of Japanese war brides to America, two more waves of Asian war brides arrived upon the western shores of the United States: Korean and Vietnamese (or Indochinese) war brides. In the midst of Japanese women following their American GI husbands, Korean women also began to move to the United States as war brides. According to one estimate, ninety thousand to one hundred thousand Korean women followed their American GI husbands between 1950 and 1989.[47] The intensive, three-year Korean War (1950–1953) and the maintenance of about thirty thousand US troops on the peninsula for more than sixty years have brought many US troops to Korea. As a result, there are twice as many Korean war brides as Japanese. For Korean women, America was far more enticing as their country was struggling for economic development and political security. Until the 1980s, America was a land of dreams.

America's ten-year (1965–1975) war in Vietnam also resulted in bringing around 8,500 Vietnamese war brides.[48] America's involvement in three major wars in Asia between 1942 and 1975 created hundreds of thousands of cross-cultural families and biracial Americans. In addition, the US military had a presence in China and the Philippines. Hundreds of Chinese and Filipino women married and followed their GI husbands home in the 1940s. These Asian women impacted not only America's demographic composition but also its culture. The legacy of Asian war brides will continue to be felt for many generations to come.

The last US census in 2010 revealed that people of Asian ancestry comprised about 5 percent of the country's total population and 13 percent in California. In the same census, the state of Hawaii was shown as having about 40 percent of the island residents with Asian ancestry. The Asian American population may continue to grow in numbers and influence in the United States. The tragedies of America's foreign wars in Asia have had many strokes in affecting the lives of millions of people on both sides of the Pacific Ocean.

NOTES

1. Elfrieda Berthiaume Shukert and Barbara Smith Scibetta, *War Brides of World War II.* (Novato, CA: Presidio Press, 1988), 187.
2. Ibid., 186.
3. Miki Ward Crawford, Katie Kaori Hayashi, and Shizuko Suenaga, *Japanese War Brides in America: An Oral History* (Santa Barbara: Praeger, 2010), xix.
4. Paul R. Spickard, *Mixed Blood: Intermarriage and Ethnic Identity in Twentieth-Century America* (Madison: The University of Wisconsin Press, 1989), 131.
5. In post-war Japan, food had to be rationed and starvation was widespread. See Chico Herbison and Jerry Schultz, "Quiet Passage: The Japanese-American War Bride Experience" (paper) (Lawrence: The Center for East Asian Studies at the University of Kansas, 1990), 3.
6. Michael Charles Thornton, "A Social History of a Multiethnic Identity: The Case of Black Japanese Americans," Ph.D. diss. (Lawrence: The University of Michigan, 1983), 89.
7. Ibid.
8. *The Japan Times,* "Numbers Tell Tale of Japan's Postwar Rise and Fall," accessed February 4, 2020, https://www.japantimes.co.jp/news/2015/01/05/national/numbers-tell-tale-japans-postwar-rise-fall/#.Xjnt4C2ZPUY.
9. Ibid.
10. *The Washington Post,* "The Untold Stories of Japanese War Brides," accessed September 23, 2016, https://www.washintonpost.com/sf/national/2016/09/22/from-hiroko-to-susie-the-untold-stories-of-japanese-war-brides/.
11. Military Intelligence Service Research Center, "Japanese American Military Intelligence Servicemen and the War in the Pacific," accessed October 20, 2020, https://www.niahs.org/misnorcal/essay.htm.
12. Shukert and Scibetta, *War Brides of World War II,* 209.
13. Ibid.
14. Thornton, "A Social History of a Multiethnic Identity," 47–48.
15. Shukert and Scibetta, *War Brides of World War II,* 216.
16. Ibid., 217.
17. Thornton, "A Social History of a Multiethnic Identity," 52.
18. Shukert and Scibetta, *War Brides of World War II,* 211–12.
19. Ibid., 206.
20. Thornton, "A Social History of a Multiethnic Identity," 93.
21. Ibid.
22. Ibid., 57.
23. Shukert and Scibetta, *War Brides of World War II,* 216.
24. Ibid.

25. Crawford et. al, *Japanese War Brides in America,* 15.
26. Shukert and Scibetta, *War Brides of World War II,* 208.
27. Ibid., 215.
28. Ibid., 205.
29. Spickard, *Mixed Blood,* 134.
30. Shukert and Scibetta, *War Brides of World War II,* 190.
31. Thornton, "A Social History of a Multiethnic Identity," 56.
32. Spickard, *Mixed Blood,* 136.
33. Thornton, "A Social History of a Multiethnic Identity," 27.
34. Ibid., 28.
35. Era Bell Thompson, "Japan's Rejected," *Ebony* (September 1967): 42–54.
36. Ibid.
37. Thornton, "A Social History of a Multiethnic Identity," 98.
38. Ibid., 97.
39. The US Census reports that 390,000 black men had white wives while 168,000 black women had white husbands in 2010. The former comprised 8.6 percent among married black men and the latter 0.3 percent among married black women.
40. Thornton, "A Social History of a Multiethnic Identity," 98.
41. Ibid., 54.
42. Ibid., 34.
43. Ibid., 125.
44. Ibid., 107.
45. Ibid., 122.
46. Shukert and Scibetta, *War Brides of World War II,* 265.
47. Association for Diplomatic Studies and Training, "Visa Fraud and GI Brides Before South Korea's Economic Boom," accessed October 20, 2020. https://adst.org/2014/07/korea-visa-fraud-and-gi-brides/.
48. Linda Trinh Vo and Marian Sciachitano, *Asian American Women: The Frontiers Reader* (Lincoln: University of Nebraska Press, 2004), 144. The US troops withdrew from Vietnam immediately when the US government had decided to end the war. In contrast, the US government has maintained around thirty thousand American soldiers in Korea since 1950.

Conclusion

In the age of gunboat diplomacy and the subsequent signing of unequal treaties imposed by the West, China, Japan, and Korea had no choice but to comply with the West's demands. These Asian nations could not hold to their closed-door policies in the face of superior Western military power in the nineteenth century. The phenomenon of Western dominance and Eastern submission continued for about one hundred years. Chinese, Japanese, and Korean immigration to the Americas before World War II as well as the mistreatment these immigrants suffered in their new resident countries were the symptoms of the asymmetrical relations between the imperial Western powers and the weak East Asian nations. Japan attempted to challenge Western dominance, but it resulted in personal tragedies for millions of Japanese at home and abroad during and after the Pacific War.

Although forced, once the latter opened up and realized the value of some Western systems, especially science and technology, they were able to catch up to the West mainly through their promotion of education at all levels. In the twenty-first century, often characterized as the Asian Century or the Pacific Century, socioeconomic and cultural gaps between the two spheres have narrowed considerably. In many respects, East Asian nations are almost at par with the West, and in a few areas, they are ahead. As a result, immigration to the Americas among Japanese and Koreans has been dwindling. Even Chinese may soon lose their enthusiasm for moving to the Americas as their standard of living has been rapidly improving.

In the last five hundred years, the center of global power has been shifting from one empire to another: Spain, Great Britain, and the United States in that chronological order. Many have predicted that the international power center will move to China in the twenty-first century, thus making a full circle as far as the one-time Middle Kingdom is concerned. To this shifting reality, America has reacted by pivoting from Europe to Pacific Asia in its military and economic concentration. The United States has formed the India-Pacific Alliance with India, Australia, and Japan against China's emergent economic and military power. China, once the most humiliated East Asian nation and often derided as a paper tiger in the West, has become not only a rival of the United States in the economic realm but also a serious military threat. China's twenty-first-century silk road project, One Belt, One Road, attempts to push it to the world's center stage. It remains to be seen whether China's ambition to become a dominant global force will come true. Nonetheless, at least the nature of relations between the East and the West in this globalized world will become more symmetrical.

Since the mid-nineteenth century, East Asian countries have transformed themselves through Westernization. Now, some developing countries, particularly in the global south, have turned to East Asia for their future development model. In retrospect, the Asian tragedy in the Americas was a part of a growing pain in the process of transforming China, Japan, and Korea. In a time where knowledge- and information-based economies thrive, these countries are poised to have a bright future. The Asian tragic stories of the past retold in this book may not repeat in the future.

Bibliography

Amemiya, Kozy K. "Being 'Japanese' in Brazil and Okinawa." *Japan Policy Research Institute, JPRI* Occasional Paper No. 13, May 1998. Accessed August 12, 2015. http://www.jpri.org/publications/occasionalpapers/op13.html.

Ancient History Encyclopedia. "Thomas Cavendish." Accessed April 2, 2020. https://www.ancient.eu/Thomas Cavendish/.

Anderson, Wanni W. and Robert G. Lee, ed. *Displacement and Diasporas: Asians in the Americas*. New Brunswick, NJ: Rutgurs University Press, 2005.

Angel Island Association. "About Angel Island." Accessed March 19, 2015. http://www.english.illinois.edu/maps/poets/a_f/angel/about.htm.

BBC. "Divinity of Emperor." Accessed January 31, 2018. http://www.bbc.co.uk/religion/religions/shinto/history/emperor_1.shtml.

Benedict, Ruth. *The Chrysanthemum and the Sword: Pattern of Japanese Culture*. Tokyo: Chrales E. Turtle Co., 1954.

Black Women of Brazil. "Brazil's Truth Commission Apologizes for Persecution and Torture of Japanese Immigrants during World War II." Accessed April 18, 2017. https://blackwomenofbrazil.co/2013/10/18/brazils-truth-commission-ap.

Charisma. "Sinchae Balbu Suji Bumo" [The Body, Hair, and Skin, All Have been Received from the Parents]. Accessed September 17, 2020. http://blog.naver.com/PostView.nhn?blogld=honesh&logNo=150141486360.

Chin, Tung Pok with Winifred G. Chin. *Paper Son: One Man's Story*. Philadelphia: Temple University Press, 2000.

China Daily. "Chinese Tourists Spend $130 Bln Overseas in 2018: Report." Accessed October 2, 2020. https://www.chinadaily.com.cn/a/201908/05/WS5d479988a310cf3e35563e6d.html.

Christopher, Emma, Cassandra Pybus, and Marcus Rediker, eds. *Many Middle Passages: Forced Migration and the Making of the Modern World*. Berkeley: University of California Press, 2007.

Churchill, Winston. *Quotefancy*. Accessed June 24, 2017. https://quotefancy.com/quote/939816/Winston-Churchill.

CIA. Country Comparison: Death Rate. *The World Factbook*. Accessed August 6, 2020. https://www.cia.gov/library/publications/the-world-factbook/rankorder/2066rank.html.

———. Country Comparison: Infant Mortality Rate. *The World Factbook*. Accessed August 6, 2020. https://www.cia.gov/library/publications/the-world-factbook/rankorder/2091rank.html.

Clyde, Paul H. and Burton F. Beers. *The Far East: A History of Western Impacts and Eastern Response, 1830–1975* (6th ed.). Englewood Cliffs: Prentice Hall, 1975.

Crawford, Miki Ward, Katie Kaori Hayashi, and Shizuko Suenaga. *Japanese War Brides in America: An Oral History.* Santa Barbara: Praeger, 2010.

Cushman, Gregory T. *Guano and the Opening of the Pacific World: A Global Ecological History.* Cambridge: Cambridge University Press, 2013.

De Azua, Mario Federico Real. "Chinese Coolies in Peru: The Chincha Islands." In *Asiatic Migrations in Latin America,* edited by Luz M. Martinez Montiel, 37–52. Mexico: El Colegio De Mexico, 1981.

Densho Encylopedia. "The Gripsholm WWII Exchanges." Accessed September 15, 2016. http://encyclopedia.densho.org/The%20Gripsholm%20wwwII%20Exchanges/.

Dongailbo, "Agricultural Immigration to Hawaii in the Last Years of Korean Empire." dongA.com February 24, 1998. Accessed July 28, 2015. http://news.donga.com/View?id=7324743&date=19980224.

DW. "Chinese Investors Chase 'Golden Visas' to the US." Accessed August 5, 2018. https://www.dw.com/en/chinese-investors-chase-golden-visas-to-the-us/a-38816291.

Encyclopedia.com. "Denis Kearney." Accessed December 17, 2019. https://www.encyclopedia.com/people/history/us-history-biographies/denis-kearney.

Enriquez, Nestor Palugod. "Manila Galleon Trade 1573–1811." Accessed December 10, 2014. http://www.philippines.tripod.com/galleon.html.

Fallon and Jacobs. "Chronology—Suspicion, Arrest, and Internment." Accessed April 14, 2016. https://www.foitimes.com/internment/chrono.html.

Foner, Eric and John A. Garraty. "The Gentlemen's Agreement." *HISTORY.* Accessed August 25, 2020. https://www.history.com/immigration/gentlemens-agreement.

Fong, Eric and William T. Markham. "Anti-Chinese Political Movement in California in the 1870s: An Intercounty Analysis." *Sociological Perspectives* 45, no. 2 (2002): 183–210.

Fraginals, Manuel Moreno. "Extent and Significance of Chinese Immigration to Cuba." In *Asiatic Migrations in Latin America,* edited by Luz M. Martinez Montiel, 53–58. Mexico: El Colegio De Mexico, 1981.

Frankopan, Peter. *The Silk Road: A New History of the World.* New York: Vantage Books, 2015.

Frodsham, J. D. *The First Chinese Embassy to the West: The Journal of Kuo Sung-Tao, Liu His-Hung, and Chang Te-Yi.* Oxford: Claredon Press, 1974.

Fukasawa, Masayuki. "Prison Island Anchieta: The Site of Numerous Tragedies-'Winning or Losing Feud,' Resulted in Imprisonment of 170 People." Translated by Mina Otsuka. *Discover Nikkei.* Accessed April 19, 2017. http://www.discovernikkei.org/en/journal/2015/1/19/anchieta.

Gardiner, C. Harvey. *The Japanese and Peru 1873–1973.* Albuquerque: University of New Mexico Press, 1975.

———. *Pawns in a Triangle of Hate: The Peruvian Japanese and the United States.* Seattle: University of Washington Press, 1981.

Garten, Jeffrey E. *From Silk to Silicon: The Story of Globalization Through Ten Extraordinary Lives.* New York: Harper, 2016.

Ghosh, Shona. "Tencent Removed Microsoft's Chinese AI Chatbot after It Posted Unpatriotic Messages." *Business Insider.* August 3, 2017. Accessed August 5, 2018. https://www.businessinsider.com/tencent-pulled-microsots-chinese-ai-chatbot-2017-8.

Gonzales, Michael J. "Chinese Plantation Workers and Social Conflict in Peru in the Late 19th Century." *Journal of Latin American Studies* 21 (1989): 385–424.

Gonzalez, Jaime. "The Japanese-Peruvians Interned in the US during WWII." *BBC Mundo,* Los Angeles. Accessed August 4, 2016. http://www.bbc.com/news/world-latin-america-31295270.

Gootenberg, Paul. *Between Silver and Guano: Commercial Policy and the State in Postindependence Peru.* Princeton: Princeton University Press, 1989.

Gordon, Bill. "47 Ships Sunk by Kamikaze Aircraft." Accessed August 7, 2015. https://wgordon.web.wesleyan.edu/kamikaze/background/ships-sunk/index.htm.

Green, Michael J. *By More Than Providence: Grand Strategy and American Power in the Asia Pacific Since 1783.* New York: Columbia University Press, 2017.

Greene, Meg and Mark G. Malvasi. "Middle Passage: Did the Treatment of Slaves During the Middle Passage Produce Excessively High Mortality Rates?" In *History in Dispute vol. 13: Slavery in the Western Hemisphere, circa 1500–1888*, edited by Ed. Mark G. Malvasi, 129–37. Detroit: St. James Press, 2003.

Guimaraes, Eloisa M. Prada Queiroz, "The Role Played by the Shinto Remmei Trial in Japanese Immigration to Sao Paulo." In *Asiatic Migrations in Latin America*, edited by Montiel, Luz M. Martinez, 113–23. Mexico: El Colegio De Mexico, 1981.

Hall, Christine Catherine Iijima. "The Ethnic Identity of Racially Mixed People: A Study of Black-Japanese." Ph.D. diss., University of California at Los Angeles, 1980.

Hecht, Johana. "The Manila Galleon Trade (1565–1815)." Accessed December 10, 2014. http://www.metmuseum.org/toah/hd/mgtr/hd_mgtr.htm.

Herbison, Chico and Jerry Schultz. "Quiet Passage: The Japanese-American War Bride Experience" (paper). Lawrence: The Center for East Asian Studies at the University of Kansas, 1990.

Higashide, Seiichi. *Adios to Tears: The Memoirs of a Japanese-Peruvian Internee in U.S. Concentration Camp.* Seattle: University of Washington Press, 2000.

Higuchi, Katsuo. "SHINDO RENMEI, a Dark Chapter in the History of Japanese Immigration in Brazil." Translated by Andre Soares. *Discover Nikke.* Accessed August 30, 2020. https://www.discovernikkei.org/en/jopurnal/2018/11/7/shindo-renmei.

Hirabayashi, Lane Ryo, Akemi Kikumura-Yano, and James A. Hirabayashi., eds. *New Worlds, New Lives: Globalization and People of Japanese Descent in the Americas and from Latin America in Japan.* Palo Alto: Stanford University Press, 2002.

History. "Battle of Attu." Accessed January 27, 2020. https://www.history.com/topics/world-war-ii/battle-of-attu.

———. "Battle of Midway." Accessed August 29, 2020. https://www.history.com/topics/world-war-ii/battle-of-midway.

———. "Firebombing of Tokyo." Accessed June 17, 2018. https://www.history.com/this-day-in-history/firebombing-of-tokyo.

———. "Treaty of Kanagawa signed with Japan." Accessed March 1, 2020. https://www.history.com/this-day-in-hisory/treaty-of-kanagawa-signed-with-japan.

Hollett, David. *More Precious than Gold: The Story of the Peruvian Guano Trade.* Madison: Fairleigh Dickinson University Press, 2008.

Hsu, Madeline Y. *Dreaming of Gold, Dreaming of Home: Transnationalism and Migration Between the United States and South China, 1882–1943.* Stanford: Stanford University Press, 2000.

———. *The Good Immigrants: How the Yellow Peril Became the Model Minority.* Princeton: Princeton University Press, 2015.

Hu-De Hart, Evelyn, ed. *Across the Pacific: Asian Americans and Globalization.* Philadelphia: Temple University Press, 1999.

———. "On Coolies and Shopkeepers: The Chinese as Huagong (Laborers) and Huashang (Merchants) in Latin America/Caribbean." In *Displacement and Diasporas: Asians in the Americas,* edited by Wanni W. Anderson and Robert G. Lee, 78–111. New Brunswick, NJ: Rutgurs University Press, 2005.

———. "Race Construction and Race Relations: Chinese and Blacks in Nineteenth-Century Cuba." In *Encounters: People of Asian Descent in the Americas,* edited by Roshini Rusatomji-Kerns with R. Srikanth and L. M. Strobel, 105–118. New York: Rowman & Littlefield, 1999.

———. "La Trata Amarilla: The Yellow Trade and the Middle Passage, 1847–1884." In *Many Middle Passages: Forced Migration and the Making of the Modern World,* edited by Emma Christopher, Cassandra Pybus, and Marcus Rediker, 166–83. Berkeley: University of California Press, 2007.

Hyun, Kyoo Whan. *Hankook Yu Iminsa* [A History of Korean Wanderers and Emigrants] vols. 1 and 2. Seoul: Hungsadan Publishing Department, 1976.

Immigration History. "Page Law (1875)." Accessed June 14, 2017. https://immigrationhistory.org/item/page-act.

Infogalactic. "Arghun." Accessed March 5, 2020. https://infogalactic.cominfo/Arghun.

The Japan Times. "Numbers Tell Tale of Japan's Postwar Rise and Fall." Accessed February 4, 2020. https://www.japantimes.co.jp/news/2015/01/05/national/numbers-tell-tale-japans-postwar-rise-fall/#.Xjnt4C2ZPUY.

———. "The Rarely, If Ever, Told Story of Japanese Sold as Slaves by Portuguese Traders." Accessed February 11, 2020. https://www.japantimes.co.jp/culture/2013/05/26/books/book-reviews/th...-if-ever-told-story--of-japanese-sold-as-slaves-by-portuguese-traders/.

Jung, Moo-Ho. *Coolies and Cane: Race, Labor, and Sugar in the Age of Emancipation.* Baltimore: Johns Hopkins University Press, 2006.

Kikumura-Yano, Akemi. *Encyclopedia of Japanese Descendants in the America: An Illustrated History of the Nikkei.* Walnut Creek: Altamira Press, 2002.

Kushner, Eve. "Japanese-Peruvian-Reviled and Respected: The Paradoxical Place of Peru's Nikkei." In NACLA. Accessed August 21, 2018. peruvian-reviled-and-respected-paradoxical-place-peru%27s-nikkei.

Lai, Him Mark, Genny Lim, and Judy Yung, ed. *Island: Poetry and History of Chinese Immigrants on Angel Island 1910–1940* (2nd ed.) Seattle: University of Washington Press, 2014.

Lanchin, Mike. "Shoichi Yokoi, the Japanese Soldier Who Held Out in Guam." *BBC Magazine.* Accessed August 4, 2015, https://www.bbc.com/news/magazine-16681636.

Lee, Erika. *At America's Gate: Chinese Immigration During the Exclusion Ear, 1882–1943.* Chapel Hill: The University of North Carolina Press, 2003.

———. *The Making of Asia America: A History.* New York: Simon & Schuster Paperbacks, 2015.

Lee, Ja-Kyung. *Hankukin Mexico Iminsa* [The History of Korean Immigration to Mexico]. Seoul: Jisik Sanup Co., 1998.

———. *Mexico Imin Yaksa* [A Brief History of Korean Immigration to Mexico: A Macro Perspective]. Unpublished Paper in Korean, 2010.

Lesser, Jeffrey. *A Discontented Diaspora: Japanese Brazilians and the Meaning of Ethnic Militancy, 1960–1980.* Durham: Duke University Press, 2007.

———. *Negotiating National Identity: Immigrants, Minorities, and Struggle for Ethnicity in Brazil.* Durham: Duke University Press, 1999.

———. "In Search of the Hyphen: Nikkei and the Struggle over Brazilian National Identity." In *New Worlds, New Lives: Globalization and People of Japanese Descent in the Americas and from Latin America in Japan,* edited by Lane Ryo Hirabayashi, Akemi Kikumura-Yano, and James A. Hirabayashi, 37–58. Palo Alto: Stanford University Press, 2002.

Lopez, Kathleen. *Chinese Cubans: A Transnational History.* Chapel Hill: The University of North Carolina Press, 2013.

The Mahathir Years. "Look East Policy." Accessed October 2, 2020. https://www.mtholyoke.edu/~teh20v/classweb/worldpolitics/LookEast.html.

Mak, Stephen. "Japanese Latin Americans." Accessed August 28, 2015. http://encyclopedia.densho.org/print/Japanese%20Latin%20Americans/.

Malvasi, Mark G, ed. *History in Dispute vol. 13: Slavery in the Western Hemisphere, Circa 1500–1888.* Detroit: St. James Press, 2003.

Marx, Karl. "British Philathropy-The Coolies at the Chincha Islands." In *New York Daily Times,* January 24, 1854.

———. *The Eighteenth Brumaire of Louis Bonaparte.* New York: Cosimo, Incorporated, 2008.

Masterson, Daniel M. with Sayaka Funada-Klassen. *The Japanese in Latin America.* Chicago: University of Illinois Press, 2004.

McFadden, Robert D. "Hiroo Onoda, Soldier Who Hid in Jungle for Decades, Dies at 91." *New York Times.* Accessed August 27, 2020. https://www.nytimes.com/2014/01/18/word/asia/hiroo-onoda-imperial-japanese-army-officer-dies-at-91.html.

Meagher, Arnold J. *The Coolie Trade: The Traffic of Chinese Laborers to Latin America 1847–1874.* Xlibris Corporation, 2008.

Military Wiki. "Gan Ying." Accessed March 5, 2020. https://military.wikia.org/wiki/Gan_Ying.

———. "German-American Internment." Accessed April 14, 2016. https://military.wikia.org/wiki/German-American_internment.

———. "James Glynn." Accessed January 27, 2020. https://military.wikia.org/wiki/James_Glynn.

Misachi, John. "World War II Casualties by Country." In World Facts. Accessed August 24, 2020. https://www.worldatlas.com/articles/wwii-casualties-by-country.html.

Miyake, Lika C. "Forsaken and Forgotten: The U.S. Internment of Japanese Peruvians during World War II." *Asian American Law Journal* 9 (January 2002):163–93.

Montiel, Luz M. Martinez, ed. *Asiatic Migrations in Latin America.* Mexico: El Colegio De Mexico, 1981.

Morimoto, Amelia. "Peruvian Nikkei: A Sociopolitical Portrait." In *New Worlds, New Lives: Globalization and People of Japanese Descent in the Americas and from Latin America in Japan,* edited by Lane Ryo Hirabayashi, Akemi Kikumura-Yano and James A. Hirabayashi, 141–58. Palo Alto: Stanford University Press, 2002.

Mungello, D. E. *The Great Encounter of China and the West, 1500–1800.* New York: Rowman & Littlefield, 2009.

Museum of Chinese in America. "Chinese Confession Program." Accessed February 10, 2020. https://www.mocanyc.org/learn/timeline/chinese_confession_program.

Nam, Andrew C. *Korea: Tradition and Transformation.* Seoul: Hollym Corp., 1988.

Namu Wiki. "Danbalyung" [Creed on Topknot Cutting]. Accessed September 17, 2020. https://namu.wiki/w/단발령.

Nelson, Mike. "Modern Henequen Production in Yucatan, Mexico." Accessed July 14, 2015. https://www.mexicomike.com/stories/henequen.htm.

New World Encyclopedia. "Overseas Chinese." Accessed October 2, 2020. https://www.newworlencyclopedia.org/entry/Overseas_Chinese.

New York Historical Society. "Picture Brides and Japanese Immigration." Accessed August 25, 2020. https://www.history.com/topics/immigration/gentlemens-agreement.

Office of the Historian. "The Burlingame-Seward Treaty, 1868." Accessed August 17, 2020. https://history.state.gov/milestones/1866-1898/burlingame-seward-treaty.

———. "Chronology of the U.S.-China Relations, 1784–2000." Accessed November 20, 2019. https://history.state.gov/countries/issues/china-us-relations.

Overseas Korean Research Institute. "Henequen Hooson-30,000 Coreanos [Henequen Descendants—About 30,000 Koreans]." *Overseas Korean Times* Special Edition on the Centennial of Korean Immigration to Mexico (KINX2005036435) (2005): 11–18.

Owen, Tess. "The Words 'Oriental' and 'Negro' Can No Longer be Used in US Federal Laws." *Vice News.* May 21, 2016. Accessed January 25, 2018. news.vice.com/the-words-oriental-and-negro- can-no-longer-be-used-in-us-federal-laws.

Pan, Lynn. *Sons of the Yellow Emperor: A History of the Chinese Diaspora.* New York: Kodansha International, 1994.

———, ed. *The Encyclopedia of the Chinese Overseas.* Singapore: Archipelago Press, 2000.

Parenas, Rhacel S. and Lok C. D. Siu, eds. *Asian Diasporas: New Formations, New Conceptions.* Stanford: Stanford University Press, 2007.

Park, Yong Suk. "The Tragedy of the First Korean Students in the United States." (in Korean) Accessed August 3, 2016. http://mijumunha.net/parkyongsuk/board_6/60014.

Park, Young Mee. "Hawaii Hanin Imin Gwa Bigyohan Mexico Chogi Iminguajunge Daehan Gochal" [An Examination of the Early Korean Immigration to Mexico in Comparison with the Korean Immigrants in Hawaii]. *Journal on the Study of Spanish Language and Culture* 28 (2002): 651–69.

Perdue, Peter C. "The First Opium War: The Anglo-Chinese War of 1839–1842. An Online Essay." Accessed July 31, 2017. https://ocw.mit.edu/ans7870/21f.027/opium_wars_01/ow1_essay01.html.

RevWarTalk. "John Kendrick." Accessed January 27, 2020. https://www.revwartalk.com/john-kendrick.

Reynolds, Gary K. CRS Report for Congress. "U.S. Prisoners of War and Civilian American Citizens Captured and Interned by Japan in World War II: The Issue of Compensation by Japan." Updated July 27, 2001.

Rusatomji-Kerns, Roshini with R. Srikanth and L. M. Strobel, eds. *Encounters: People of Asian Descent in the Americas.* New York: Rowman & Littlefield, 1999.

———. "Introduction." In *Encounters: People of Asian Descent in the Americas*, edited by Roshini Rusatomji-Kerns with R. Srikanth and L. M. Strobel, 1–9. New York: Rowman & Littlefield, 1999.

The Samurai Archives. "Gregorio de Cespedes." Accessed February 2, 2020. https://wiki.samurai-archieves.com/index.phd?title=Gregorious_de_Cespedes.

———. "Japanese Immigration to Hawaii." Accessed May 20 2020. https://wiki.samurai-archives.com/index.php?title=Japanese_immigration_to_Hawaii.

Shiraishi, Kaori. "The Kachigumi/Makegumi Conflict in Brazil: Its Social and Psychological Influence on the Japanese Community." BA thesis, Sophia University in Tokyo, 2015.

Shukert, Elfrieda Berthiaume and Barbara Smith Scibetta. *War Brides of World War II*. Novato, CA: Presidio Press, 1988.

Skagg, Jimmy M. *The Great Guano Rush: Entrepreneurs and American Overseas Expansion*. New York: St. Martin Press, 1994.

Spickard, Paul R. *Mixed Blood: Intermarriage and Ethnic Identity in Twentieth-Century America*. Madison: The University of Wisconsin Press, 1989.

Statistica. "Number of Chinese Students Studying Abroad 2008–2018." Accessed October 2, 2020. https://www.statistica.com/statistics/227240/number-of-chinese-students-that-study-abroad/.

Stewart, Watt. *Chinese Bondage in Peru: A History of the Chinese Coolie in Peru, 1849–1874*. Westport, CT: Greenwood Press, 1951.

Suh, Sung Chul. "Mexico Hanin Iminsa Hyunwhanggwa Munjaejum [The State of the History on the Korean Immigrants in Mexico and Its Problems]." *Jaeoe Hanin Yungoo* [*Study of Overseas Koreans*] 5 (1996): 198–218.

Takenaka, Ayumi. "Transnational Community and Its Ethnic Consequences: The Return Migration and the Transformation of Ethnicity of Japanese Peruvians." *American Behavioral Scientist* 42 (1999): 1459–74.

Tawil, Jesse. "An Analysis of the Conditions of Life of Japanese Americans during World War II." Accessed April 12, 2017. http://essaymixture.com/an-analysis-of-the-conditions-of-life-of-japanese/.

Thompson, Era Bell. "Argentina: Land of the Vanishing Blacks." *Ebony* (October 1973): 74–85.

———. "Japan's Rejected." *Ebony* (September 1967): 42–54.

Thornton, Michael Charles. "A Social History of a Multiethnic Identity: The Case of Black Japanese Americans." Ph.D. diss., The University of Michigan, 1983.

Tigner, James L. "Japanese Immigration into Latin America: A Survey." *Journal of Interamerican Studies and World Affairs* 23, no. 4 (1981): 457–82.

Timenote. "Teruno Nakamura." Accessed August 4, 2019. https://timenote.info/en/Teruno_Nakamura.

Trout, Robert. *Brainy Quote*. Accessed July 19, 2017. https://www.brainyquote.com/quotes/robert_trout_279512.

Truman, Harry S. "Proclamation 2662—Removal of Alien Enemies," 1945. Accessed April 5, 2017. http://www.presidency.ucsb.edu/ws/?pid=87040.

Turner II, Christy G. "Teeth and Prehistory in Asia." *Scientific American* (February 1989): 88–96.

Uehara, Alexandre and Guilherme Casaroes. "Brazil, East Asia, and the Shaping of World Politics." *Perception* 18, no. 1 (2013): 75–100.

U.S. Congress. "An Act to Authorize Protection to be Given to Citizens of the United States Who May Discover Deposits of Guano." 34th Congress. CLXIV August 18, 1856. Accessed March 19, 2017. www./loc.gov/law/help/Statues-at-large/34th-congress/c34.pdf.

U.S. Senate. "Expressing the Regret of the Senate for the Passage of Discriminatory Laws against the Chinese in America, Including the Chinese Exclusion Act." Congressional Bills 112th Congress, May 26, 2011.

Waters, Mary-Alice. "The Unique History of Chinese in Cuba: From Independence War to Socialist Revolution." *The Militant* 75, no. 30 (August 2011): 1–11. Accessed August 2, 2016. http://www.themilitant.com/2011/7530/753050.html.

Watts, Jonathan. "Brazil's Japanese Community Gets Apology for Abuse." *The Guardian.* Accessed April 9, 2017. https://www.theguardian.com/world/2013/oct/11/brazil-japanese-community-apology-abuse.

Westad, Odd Arne. *Restless Empire: China and the World Since 1750.* New York: Basic Books, 2012.

Williamson, Samuel H. and Louis P. Cain. "Measuring Slavery in 2011 Dollars." Accessed November 29, 2017. https://www.measuringworth.com/slavery.php.

Wright, Giuseppina. "WWII Secret: Italian-American Internment as Alien Enemies." Accessed April 14, 2016. http://www.ejjournalncrp.org/wwii-secret-italian-americans-internment-as-alien-enemies/.

Yoo, Young Ryul, ed. *Jungnammi Haninei Yuksa* [The History of Koreans in Central and South America] vol. 6. Seoul: The Editorial Board of Korean History, 2007.

Yoon, Won K. *Global Pulls on the Korean Communities in Sao Paulo and Buenos Aires.* Lanham, MD: Lexington Books, 2015.

———. *The Passage of a Picture Bride.* Loma Linda: Loma Linda University Press, 1989.

Young, Elliott. *Alien Nation: Chinese Migration in the Americas from the Coolie Era through World War II.* Chapel Hill: The University of North Carolina Press, 2014.

Yun, Lisa. *The Coolie Speaks: Chinese Indentured Laborers and African Slaves in Cuba.* Philadelphia: Temple University Press, 2008.

Index

Afong Moy, 121–122
Ahn Chang Ho, 147
Alvares, Jorge, 20
American civilian detainees during World War II, 193
American Civil Liberty Union, 199
American surrogate mothers preferred, 128
America's domino effects in the sphere, 5–6
Angel Island, 115–118; family separation, 115–116; information exchange, 117; interrogation, 116–119
apology of US government to: Japanese Americans, 198; Peruvian Japanese, 199
Arrow War. *See* Opium War, Second
Asian laggard, 6–7
Asian success story, 2
Asian war brides: Japanese, 225–231; Korean, 241; other, 241; Vietnamese, 241
Asiatic threat, 34
asymmetric relations between East and West, 6
Axis nations, 187, 190, 191, 197, 208, 209

barbarian, 6, 24
barbarian foreign affairs. *See Zongli Yamen*
barracoon, 43, 44, 49
Battle of Midway, 212

Benedict, Ruth, 205
blackbirding, 93–94
Black Fleet of US Navy, 5
black-Japanese couple in America, 236–238; double rejection, 232–234; triple rejection, 234–235
bound feet, 118
Boxer Rebellion, 25, 34
Buy British Last Policy, 36

Californianos, 75
Catholic church establishment in: China, 20; Japan, 27; Korea, 29–30
Catholic practice among coolies, 67
century of Asian humiliation, 4–5, 7
child labor, 140; climate, 84; *guano* deposit, 84; location, 84; Spanish attempt, 96
China-Cuba relations at present, 79
China-Latin America relations at present, 79
Chinatown in: Havana, 75; San Francisco, 109, 110
Chincha Islands, 84
Chinese: concubine, 112; confession program, 126–127; diaspora communities, 56–57; earning in America, 114; Exclusion Act, 5, 75, 105–107, 158, 207; foreign activities, 57; freedom fighters in Cuba, 80; laborers to different countries, 17, 54;

prostitute, 122, 123
Chung Bong Woon, 171–172
Churchill, Winston on coolies, 99
civilized West, 6
Civil War, 2
Columbus, Christopher, 14, 20
coolie: cost of transportation, 52; from Cuba to Louisiana, 76; ownership change, 68; purchasing price, 64; rehabilitation, 67; replacement of slave, 55; reselling, 67, 68; tension with slaves, 65–66
coolie trade: China-Cuba voyage route, 44–45; China-Peru voyage route, 45–46; comparison with slave trade, 54–56; coolie mortality compared with slave mortality, 55–56; lucrative business, 52–54; mortality at sea, 2, 47, 63; mutiny at sea, 49–52; passenger capacity, 46; voyage distance, 61
Creoles in Yucatan, 138–139
Cuba: slavery, 62; sugar plantation working condition, 66; sugar production, 66

da Gama, Vasco, 14, 20
de Gobineau, Joseph Arthur Comte, 16
denial of Japanese defeat in World War II, 212
deportation of Japanese to America, 5; countries involved, 190; transport route, 191–192
diplomatic relations established between Peru and: China, 99; Japan, 98
discovery of: Japan by Portuguese, 27; Korea by Dutch, 29
Dutch: learning in Japan, 27; traders in Japan, 27, 234
dynasty rule ended in: China in 1911, 4, 25, 35; Korea in 1910, 4, 131, 145

Easter Island, 94
EB-5 investor visa, 127
Ellis Island of New York, 115
Ellis Island of the West. *See* Angel Island
enemy alien, 186, 193, 197, 199, 211, 213
Enlightenment, 15
escape attempts by Koreans in Yucatan: difficulty, 141; penalty, 142; punishment, 141; success, 142
Executive Order 9066, 183, 198

faction in Japanese community in Brazil: defeat faction, 212; victory faction, 212
Filipinos, 62
first Asian tour to the West by: Chinese, 33; Japanese, 32; Korean, 33
first Chinese settlement in Mexico, 21
food shortage in post-war Japan, 223–224
foreign devils, 24
foreign language restriction in Brazil, 208
fraudulent identity: coaching book, 113–114; coaching specialist, 114; cost of bringing Chinese to America, 114; creation of bogus family, 111–114; entry coaching, 112–114
freedom payment in Yucatan, 142

Gentlemen's Agreement, 157–158
golden visa. *See* EB-5 investor visa
Gold Mountain, 77; attraction, 103–104; earning, 108; wife, 108
Great East Asian War, 182, 203
Greater East Asian Co-Prosperity Sphere, 181–182
Gripsholm World War II Exchange of Civilian, 193–194
guano: American desire, 96; British attempt, 97; brown gold rush, 95–97; danger, 88; deposit, 84–85; export, 95; labor shortage, 85; national revenue, 95–96; Spanish attempt, 96
Guano Islands Act in the United States, 96
gun-boat diplomacy, 14

Haiti slave rebellion, 1, 71
half-black children in: America, 236–237, 238–240; Japan, 235
Hamel, Hendrik, 29
hearing board, 116
henequen, 132–133; cutting, 132–141; decline, 151; demand, 133; made Merida rich, 133; major producer of Yucatan, 133
henequen Koreans, 154, 155
Hermit Kingdom, 133, 138
homogenization attempt in Brazil, 208
Hong Kong, 107, 120, 124

Index

Honolulu, 161; entry interview, 166–167; first impression, 165; first night, 170–171; immigration station, 165

indentured laborers: Chinese, 66–67; Korean, 141
Industrial Revolution, 6
immigration: admission of Chinese women into America, 122; Chinese to America, 104; Chinese to Cuba, 62–63; denial rate at USA, 119; fraud, 108–110; impression gimmicks, 118; Korean to Mexico, 135; Japanese to Peru, 188–189
Immigration Amendment Act, 126
Indo-Pacific Security Alliance, 220
intermarriage: among Japanese, 227–228; among Koreans, 145–146; legal barriers to intermarriage in USA, 228–229; military tactics to discourage, 229–230
internal relocations during World War II in: America, 183–186; Brazil, 190; Mexico, 190
internment in America during World War II: German, 197–198; Italian, 198; Japanese Americans, 183–186; Peruvian Japanese, 190–192
interpreters for: Chinese immigrants, 113, 116; Korean immigrants, 144, 166

Jaemulpo in Yucatan, 135, 146
Japanese and Korean Exclusion League, 158
Japanese community in Brazil, 206
Japanese immigration to the Americas, 17–18
Japanese in Peru: anti-Japanese legislation, 189; anti-Japanese riot, 189; deportation to America, 190–192; Japanese Exclusion Law, 192; Japanese population, 189
Japanese Regiment in WWII, 185–186
Japanese stragglers of WWII, 204
Japanese war bride to America, 231
Japanese war efforts for Japan in Brazil, 215
Japan's military victory over: China in 1895, 25, 28, 181; Russia in 1905, 28, 181

Jeju Island in Korea, 29

kamikaze, 219
Keynes, Maynard, 99
kibei soldiers in Japan, 228
King Kojong, 132, 138, 145
Korean American Resident Association, 147, 152
Korean freedom fighters in: Guatemala, 149; Mexico, 149
Korean immigration to the Americas, 18
Korean independence movement in: America's mainland, 150; Hawaii, 177; Mexico, 147, 155
Korean innkeepers in: Honolulu, 168, 171; Yokohama, 163–164
Korean journey to Yucatan, 135
Korean remigration to Cuba, 151–152
Korean school in Yucatan, 146
Korean War, 126, 223, 241
kowtow, 24, 33

labor contract, 43, 66, 134
labor recruitment: Chinese, 42–44; Korean, 133–134
Latin American internment in America, 183, 197–198
Lee Young Oak, 160–179
life on plantations: sugarcane plantation in Cuba, 65–74; sugarcane plantation in Hawaii, 172–174; henequen plantation in Yucatan, 138–148
Look East Policy, 36

Macao, 14, 20, 42, 44, 45, 107
MacArthur, Douglas, 214, 217, 223, 224
Manchukuo, 206–207, 211, 220
Manila Galleon Trade, 20–21
maquiladoras, 154
Marx, Karl on Chinese, 91, 93
match-lock long rifle introduced to Japan, 14
Mayan, 62, 133, 138, 140, 145
McCarran-Walter Act, 229
McCarthy Era, 126
Meiji Reform, 5, 138
Merida, 133, 146
mestizos, 6
Meyer, John, 132, 133, 134

NAFTA. *See* USMCA
Nagasaki, 27, 234
name change among: Chinese in Cuba, 67; Koreans in Mexico, 145
National Origin Act, 126, 207
National Truth Commission of Brazil, 219
Naturalization Act, 76, 109–110, 197
Nestorian Christians, 21, 32
New York Times, 54

Olympic games in East Asia, 36; significance to Japanese, 203; significance to Koreans in Mexico, 154
One Road, One Belt (OROB), 37
Opium trade, 23
Opium War: First, 22, 42; first treaty, 22; Second, 23, 33; second treaty, 23–24
Oriental Exclusion Act, 5, 177, 178, 207, 228–229

Pacific Islanders, 93
Pacific War, 4, 188, 209, 213
Page Act of 1875, 123–124
Panama Canal, 44, 188, 191
Pearl Harbor attack, 183, 187, 189, 191, 198, 203, 208, 210, 211, 229
Perry, Mathew, 27
Persecution of Catholics: in Japan, 27; in Korea, 30
Peruvian Japanese: legal issues, 194–197; life at the relocation camp, 192–194; remained in America, 196–197
picture marriage: advantages, 158; angry brides, 168, 171; match-makers, 158; picture exchanges, 159–160; wedding ceremony, 168–170; wedding reception, 170
Pisco, Peru, 90
plantation: earning in Cuba, 65; earning in Hawaii, 176; earning in Yucatan, 140–141; hierarchy in Cuba, 71
Polo, Marco, 20, 25
probing questions on Chinese immigrants, 117

Qing dynasty of China, 21–25, 28
Quad. *See* Indo-Pacific Security Alliance

racial hierarchy, 6–7, 16, 72

racial tension between black and Chinese, 92
red scare, 126
reentry permits to US, 110
relocation camp life, 192–194
remigration attempts by Koreans, 152–153
repatriation to Japan, 196
reports on laborer's misery: Chinese in Chincha Islands, 97–98; Chinese in Cuba, 77; Korean in Yucatan, 143–144
returning home among: Chinese, 77–78; Koreans, 132, 142
revolution in the twentieth century: China, 79; Cuba, 79; Guatemala, 149; Mexico, 149; Russia, 153
Rhee, Syngman, 177
Ricci, Matteo, 21
Roosevelt, Franklin, 187, 197, 198
Russo-Japan War, 34, 132, 148

San Francisco earthquake, 110–111
sex ratio of: Chinese in America, 3; Koreans in Hawaii, 157, 178; Koreans in Mexico, 134
Shindo Renmei, 213–217; assassination squad, 215–216; fraudulence, 215; imprisonment, 218–219; membership, 213; misinformation campaign, 214; ridicule, 215; sabotage, 215; violence, 215–216
Silk Road, 13; New Silk Road, 37; Silk Road of the Sea, 20
Sino-Japan War, 34, 35, 132, 220
Sinophilia, 15
Sinophobia, 16
slave: price in America, 64; price in Cuba, 63–64; profit of slave trade, 53; smuggle, 68–71
Social Darwinism, 16
sojourner mindset, 3
Soldier Brides Act, 229
special hearing board, 119
Suez Canal, 45
suicide among Chinese laborers: on Chincha island, 90; in Cuba, 73; during voyage, 47

Taiping Rebellion, 22
Tencent chatbot, 127

3D jobs, 3
topknot: cut-off in Yucatan, 136–138; king's decrees, 138; social significance, 137
Toyotomi Hideyoshi, 27
trail of tears, 200
treaty of: Burlingame, 76; Chemulpo, 30; Kanagawa, 27; Nanjing, 22; Tianjin, 23–24, 76; Todesillas, 14
treaty ports, 22, 24
Truman, Harris, 214, 217, 229
Twain, Mark, 129

unequal treaties, 14–15
USMCA (United States, Mexico, Canada), 154
US Supreme Court rule on: Chinese Exclusion Act, 128; Japanese internment, 186; *Loving vs. Virginia*, 229

war bride, 225–240; left behind in Japan, 231–232; public attitude to, 231–232; school in Japan, 231, 232

wartime control in Brazil, 211
Western imperial activities in Asia, 4
Westernization of Japan, 138

Xavier, Francis, 33
Xi Jin Ping, 57

yellow peril, 4, 34–35, 135
yellow slave, 68
yellow terror, 34
yellow wife, 230
Yi Dynasty, 4, 28, 131, 145
YMCA for war bride, 231
Yokohama, 98, 120, 163–164; farewell party, 164; medical examination, 163; waiting for ticket, 163
Yuan Dynasty, 13, 20, 219
Yucatan, 132, 136
YWCA for war bride, 231

Zongli Yamen, 33
Zulueta, Pedro, 42

About the Author

Won K. Yoon is retired and was a longtime professor of sociology at La Sierra University and Loma Linda University. His academic interests focus on the life experiences of Korean immigrants in particular and people of East Asian ancestry in general throughout the Americas. Over the years, his writing has evolved in a concentric manner, from the experiences of individuals (*The Passage of a Picture Bride*, 1989) to national groups (*Context and Continuity: The Korean Adventist Church in North America and Its Future Generations*, 2008 and *Global Pulls on the Korean Communities in Sao Paulo and Buenos Aires*, 2015) and regional groups (the forthcoming *Asian Tragedies in the Americas: Chinese, Japanese, and Korean Stories*, 2021). The author's interests continue to evolve as he examines the Western impacts upon the structural changes of East Asian societies during the modernization period. He enjoys travel and has visited more than fifty countries in five continents. He and his wife have two children and three grandchildren, all of whom live in California.